Southeast Missouri
from Swampland
to Farmland

ALSO OF INTEREST

Food in the American Military: A History,
by John C. Fisher *and* Carol Fisher
(McFarland, 2011)

Southeast Missouri from Swampland to Farmland

The Transformation of the Lowlands

John C. Fisher

McFarland & Company, Inc., Publishers
Jefferson, North Carolina

LIBRARY OF CONGRESS CATALOGUING-IN-PUBLICATION DATA

Names: Fisher, John C., 1949– author.
Title: Southeast Missouri from swampland to farmland : the transformation of the lowlands / John C. Fisher.
Description: Jefferson, North Carolina : McFarland & Company, Inc., Publishers, 2017. | Includes bibliographical references and index.
Identifiers: LCCN 2017008610 | ISBN 9780786479955 (softcover : alkaline paper) ∞
Subjects: LCSH: Reclamation of land—Missouri—History. | Drainage—Missouri—History. | Little River Drainage District (Mo.)—History. | Swamps—Missouri—History. | Geology—Missouri—History. | Missouri—Geography. | Cape Girardeau Region (Mo.)—Geography. | Missouri—Environmental conditions. | Missouri—Social conditions. | Missouri—Economic conditions.
Classification: LCC TC977.M8 F57 2017 | DDC 333.73/153097789—dc23
LC record available at https://lccn.loc.gov/2017008610

BRITISH LIBRARY CATALOGUING DATA ARE AVAILABLE

ISBN (print) 978-0-7864-7995-5
ISBN (ebook) 978-1-4766-2791-5

© 2017 John C. Fisher. All rights reserved

No part of this book may be reproduced or transmitted in any form or by any means, electronic or mechanical, including photocopying or recording, or by any information storage and retrieval system, without permission in writing from the publisher.

On the cover a logging camp in Southeast Missouri about 1910 (Himmelberger-Harrison Lumber Company Records, Special Collections and Archives, Southeast Missouri State University); *background image* Refugees from the 1927 Mississippi River flood crowded into Red Cross tents set up on levees (photograph from the collections of the St. Louis Mercantile Library, University of Missouri–St. Louis); *background map* landforms that make up the southeast Missouri lowlands (map from John G. Grohskopf, *Subsurface Geology of the Mississippi Embayment of Southeast Missouri*)

Printed in the United States of America

McFarland & Company, Inc., Publishers
Box 611, Jefferson, North Carolina 28640
www.mcfarlandpub.com

To my wife
and to the memory of my father and mother,
who loved the land

Table of Contents

Acknowledgments   ix
Introduction   1

1. Geology and Geography of the Lowlands   5
2. The First Inhabitants   15
3. Euro-American Settlement to 1811   28
4. The New Madrid Earthquakes   39
5. Settlement, Early Agriculture and Civil War   56
6. Transportation   67
7. Timber   78
8. Beginning Reclamation   90
9. Little River Drainage District: Organization and Opposition   107
10. Little River Drainage District: Planning and Construction   120
11. Little River Drainage District: Floods, the Great Depression, Financial Failure and Recovery   135
12. Land Promotion, Post-Drainage Agriculture and Social Change   159
13. New Political and Religious Movements and the Sharecropper Demonstration   176

14. Politics and Farm Labor Changes 202
15. End of an Era 212

Chapter Notes 217
Bibliography 231
Index 239

Acknowledgments

In many ways the history of the southeast Missouri lowlands is unique and has not been chronicled in one volume that places the changes in the lowlands made during the first half of the twentieth century in the context of its geology, Native American history, agriculture, and sociology. But in attempting that, one has to rely on the foundations that have been laid. There have been some older excellent histories written such as *The History of Southeast Missouri* by Sydney Douglass and two multivolume sets of works by Louis Houck, *History of Missouri* and *Spanish Regime in Missouri*. Local historical societies have also compiled valuable histories and accounts. More recent scholarship has focused on some specific areas of the region's history such as railroad building, religious movements, labor unrest, and a re-examination of the effects of geographical changes brought about by drainage and land clearing through the lives of individuals such as Mississippi County planter and social reformer Thad Snow and railroad builder Louis Houck.

I want to thank the State Historical Society of Missouri for the Brownlee Research Grant received in 2007 used in researching the Little River Drainage District Records. This started the process that led to this publication. The staff of the Southeast Missouri State University Special Collections and Archives was particularly helpful as I searched for material in this collection which at the time had not been completely cataloged as well as in other collections in their archives. Personnel at the Missouri Historical Society in St. Louis provided valuable assistance in researching the Otto Kochtitzky Papers housed there. The Dunklin County Library accommodated my constant requests for interlibrary loan material. I want to especially thank my good friend Tony Byrd who serves as a volunteer researcher at the Dunklin County Library. Tony was constantly on the lookout for material that might be useful. He was especially helpful as I scoured the pages of newspaper microfilms. We also enjoyed many discussions of local and regional history which gave new perspectives. Another friend, Van Byrd, who has a deep knowledge of the Native American history of southeast Missouri, provided insights that helped shape that part of the manuscript.

Images provide an added dimension to any work of history. Staff at the State Historical Society of Missouri, the Southeast Missouri State University Special Collections and Archives, the Mercantile Library at the University of Missouri–St. Louis, and the Missouri State Archives provided assistance in locating and securing images. Images were also obtained through the Library of Congress, the United States Geological Survey, and the Agricultural Research Service of the United State Department of Agriculture.

Introduction

The southeast Missouri lowlands, located in the extreme southeast corner of the state, includes four counties entirely, Dunklin, Pemiscot, New Madrid, and Mississippi, and parts of three additional counties, Scott, Stoddard, and Butler. Often this area is referred to as the Bootheel, but in a strict geographical sense, the Bootheel would include only Dunklin, Pemiscot, and New Madrid counties. The southeast Missouri lowlands lie within the abandoned flood plains of the Mississippi and Ohio rivers and the present active Mississippi River flood plain. They have been shaped in part by the subsurface geological structures comprising the New Madrid Seismic Zone as well as the migration of the Mississippi and Ohio rivers across the Bootheel as water and sediment inundated the region during the Pleistocene and early Holocene epochs.

The earthquakes occurring along the New Madrid Seismic Zone in 1811 and 1812 deterred settlement for a time and caused some settlers to leave when the federal government allowed them to exchange land in the lowlands for other public land in Missouri. These earthquakes still rank as some of the strongest ever experienced in the United States.

Because dense, poorly drained hardwood forests covered much of the area referred to as the southeast Missouri lowlands, settlement came later than other regions in the state excepting perhaps the more rugged regions of the Ozarks. Economist Gary Lane McDowell described the lowlands this way: "The westward advance of agriculture in the 19th century left large areas of wetlands in the United States partially developed or undeveloped and outside of an established agriculture. The wetlands became a frontier behind the Frontier."[1] This describes the southeast lowlands well.

While the other farming regions of the state had been well developed for decades, much of southeast Missouri could still be described as wilderness at the beginning of the twentieth century. The vast area of swampland covered with cypress, oak, gum and other trees impeded easy east to west movement of settlers. Although settlers carved out isolated homesteads as early as the 1840s over much of the region and even earlier in areas along the Mississippi River, only with the spread of railroads could entrepreneurs tap the valuable timber resources, changing the landscape forever.

The transformation of the landscape of Missouri's southeast lowlands in the first four decades of the twentieth century stands as an amazing feat of human activity. Within the first two decades, the region, once dominated by poorly drained swamps containing magnificent virgin forests, became a land of depleted accessible resources, full of head-high stumps, overgrown with brush and vines, and holding such little value that often owners could not even afford to pay their property taxes. Much of its legendary wildlife, which had once attracted numerous hunters from St. Louis and other distant cities to organized hunting clubs, disappeared as well, a consequence of over-hunting and habitat changes. Fertile soil lay beneath, but without a means to remove excess water, it could not be utilized.

Drainage afforded by the construction of the Little River Drainage District and other smaller drainage districts changed the landscape again, helping, in the next two decades, to turn the lowlands into one of the nation's most productive agricultural areas. The contribution of the seven southeast Missouri counties to the state's total agricultural production is phenomenal. Occupying only about 6 percent of the state's total land area, these counties produce approximately 25 to 30 percent of the state's total agricultural output. Several smaller drainage districts had been dug before Little River, but in a sense it was the last piece of the puzzle, because that system removed excess water entirely from the region rather than simply moving water from higher to lower locations within the lowlands as earlier drainage projects had.

The Little River Drainage District today consists of 957.8 miles of ditches and 304.43 miles of levees. It is some 90 miles in length from Cape Girardeau to the Arkansas line with the width varying from ten to 20 miles. The district is made up of 540,000 acres but in effect drains 1.2 million acres. The upper district consists of the diversion channel system which receives water from nearly 1,130 square miles in the Ozarks and diverts this water directly to the Mississippi River. There are 50.25 miles of channels and 44.73 miles of levees and three water detention basins. The lower district furnishes drainage for 1,710 square miles or 1,094,400 acres. This is accomplished through 849.6 miles of ditches, 241.6 miles of levees, and three detention basins. The longest ditch extends approximately 100 miles, running the entire length of the district. There are also five ditches paralleling this ditch. This set of ditches is locally referred to as the floodway ditches.[2]

It is interesting to ponder some possibilities under a different set of circumstances. Certainly today such a massive drainage project could never be accomplished because of regulations in place to protect wetlands. This is not to argue the rightness or wrongness of these regulations just that in another time the transformation brought by drainage would likely not be permitted. Likewise, without the cooperation and dedication of some farsighted landowners, such an undertaking could not have been carried out. While these landowners were certainly capitalists and driven by their hope to profit from the increased value of their holdings, it required vision to see the possibilities for the region that good drainage could bring.

This book chronicles the changes wrought by one of the greatest land reclamation projects ever attempted and the path agriculture followed in this region. These changes can best be understood in the context of the geological forces forming the area, the Native American inhabitants' use of its resources, and the settlement history. The changes were not limited to the physical geography. Major sociological changes took place as well through changes in agriculture. Agriculture shifted from primarily a diversified Midwestern type of agriculture to one focused on cotton and the development of the sharecropper system brought from the South. The influx of large numbers of both African American and white workers and sharecroppers in the 1920s produced racial conflict as well. Protests by tenants over land rents and by workers over wages led to some extensive periods of violence. A demonstration by sharecroppers in 1939 brought changes to federal programs designed to help farmers during the Great Depression. Mechanization of agriculture brought more change, ending the sharecropper system and reducing the demand for farm labor.

A variety of resources have been mined to piece together this history. First of all, the Little River Drainage District kept exquisite records from its inception. All of the past records have now been archived at Southeast Missouri State University. Additionally, records from some of the large lumber companies working in the area such as Himmelberger and Harrison and Gideon-Anderson have also been preserved at Southeast Missouri State University and the University of Missouri, respectively. The first engineer of the district, Otto Kochtitzky, has his papers archived at the Missouri Historical Society in St. Louis. Early local histories provide a wealth of information about the settlement of towns across the region. Local historical societies have also published works which give accounts of individuals and communities in the region. Government documents have also been utilized for information related to the disposition of swamplands and their drainage. Census data contain a wealth of information about population make-up, land tenancy, and crop production. Newspapers provide yet another primary source of information. Primary and secondary resources in the areas of agriculture, sociology, geography, and geology have added depth to the study. Within the past decade, excellent research by scholars such as Joel Rhodes, Bonnie Stepenoff, and Jarod Roll have resulted in publications that have been especially helpful and have contributed much to the understanding of the region's history.

CHAPTER 1

Geology and Geography of the Lowlands

The casual observer traveling the roadways of Missouri's Bootheel primarily sees continuous fields of cotton, soybeans, wheat, corn, or rice and a relatively level surface which conceals the geological complexities that lie below. It is also difficult to imagine the vast swampland filled with towering cypress and other trees which once covered much of its landscape. The present day landforms in the southeast lowlands are the result of complex geological processes occurring over millions of years. Understanding how the landscape of the southeast lowlands evolved takes us on a journey into the distant geologic past of the region where we see continents dividing, mountains uplifted, sea levels fluctuating, and rivers constantly changing their course.

Three types of landforms make up the surface of the Bootheel region. Most of the surface is made up of lowlands which consist of a relatively level surface with occasional low ridges and some distinct relic channels. These surfaces resulted from both erosion and deposition by the Mississippi and Ohio rivers. They occupy the lowest elevations in the region and made up the majority of the swampland before drainage. Two types of ridges make up the remaining landforms. One is Crowley's Ridge, an erosional remnant lying on the western side of the region. It extends from the Mississippi River near Commerce southwestward into northeastern Arkansas. Crowley's Ridge displays as much as 250 feet of local relief and averages ten miles in width. It is composed of sands and clays deposited during parts of the Cretaceous Period (144–65 million years B.P.) and the Tertiary Period (65–1.8 million years B.P.). While most geologists consider Crowley's Ridge to

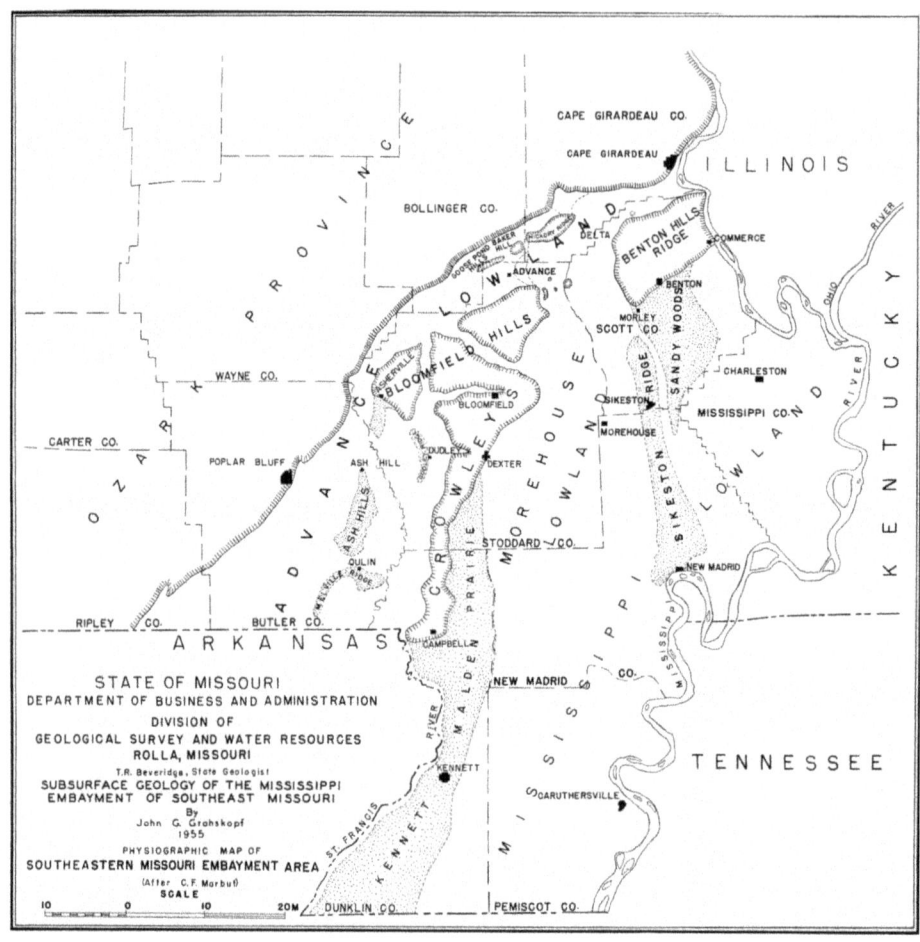

Map showing the landforms that make up the southeast Missouri lowlands (Grohskopf, *Subsurface Geology of the Mississippi Embayment of Southeast Missouri*).

be erosional in origin, some recent studies have identified faults bounding each side of it in certain sections, suggesting that it may in part be structural in origin.[1] The other type of landform is sandy ridges or terraces resulting from deposition by the Mississippi and Ohio rivers during the Pleistocene Epoch. The two most prominent sand ridges are the Sikeston Ridge and the Kennett-Malden Prairie. Lying on the eastern side of the area and extending from New Madrid to Sikeston, the Sikeston Ridge is about two miles wide and lies about 20 feet above the elevation of the surrounding land. To the west lies the Kennett-Malden Prairie, sometimes referred to as the Malden Plain, located just east of Crowley's Ridge. It has elevations ten to 20 feet above the surrounding area and extends from the southern boundary of Dunklin County to just south of Dexter, a distance of about 50 miles. It varies in width from five to 12 miles. The Ash Hills and the Mehlville Ridge are two smaller ridges in Butler County. East of the Sikeston Ridge and adjoining the Benton Hills (part of Crowley's Ridge) lies Sandy Woods, also known as the Charleston Alluvial Fan. All of these ridges contain sandier soils than those found at lower elevations. Because of their drier soils and higher elevation these ridges were some of the first land to be inhabited and farmed. The Sikeston Ridge and the Kennett-Malden Prairie also provided travel lanes in a north-south direction which allowed travelers to avoid crossing the swamps.

Geologists refer to the area occupied by the southeast Missouri lowlands as being a part of a structural trough or down-warped area known as the Mississippi Embayment, which has its origin in the distant past. To fully understand the origins of this structure we need to go back even further in geologic time. About one billion years ago all of the continents were joined together in one land mass geologists call Rodinia. Approximately 725 million years ago this supercontinent started breaking apart. Geologists refer to those areas where continents separate as rift zones. The land area comprising the North American continent started to break apart in what is now the Mississippi Valley. The process failed to completely break apart the continent, leaving instead two large fractures in the earth's crust called the Reelfoot Rift. A block between then moved down-

GEOLOGIC TIME SCALE

ERA	PERIOD	
CENOZOIC ERA 65.5 MILLION YEARS AGO TO PRESENT	QUATERNARY PERIOD 1.8 MILLION YEARS AGO TO THE PRESENT	
	TERTIARY PERIOD 65.5 TO 1.8 MILLION YEARS AGO	
MESOZOIC ERA 251 TO 65.5 MILLION YEARS AGO	CRETACEOUS PERIOD 145.5 TO 65.5 MILLION YEARS AGO	
	JURASSIC PERIOD 199.6 TO 145.5 MILLION YEARS AGO	
	TRIASSIC PERIOD 251 TO 145.5 MILLION YEARS AGO	
PALEOZOIC ERA 542 TO 251 MILLION YEARS AGO	PERMIAN PERIOD 299 TO 251 MILLION YEARS AGO	
	CARBONIFEROUS PERIOD 359.2 TO 299 MILLION YEARS AGO	PENNSYLVANIAN 318 TO 299 MILLION YEARS AGO
		MISSISSIPPIAN 359 TO 318 MILLION YEARS AGO
	DEVONIAN PERIOD 416 TO 359.2 MILLION YEARS AGO	
	SILURIAN PERIOD 443.7 TO 416 MILLION YEARS AGO	
	ORDIVICIAN PERIOD 488.3 TO 443.7 MILLION YEARS AGO	
	CAMBRIAN PERIOD 542 TO 488.3 MILLION YEARS AGO	
PRECAMBRIAN ERA 4.5 BILLION YEARS A GO TO 542 MILLION YEARS A GO		

Geologic time scale (illustration by the author).

ward, creating a trough.[2] This trough became the site of the accumulation of thick deposits of sandstone, limestone, and dolomite during the early to mid Paleozoic Era.[3]

During the mid to late Paleozoic Era, 300 to 250 million years before the present (B.P.), gradual uplift occurred over the region forming the Ozarks to the west and the Nashville Dome to the east. Between the Ozarks and the Nashville Dome, the Pascola Arch formed, uplifting much of the Paleozoic rocks in the area. This uplift resulted in erosion of large amounts of the Paleozoic sediments in the Mississippi Embayment.[4] Because of the extensive erosion, the Pascola Arch now has no surface expression and can only be recognized in the subsurface. During the Cretaceous Period, 144 to 65 million years B.P., as the present day Atlantic Ocean and Gulf of Mexico were opening, regional stress in the crust caused rifting to resume, resulting in subsidence and the creation of a large trough. This allowed an arm of the Gulf of Mexico to extend northward to just south of Cape Girardeau, Missouri. This trough or syncline became the site of the accumulation

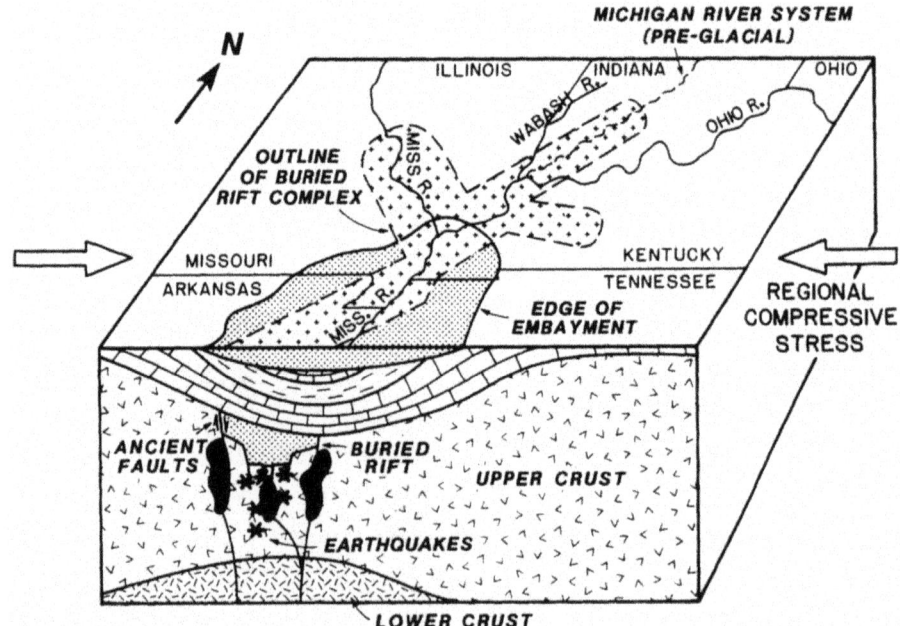

Block diagram showing the subsurface structures of the New Madrid Seismic Zone and where earthquakes occur along the zone (by Braile, Hinze, Sexton, Keller, and Lidiak published in United States Geological Survey Open File Report 84-770, "Proceedings of the Symposium on 'The New Madrid Seismic Zone,'" Reston, Virginia, 1984).

of thick deposits of both marine and nonmarine sediments during the Cretaceous and Tertiary Periods.[5] Along some of the fractures created in the crust by the rifting, magma from deep within the crust was forced into the surrounding rocks creating large masses of granite-like rock below the surface. The rifting again failed to break apart the continent but left a zone of weakness in the crust with numerous fractures and some complex structures. Geologists now refer to this area of fractured crust as the New Madrid Seismic Zone. It has produced numerous large earthquakes, most notable in historic times, the New Madrid Earthquake of 1811-1812. This earthquake and its impact will be discussed in detail in Chapter 4.

A drop in sea level and subsidence of the Mississippi Embayment left a valley which provided a natural drainage route through the middle of North America. According to geologist Roger T. Saucier, "By the end of the Tertiary Period [2.5 million years B.P.], most of the [Mississippi] Embayment had been filled with sediment, and the ancestral Mississippi was probably established in a well defined but rather narrow and shallow valley. That marks the first manifestation of a Mississippi alluvial valley."[6] The ancestral Mississippi River flowed on the western side of Crowley's Ridge while the ancestral Ohio River occupied the valley east of Crowley's Ridge. The two did not join until some point south of Helena, Arkansas.[7]

Early Pleistocene glaciations disrupted northward flowing streams and diverted more flow southward through the Mississippi Valley. The end of the first Pleistocene glacial advance, about two million years ago, brought enormous amounts of glacial meltwater and sediment into the region resulting in widening and deepening of the valley, marking, according to Saucier, "the effective beginning of the Mississippi alluvial valley." Saucier further notes that this alluvial plain "was 100 ft or more above the level of the present floodplain."[8]

The cycle of glacial advance and retreat through the Pleistocene resulted in alternating periods of erosion and entrenchment of the river courses along with periods of sediment deposition. During episodes of glacial advance, the lower sea levels produced increased stream gradients, allowing them to more effectively erode their valleys. As glaciers recede, sea levels rise, reducing stream gradients, causing more deposition of the stream's sediment load. Another factor affecting the development of Mississippi alluvial valley through the southeast Missouri lowlands was the volume of water coming from melting glaciers and the massive amount of sediment it carried. When glaciers melt, ice margin lakes often form and fill until the water can no longer be contained. This water is then released in outburst floods of enormous magnitude. Such near-catastrophic floods contributed to the

THE QUATERNARY PERIOD AND PLEISTOCENE GLACIAL STAGES

QUATERNARY PERIOD 1.8 MILLION YEARS AGO TO THE PRESENT	HOLOCENE EPOCH 11,477 YEARS AGO TO THE PRESENT	NORTH AMERICAN PLEISTOCENE GLACIAL AND INTERGLACIAL STAGES	WISCONSINAN GLACIAL 75,000 TO 11,477 YEARS AGO
	PLEISTOCENE EPOCH 1.8 MILLION TO 11,477 YEARS AGO		SANGAMONIAN INTERGLACIAL 120,000 TO 75,000 YEARS AGO
			ILLINOIAN GLACIAL 170,000 TO 120,000 YEARS AGO
			YARMOUTHIAN INTERGLACIAL 230,000 TO 170,000 YEARS AGO
			KANSAN GLACIAL 480,000 TO 230,000 YEARS AGO
			AFTONIAN INTERGLACIAL 600,000 TO 480,000 YEARS AGO
			NEBRASKAN GLACIAL 800,000 TO 600,000 YEARS AGO
			PRE-NEBRASKAN 1.8 MILLION TO 800,000 YEARS AGO

Chart showing the dates of the various glacial stages (illustration by the author).

development of outwash deposits forming the braided stream deposits in the southeast lowlands. It has been estimated that during late glacial times, the average flow through the lower Mississippi Valley exceeded the present flow by a factor of five and during flood events the flow would have been even higher.[9]

The Mississippi Valley through the southeast Missouri lowlands evolved as the ancestral Mississippi and Ohio rivers migrated from west to east across the region, alternating between eroding and depositing sediment. The two river systems broadened and filled their valleys with a blanket of rich soil. The sequence of events that lead to the development of the present day landforms in the upper lower Mississippi Valley has been studied by numerous geologists beginning with a landmark study by H.N. Fisk in 1944. More recent studies have been made by Saucier, 1974 and 1994; Blum, Guccione, Wysocki, Robnett, and Rutledge, 2000; and Rittenour, Blum, and Goble, 2007. While scientists have differed in the exact dating of the time of formation of various landforms and deposits, the understanding of the general sequence of changes in the evolution of the Mississippi and Ohio river valleys through the lowlands has changed only slightly. More recent scholarship utilizing newer dating techniques such as optical luminescence have helped to refine the determination of the time of formation of various features of the landscape. The following two paragraphs provide a general summary of the chronology of the development of the Mississippi valley in southeast Missouri and the formation of the present landforms.

During the late Illinoian glacial period, about 130,000 years B.P., the Mississippi River flowed on the western side of Crowley's Ridge through the Advance Lowland forming several braided stream terrace deposits such as the Ash Hills and the Mehlville Ridge while the Ohio River flowed to the east of Crowley's Ridge in a nearly parallel course. The large amount of sediment these streams carried from the melting glaciers in the form of glacial outwash caused both the Mississippi and Ohio to flow in a braided pattern. Braided streams flow in a network of channels which split and flow around islands or bars and then rejoin. This pattern is characteristic of streams carrying a heavy sediment load. Geomorphologists can recognize these relict braided stream patterns from aerial and satellite photos.

Both the Mississippi and Ohio continued to change courses as they filled their channels with sediment. Near the end of the maximum of the Wisconsin glacial period ice sheet advance, about 20,000 years B.P., the Mississippi River abandoned the Advance Lowland and most of its flow cut through Crowley's Ridge at the Bell City-Oran Gap and then came down the eastern side of Crowley's Ridge. Only during periods of extremely large floods would a portion of the Mississippi's flow follow channels west of Crowley's Ridge. The Ohio River had left a large area of sandy, braided stream deposits known as the Sikeston Braid Belt between Crowley's Ridge and the present day course of the Mississippi River as it shifted eastward. These deposits were made mostly between 19,000 and 17,000 years B.P. As the Mississippi flowed on the east side of Crowley's Ridge it made new braided stream deposits forming the Kennett-Malden Prairie between 16,000 and 15,000 years B.P.[10] The Mississippi River's course continued to migrate eastward, first eroding then depositing sediment to form deposits referred to as the Morehouse Braid Belt which make up today's Morehouse Lowland. The Morehouse Lowland surface rests at a lower elevation than both the Kennett-Malden Prairie and the Sikeston Ridge. A distinct escarpment marks the boundary between the two ridges and the adjacent lowlands. A remnant of the earlier Ohio braided stream deposits remained in the form of the Sikeston Ridge. Between 11,000 and 12,000 years ago the Mississippi changed courses again, this time diverting its flow through the Thebes Gap allowing it to intersect the Ohio River near present day Cairo, Illinois.[11] Prior to its capture of the Ohio River at Cairo, the Mississippi River, flowing through the Thebes Gap, entered the lowlands at the northeast edge of the Sikeston Ridge and adjacent to the Benton Hills. It left an area of sandy deposits referred to as the Charleston Alluvial Fan.

Rivers entering the lowlands from the Ozark escarpment have occupied the abandoned channels of the Mississippi and Ohio rivers. The Black River flows through an abandoned Mississippi River course in the Advance Lowland. The St. Francis River flows through the Advance Lowland until in cuts through Crowley's Ridge near Campbell and then flows on the eastern side of Crowley's Ridge and along the western edge of the Kennett-Malden Prairie. Further east, Castor River and Little River each occupy abandoned channels in the Morehouse Lowland.

The vast amount of glacial outwash deposited in the region by the Mississippi and Ohio rivers provided a source of material for loess or wind blown deposits. Before vegetation became established on these new deposits, prevailing west-northwest winds picked up and deposited these mostly silt-sized materials on the tops of upland areas adjacent to the valley including Crowley's Ridge and the upland areas of western Tennessee. In addition, several areas of sand dunes formed which are still evident. Dune fields are recognizable in the Advance Lowlands close to the Ozark Escarpment and in the Eastern Lowlands dunes occur east of and parallel to the Sikeston Ridge.[12]

Scientists use a variety of methods to reconstruct past climatic and vegetation patterns. These include pollen from sediment cores, plant and animal fossils, oxygen isotope ratios in the shells of foraminifera found in deep-sea sediment cores and in ice cores. Oxygen exists in two isotope forms, ^{16}O and ^{18}O. The ratio between the two isotopes varies depending upon water temperature thus this ratio can be useful in determining past climatic conditions. Such techniques have allowed the determination of vegetation patterns for various time periods during the Pleistocene and Holocene in the lower Mississippi Valley. The vegetation of the southeast lowlands looked vastly different during the Pleistocene and early Holocene than today. The periods of glacial expansion and retreat brought about wide shifts in the climate around the world.

Changes in plant communities accompanied these sharp variations in the climate. The greatest extent of glacial ice coverage of North America occurred during the Illinoian glacial period when the Laurentide ice sheet reached near the current location of the Missouri and Ohio rivers. The last glacial maximum occurred during the Wisconsinan glacial period about 20,000 to 18,000 years ago. At this time the Laurentide ice sheet extended southward to about 40° north latitude.[13] Most of the southeast Missouri lowlands lie between 36° and 37° north latitude. The direction of the southern jet stream at the time would have caused much cooler temperatures and greater precipitation in the winter from 33° north latitude to the ice margin. During the time of the maximum Wisconsinan glacial advance, south of the Laurentide ice sheet to about 34° north latitude, which includes the southeast Missouri lowlands, the predominate vegetation would have been boreal forests.[14] Such forests consist primarily of evergreen coniferous trees such as pine, spruce, fir, and larches. Today similar conditions exist between 50° and 60° north latitude which covers large areas of Canada, the interior of Alaska, and the extreme northern portions of the contiguous 48 states. Tundra, which does not support tree growth, occurs above the boreal forest regions.

Spruce, fir, and tamarack forests covered most of the western lowlands while a spruce-willow forest grew on the valley train or braided-stream deposits derived from glacial outwash in the Eastern Lowlands. Crowley's Ridge had a Spruce-Oak forest and a Spruce-Jack Pine forest covered sandier abandoned valley train terraces just east of Crowley's Ridge. By 14,000 years B.P. in response to climate warming, temperate climate deciduous species began to dominate the vegetation. Oak-Hickory forests began replacing Spruce-Willow forests on braided stream terraces in both the Western and Eastern Lowlands although the Spruce-Willow vegetation remained in active areas of braided stream deposition. By 12,000 years B.P., Oak-Hickory forests covered most of the abandoned braided stream terraces in both the Western and Eastern Lowlands. Spruce-Willow growth declined and became confined to areas along the active channel of the Ohio River.[15]

Beginning at 10,000 years B.P., vegetation cover changed from temperate to warm-temperate characteristics, similar to present day natural vegetation, as the climate continued to warm. Sweet gum first appeared at this time as did bald cypress and tupelo gum, both common trees in the lowlands at the time of settlement. Oak-Hickory Forests expanded and Willow-Cane Forests developed on natural levees which the Mississippi River constructed along its now meandering flow pattern. Around 8,000 years B.P., the climate continued to warm, favoring warm temperate species like oaks. After 8000 years B.P. the lower Mississippi Valley entered a warm dry period known as the Hypsithermal which lasted to about 4000 years B.P. During this time Oak-Hickory Savanna expanded in both the Western and Eastern Lowlands while Willow-Forest and Cypress-Tupelo Forest remained confined to the easternmost parts of the Eastern Lowlands along the active Mississippi River meander belt. Savannas are characterized by scattered trees interspersed with wide expanses of flowering plants and grass.

Unlike a forest, the tree canopy is less than 50 percent. Grazing animals and natural fires caused by lightning strikes tend to control understory growth in savannas. A study of pollen from the Old Field Swamp near Advance in Stoddard County, Missouri, which is situated in the Morehouse Lowland indicates that between 8700 and 5000 year B.P. the southeast lowlands experienced a warm dry climate with low water levels. Between 8700 and 7000 years B.P. the grass pollen dominates the record. By 6500 years B.P. a shift to increased tree pollen occurs and after 5000 years B.P. pollen shows renewed growth of bottomland forest vegetation, especially oaks.[16]

By 2000 years B.P. the climate had shifted from warm and dry to warm and wet allowing the expansion of Willow-Cane Forests to broader areas along meander belts.[17] Large expanses of Cypress-Tupelo Forest also developed in the lowland areas such as the Morehouse Lowland and the Advance Lowland. On parts of the Sikeston Ridge and Kennett-Malden Ridge, some true prairie land also developed.[18] At 1000 years B.P. the vegetation cover remained virtually the same and is basically the cover existing at the time human activity began to significantly impact vegetative cover.

If we had wandered through the boreal forests covering the southeast lowlands during the Pleistocene we would have encountered an unusual array of animals compared to today. During the Pleistocene, large mammal species dominated the fauna of North America however, most of these so-called mega-fauna became extinct before end of the Pleistocene. Of course the animals most people think of in relation to the Ice Ages are the mammoths and mastodons. Mammoths were primarily grazing animals feeding mostly on grasses thus most of their remains come from the western part of the state. Mastodons fed by browsing on twigs and tree branches in boreal forests. This type of vegetative cover predominated in the southeast lowlands and the eastern part of the state thus only mastodon remains have been found in these areas. Other large mammals that roamed the region include bison, musk-oxen, ground sloths, tapirs, llamas, flat-faced bears, saber-toothed tigers, and horses.

After 10,000 years B.P. these animals had become extinct in the central and lower Mississippi Valley as more familiar species became the dominant animal life including elk, deer, rabbits, squirrels, raccoon. All of these along with fish and turtles made up an important part of diet of the first human inhabitants of the region.

Chapter 2

The First Inhabitants

When did the first human inhabitants arrive in the southeast Missouri lowlands and hunt along its waterways? The rich alluvial valley undoubtedly would have been home to a wide variety of animals making it an attractive location to its first inhabitants. However, the question of when the first humans inhabited North America has been a much debated topic among archaeologists for many years. Traditional thought has been that these ancestors came from Siberia across the Bering Strait into Alaska during the Wisconsin Glacial Period when continental glaciation lowered sea level enough to expose a strip of land referred to as Beringia. The oldest verified evidence of human habitation in North America comes from Clovis sites. Clovis sites date from around 13,000 years B.P.[1] Archaeologists first found the distinctive projectile points made by the Clovis people near Clovis, New Mexico, in the early 1930s. Points were found in direct association with mammoth bones thus demonstrating that North America held a human population before the extinction of mammoths, mastodons, and other large Pleistocene fauna. Clovis points have since been identified over a vast area ranging from the Atlantic to the Pacific coast and from southern Canada to Central America.[2]

A new hypothesis has emerged recently, linking the Clovis tool making technology to the Solutrean culture in northern Spain and southern France. The similarity of the Clovis points to those made by the Solutreans in southwestern Europe have led to suggestions that pre–Clovis people may have arrived in America by crossing the Atlantic in front of the ice which closed off the north Atlantic instead of coming across the Bering Strait. The Clovis and Solutrean points resemble each other not only in shape but in the flaking techniques employed to produce them. Bruce Bradley and Dennis Stanford, leading proponents of the European origin of the Clovis people, state that "all Clovis tool types including fluted bifaces occur in Solutrean assemblages. By contrast, only a few ubiquitous flaked tool types are shared between Clovis and any Siberian technology."[3] Evidence has been mounting that humans inhabited North America earlier than the Clovis period. Bradley and Stanford note that three sites in eastern North America, Meadowcroft Rock Shelter in Pennsylvania, Cactus Hill in Virginia, and Page-Ladson in Florida, have all yielded radiocarbon dates in excess of 13,000 years B.P. These and two other sites, one in Wisconsin and another in Oregon, appear to be the oldest sites in North American with evidence of human habitation and strongly suggest human presence before Clovis occupation.[4] Bradley and Stanford also observe that the oldest radiocarbon dates for Clovis sites are in the southeast and become progressively younger to the west.[5] However archaeologist Julie Morrow points out that work done by other archaeologists on linguistics, DNA, dental studies, and radiocarbon dates indicate that the earliest Paleoindians came from Asia.[6]

Clovis points have been found in more than half of all Missouri counties. In the southeast lowlands, Clovis points have been collected in all of the southeast lowland counties except Pemiscot and Mississippi. The Clovis people hunted large Pleistocene animals such as bison, mastodon, and horse. Definitive evidence of their hunting mastodons in Missouri came from a location in Jefferson County known as the Kimmswick Bone Bed, now known as Mastodon State Historic Site. As far back as the early 1800s bones of mastodons and other extinct Pleistocene animals were found at the site. Archaeologists made excavations in 1839 and in the early 1900s. An excavation in 1979 by the Illinois State Museum discovered a Clovis point in direct association with mastodon bones demonstrating for the first time definitive proof that Clovis people hunted these now extinct creatures in Missouri.

The role of Clovis hunters in the extinction of large species especially mammoth and mastodon has received attention from archaeologists since most of these large species became extinct after 11,000 years ago. While early Native Americans certainly hunted these animals, other factors involved in their extinction relate to changes in climate and habitat. For example, the area of boreal forests favored by the large Pleistocene species became reduced in extent as the climate warmed and deciduous species such as oak and hickory replaced the spruce and fir forests. New diseases might also have been a factor. Archaeologists Donald K. Grayson and David J. Meltzer conclude that "there is no evidence provided by the North American archaeological record to support the argument that people played a significant role in causing Pleistocene extinctions here."[7]

Archaeologists sub-divide the Paleoindian period based on the type of projectile points and blades these early inhabitants manufactured. Following the Clovis, other fluted points, mainly Folsom and Dalton became the dominant forms. Archaeologists Michael J. O'Brien and W. Raymond Wood observe that "the Paleoindian period contains a bewildering array of technological innovations."[8] These people obviously became more efficient in utilizing the resources of their environment although details of the daily life of the Paleoindians remain sparse. Evidence suggests that they lived nomadic lives as hunters, following the herds of animals they preyed on and as gatherers of wild food. While they utilized mastodon and other megafauna, by the beginning of the Holocene, about 11,000 years B.P., these had disappeared to be replaced by more modern forms such as bison and deer which became important parts of their diet. Archaeologists Dan and Phyllis Morse speculate that the Paleoindians lived in bands rather than tribes. They define bands as "a loosely defined group of people who recognize kinship with one another." Several families within a band might come together to form seasonal hunting parties.[9] O'Brien and Wood observe that Dalton points "occur in quantities so large as to suggest that the mid-continent was well populated by the beginning of the ninth millennium B.C."[10] Archaeologists usually consider the Paleoindian period as ending about 9500 years B.P.

The early Archaic cultural period represents a transition from the Paleoindian during the Hypsithermal period. During the Hypsithermal, the climate warmed and became drier. Evidence from pollen studies suggests spreading of prairie grasses in response to the drier climate. Warming reached its maximum between 7,500 and 5,000 years B.P. Dan and Phyllis Morse note that classic Dalton points, a characteristic point of the late Paleoindian period, "ceased being made some time between 9,000 and 7500 B.P."[11] The type of points manufactured evolved throughout the Archaic period. O'Brien and Wood note a change "to a host of notched forms and at least one stemmed form, the ubiquitous Hardin barbed point."[12] Much of this change is attributable to a change in the animals hunted. The need for the very large spear points used in hunting the large Pleistocene mammals diminished as smaller species such as deer, raccoon, and rabbits replaced them. According to O'Brien and Wood, archaeological evidence indicates that the Early Archaic people lived in "small groups who pursued a generalist foraging strategy."[13] Dan and Phyllis Morse believe that during

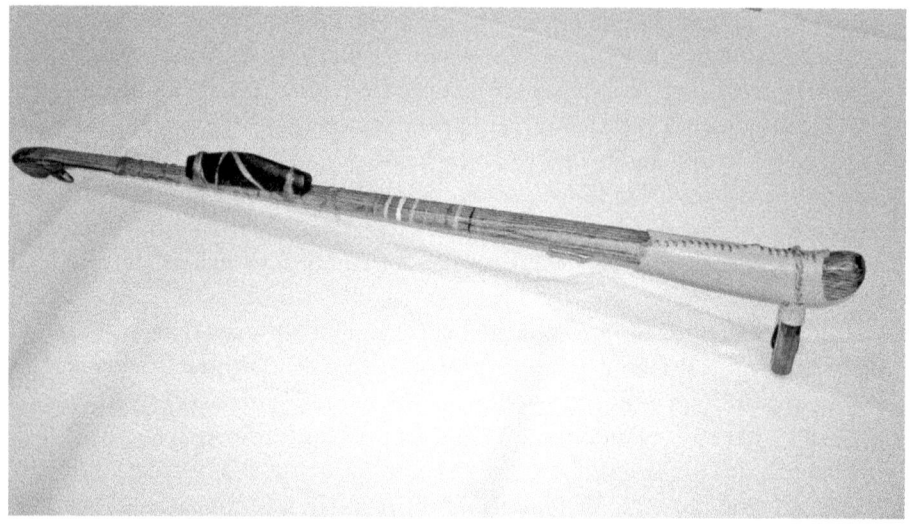

Modern-day atlatl. Notice the stone tied to it. Archaeologists believe that bannerstones first found in Archaic sites were used as atlatl weights. The atlatl increases the force and accuracy of a spear. The atlatl is used by some hunters to take deer during Missouri's archery season (photograph by the author).

the Hypsithermal in the central Mississippi valley region most of the human population concentrated in the Ozark uplands rather than the lowlands. However, following the Hypsithermal the population and permanent camps significantly increased in the lowlands based the number of Late Archaic remains found.[14]

The human population expanded and greatly increased during the Late Archaic Period (5000 years B.P. to 2700 years B.P.), particularly in the southeast Missouri lowlands. In addition to spear points and blades, the Archaic people manufactured a variety of other stone pieces. These include adzes, celts, grooved axes, beads, and bannerstones. Archaic people apparently used bannerstones, polished stones with a hole drilled through them, as atlatl weights. Bannerstones occur in a variety of shapes and some even have effigy figures of animals carved on them. The atlatl or spear thrower increased the force and accuracy of a spear and became the major weapon for both Archaic and Woodland cultures.[15] Because the atlatl and spears were made of wood, usually only the bannerstone and spear point is found in archaeological sites. Hunters today have begun to make and use atlatls for taking deer and other game.

The Woodland Period designates the next cultural period of North American Native populations. According to O'Brien and Wood, Early and

Middle Woodland sites in the southeast lowlands occur on the older braided stream deposits of the ancestral Mississippi and Ohio rivers or on relict point bars and levees related to more recent Mississippi River meandering.[16] Woodland Period sites occur throughout the southeast lowlands. Some of the important sites of this period include Weems and Burkett in Mississippi County and the Pascola site in Pemiscot County. The Old Varney River site in Dunklin County represents a late Woodland settlement. The Early and Middle Woodland, 2600 B.P. to 450 B.P., marks a time of major change in life style for Native Americans. During this time, agriculture, burial mounds, and pottery first appear. The manufacture of pottery ushered in a change in their way of cooking. Morse and Morse note that with the manufacture of pottery "a whole new cuisine would have been possible, with an emphasis on cooking of soups and stews."[17] The manufacture of pottery might also indicate groups becoming more tied to one location since pottery required and extended amount of time to produce and transporting pots would be difficult.

Early to Middle Woodland pottery typically exhibits decorations and cord marks. The Woodland people used easily obtainable backswamp clay for making their pottery. This clay however has a high rate of shrinkage when it dries thus requires the addition of some material to temper the clay so that it will not crack as the piece dried. During the Woodland period, pottery makers used primarily sand to mix with the clay to reduce shrinkage. Sand would have been readily available from the braided stream terrace surfaces in the lowlands. Cord marking, characteristic of Woodland pottery, was accomplished by using a cord wrapped wooden paddle. Archaeologists suggest that the cord marks may have been added to keep the jars from slipping through the hands when handled.[18] Following what was a long drying process, Woodland Period pottery makers fired their pieces in shallow pits containing wood coals. The style of markings and decorations used on pottery evolved with time and serve as good chronological markers when studying this period.

Evidence such as discoveries at a site in Benton County, Missouri, suggests that Late Archaic people began cultivating plants. At this site archaeologists found wooden digging sticks and seeds of squash.[19] Woodland Period people greatly expanded the use of cultivated plants. Plants cultivated and making an important part of the diet during the Woodland Period included goosefoot or lambsquarter (*Chenopodium sp.*), little barley, maygrass, knotweed, marsh elder, sunflower, and squash.[20] In addition to these plants, they also made use of seasonal wild fruits and nuts such as plum, blackberry, walnut, pecan, and hickory. Cultivation of corn may have

Saul's Mound in the Pinson Mounds complex near Jackson, Tennessee, just east of the southeast Missouri lowlands. This Middle Woodland mound is 72 feet tall and may have been used for observation of the summer solstice and equinox (photograph by the author).

begun during the late Woodland time but it does not appear to have been a major part of the diet.[21]

Mound building became a part of the culture by the Middle Woodland time. Mounds were used for both ceremonial and burial purposes. Robert C. Mainfort notes that some mound complexes although covering several acres did not support a large population, rather they "appear to have served as a location where people from many different groups or over large areas came together to participate in collective ceremonies."[22] The Pinson Mounds in west Tennessee are an example of this type of mound complex. O'Brien and Wood observe that some Middle Woodland mounds contain log-lined or log roofed burial chambers.[23]

The bow and arrow appears to have come into use during the Late Woodland period based the increase in the number of projectile points small enough to be used on an arrow. By about A.D. 750, the bow may have replaced the atlatl and spear as the primary weapon. Although, the change most likely took place gradually and may not have occurred in all areas at the same time.[24]

The Hoecake Site, located in the Cairo Lowland in Mississippi County, contains artifacts of both the Late Woodland and Early Mississippian periods. Before destruction by land leveling, the site has been estimated to have contained between 31 and 54 mounds and perhaps covered as much as 200 acres and is believed to have been a large community for a period of 500 to 600 years. Houses excavated at Hoecake measured between 10.5 and 14.5 feet in length and 6.5 and 9.5 feet in width. While archaeologist discovered a few burials near houses, most burials at the site were located in what is referred to as Story Mound I. Two other important southeast Missouri Late Woodland sites are located in the Little River Lowland. One is the Double Bridges site found in New Madrid County and the other is the Kersey site located in south-central Pemiscot County.[25]

The Mississippian Period (A.D. 900 to historic contact) begins a time of important changes in the lifestyle and land utilization by the first inhabitants of the southeast lowlands. They left important marks on the landscape of the central Mississippi valley and southeast Missouri lowlands in the form of earthen mounds and numerous artifacts of pottery and stone tools. Archaeologist J.E. Kelley lists five characteristics that define what is meant by the Mississippian Period: "1. Dramatic changes in technology and material culture, 2. A shift to maize-dominated field agriculture, 3. Interregional exchange, 4. An increase in the size and organization of sociopolitical units, 5. A marked increase in social differentiation."[26]

Other archaeologists would add to that list the manufacture of shell-tempered pottery. The use of the ground up shells of mollusks to temper pottery instead of sand often is considered a marker for the beginning of the Mississippian Period.[27] Although, there may have been a transition from sand-temper to shell-temper during the late Woodland Period as suggested by evidence from the Old Varney River site in Dunklin County.[28] Debate has also centered on whether the Mississippians represented a new group moving in to displace the Woodland people or whether they were simply the same inhabitants changing their culture over time. Archaeologists subdivide the Mississippian period into three categories, early, middle, and late although there are few hard and fast markers between these three as O'Brien and Wood note that the choice of beginning and ending dates for these subdivisions is really "an artifice of convenience."[29]

Archaeologists usually ascribe A.D. 900 as the beginning date for the Mississippian period and the time of historical contact as the ending date but as noted above, these dates are more for convenience than distinct markers. Sites such as Hoecake and Kersey exhibit pottery representative of both Late Woodland and Early Mississippian periods. However, the

Mississippian temple mound located at Towosahgy State Historic Site in Mississippi County. Such large central mounds in Mississippian sites were possibly used for ceremonial purposes, not for burials (photograph by the author).

archaeological record shows that after A.D. 900 the distribution of settlements changed in dramatic ways. Archaeologists use A.D. 1200 as the beginning point of the Middle Mississippian period. It is then that nucleation and fortification of settlements began. Mississippian builders accomplished fortification by constructing a walled palisade of posts set vertically on top of an embankment around the perimeter of the village. Usually a ditch or trench encircled the exterior of the wall. Small scattered villages began to merge into larger population centers.[30] Cahokia, situated on the Mississippi River floodplain just east of St. Louis and less than 200 miles north of the southeast Missouri lowlands, is the best known example of this nucleated and fortified town. Between A.D. 1100 and 1200 as many as 20,000 people may have lived in an enclosed city covering nearly six square miles.

Anthropologist Robbie Ethridge believes that a political system referred to as the chiefdom was the primary form of government for Mississippian settlements. Ethridge defines the chiefdom as "a political order with basically two social ranks determined by kinship affiliations: ruling elite lineages and non elite lineages. Generally speaking, the members of the chiefly lineage were considered related to supernatural beings, which gave them religious

Many Mississippian sites were enclosed with fortified walls. These posts show the location of part of the fortification wall at Towosaghy State Historic Site in Mississippi County (photograph by the author).

sanction for their status, prestige, and political authority."[31] The peak of this process of nucleation and fortification occurred around A.D. 1300 to 1350 after which residents abandoned these large population centers and smaller settlements as well. Archaeologists refer to this large-scale abandonment of areas in the Ohio and Mississippi valleys as the Vacant Quarter.

Three fortified sites in the southeast lowlands that have been well studied include Power's Fort in Butler County, Lilbourn in New Madrid County, and Beckwith's Fort in Mississippi County. The latter location is now known as Towosaghy State Historic Site. The fortified settlements consisted of houses built with wattle and daub construction and mounds for ceremonial and burial use. However, not all burials were made in mounds and many mounds contain no burials. Archaeologists generally believe that smaller villages and individual farmsteads surrounded each fortified center thus producing a hierarchy of settlements.[32]

The Middle Mississippian time brought an increase in population and the number of settlements and also an increase in their dependency on agriculture, especially corn for food. The size of the area cultivated expanded with the development of larger nucleated settlements. Instead of growing garden-sized plots, they began cultivating larger fields. The easily tilled alluvial soils of the southeast lowlands proved ideal for the Mississippian farmers. Besides corn they also grew beans and squash. Fish, turtles, frogs, and mussels along with deer, rabbit, squirrel, raccoon, muskrat, beaver, and waterfowl contributed to their diet. As the population grew and became more concentrated in fortified centers, the dependence on cultivated crops, especially corn grew which made the food supply more susceptible to disruption by changing weather patterns.

A study of their pottery reveals much about the life of the Middle and Late Mississippian people. Pottery makers depicted a variety of animals on their pottery. Some vessels represent human figures. In some cases the shape of a human head may form the top of a water bottle while in others the whole container may be shaped like a human head. Archaeologists refer to these as head pots. Such ceramics show hairstyles and facial decorations.[33] Archaeologists have identified several different types of pottery based on construction and painting and decoration of the individual pieces. The types and forms of pottery and the manner of its decoration became increasingly complex into the Late Mississippian time.

In addition to the Madison and Nodena projectile points found widely on Mississippian sites in southeast Missouri, other stone artifacts such as chert blades, celts, discoidals and chert hoes. Because of their dependence on field agriculture, chert hoes are particularly characteristic of the middle and late Mississippian time. These artifacts are invariably made from either Mill Creek which is found in southern Illinois or Dover Chert occurring in northwestern Tennessee. Archaeologist Charles R. Cobb notes that "the most common and widely exchanged stone hoes during the Mississippi period were manufactured from Mill Creek chert." He further observes that "the ubiquity of hoes and hoe fragments made from this distinctive chert makes these artifacts almost as much a defining characteristic of Mississippian as such traditional criteria as wall trench structures and shell-tempered pottery."[34] Archaeologists generally believe that the hoes were traded as a finished product. Hoes made from Dover Chert appear to be chronologically later, becoming the dominant type after A.D 1350.[35]

One intensely debated issue related to the Late Mississippian period has been the abandonment of the large fortified centers after 1350 particularly in the Cairo Lowland. Morse and Morse propose than rather that disappearing, the population "shifted into the meander belt areas of the Mississippi and St. Francis rivers, Little River-Pemiscot Bayou crevasse channel of the Mississippi, and the alluvial soils of the White River."[36] O'Brien and Wood conclude that "the archaeological record for the Cairo

Lowland and the Western Lowlands clearly indicates that ca. A.D. 1350–1375 many if not all of the large fortified centers were either abandoned or witnessed significant declines in population. In addition it appears that many of the smaller communities peripheral to the centers also were abandoned."[37] The reasons for this abandonment remain murky. Some suggestions include a decline in health resulting from over dependence on corn, other diseases, or a change in weather patterns resulting in corn cop failures making it difficult to support concentrated populations thus a reversion to more dispersed tribes.

Late Mississippian occupation in southeast Missouri is concentrated along the Pemiscot Bayou. O'Brien and Wood discuss six southeastern Missouri sites, Campbell, Brooks, Berry, Cagle Lake, Denton Mounds, and Murphy which represent the last prehistoric settlement prior to historic contact with the Spanish in the 1500s.[38] A study of skeletons from several of the Pemiscot Bayou sites has revealed details about the life and health of the region's early residents. The average individual appears to have lived to about 30 years. Dental studies reveal a high incidence of caries indicating a diet utilizing large amounts of corn. Skeletons also displayed a high incidence of cribra orbitalia.[39] This condition produces spongy, porous bone in the roof of orbits in the cranium. Cribra orbitalia has complex causes but is considered by anthropologists to be a marker of stress in prehistoric populations. It is related to a type of anemia which causes the body to try to compensate for a loss of red blood cells resulting in hypertrophy of bone marrow. One major factor in producing this disorder is multiple nutritional deficiencies.[40] Other conditions that may contribute to cribra orbitalia include, infectious diseases, especially gastro-intestinal infections, parasites, and even traumatic injury.[41]

It can be concluded that these Late Mississippian dwellers in the southeast Missouri lowlands depended heavily on corn for sustenance but this over reliance on the carbohydrate and calorie rich corn resulted in nutritional deficiencies affecting the health of the population. A lack of animal protein in the diet can lead to vitamin B_{12} deficiencies, particularly in children.[42] Concentrated populations must rely more heavily on plant agriculture because animal resources in a given area may be over used and their population reduced. The animal protein utilized would have included fish and other animals living in or near waterways since they lived on or in close proximity to abandoned Mississippi River channels. Despite obvious nutritional deficiencies, O'Brien concludes that overall, based on currently available evidence, "the populations appear to have been in good health."[43]

Artifacts of Spanish origin occur in some of the Pemiscot Bayou sites, especially the Campbell and Brooks sites. Whether these residents acquired the articles through direct contact with the Spanish or through trading with other indigenous groups can't be established with certainty. Between 1540 and 1543 the de Soto expedition explored what was to become the southeastern United States. They reached northeast Arkansas in 1541, encountering several Native American groups there. Journals written by members of the expedition have provided important information about these groups including the names or at least the Spanish interpretation the Indian names of towns and chiefs. Spanish items discovered there and journal descriptions point to the Parkin Site as the location of the town of Casqui where the chief of the same name lived. De Soto died of illness in 1542. Members of his expedition sank his body in the Mississippi River to avoid its discovery by the Indians. Following de Soto's death, the remaining members of his force wandered for a time trying to find an overland route to Mexico before returning to the Mississippi River and traveling southward to the Gulf of Mexico. Although stories persist of his expedition traveling into Missouri, historians generally doubt that they ventured north of Arkansas.[44]

Following departure of the de Soto expedition in 1543 we have no further record of European contact with native populations in the middle Mississippi valley until Jacques Marquette and Louis Joilet make their voyage down the Mississippi in 1673. Archaeologists have long debated the connections between the Mississippian people and historic Indian tribes such as the Osage, Quapaw, and Chickasaw encountered by Marquette and Joilet and other European explorers. By the end of the 1400s large areas of the Mississippi Valley appear to have become depopulated, a part of what has been referred to as the Vacant Quarter. Ethridge notes that early French expeditions down the Mississippi River "found the region between the Missouri River and north of present-day Memphis thinly populated."[45] O'Brien and Wood observe that some Osage legends claim their ancestors originated in the central Mississippi valley and moved westward.[46] Historian Louis F. Burns references the disagreement about Osage origins but believes the evidence points to areas east of the Mississippi River as their area of origin, especially the Ohio River valley. The Osage, Quapaw, Ponca, Omaha, and Kansas all have a similar Dhegiha Sioux language. Quapaw legend suggests that they also moved from the Ohio River valley down the Mississippi through southeast Missouri and eventually settling in the vicinity of the confluence of the Arkansas and the Mississippi rivers.[47]

Other historic tribes with a significant presence in the southeast lowlands included the Shawnee and Delaware who had been pushed westward from their original homelands in the East. In 1787, during the time of Spanish control of Missouri, the Spanish government asked Louis Lorimer to bring members of the Shawnee and Delaware tribes from the Ohio valley to the west side of the Mississippi River to serve as a buffer to the Osages to the west, living primarily in the Ozarks, who made frequent attacks on settlers and as a deterrent to American encroachment from the east. While the greatest concentration of these two tribes settled between Ste. Genevieve and Cape Girardeau, others dispersed throughout the lowlands where they engaged in fur trade.[48] In Stoddard County, the Shawnee located a village on Castor River and the Delaware had a settlement near present day Bloomfield. A group of Delawares under Chief Chilliticaux settled at the present site of Kennett in Dunklin County. A legend about Chief Chilliticaux is part of the oral folklore tradition in Dunklin County. According to the folklore, Chilliticaux chose Kennett as the site for his village because he believed it would not be destroyed by strong storms. He supposedly referred to the area as "land of the dividing winds," meaning that storms would pass either to the north or south of his village. The Indians most often encountered by Euro-American settlers in southeast Missouri lowlands were members of one of these two tribes.

It is these indigenous people who for thousands of years before Euro-American settlers arrived, hunted game, cut timber, tilled the soil, and grew crops in the southeast Missouri lowlands. Historian Robert Sidney Douglass makes what is an excellent summary of the first inhabitants of the southeast Missouri lowlands although he wrote in 1912, an era when sensitivity to Native American issues was not a high priority.

> Most of those now living with the borders of the state never saw an Indian in his native haunts, and cannot reconstruct the life of the time when he formed an important part in the making of the history of the country. And yet we cannot give more than mere casual attention to the story of the development of Southeast Missouri, without discovering that the Indian once played a great part here. He has left ineffaceable traces of his life, and no one can ever hope to come to a complete understanding of our history without a study of Indian life and character.[49]

Chapter 3

Euro-American Settlement to 1811

Jesuit priest Jacques Marquette and trader Louis Joliet were probably the first Europeans to see the area of the southeast Missouri lowlands when they made their trip down the Mississippi River as far as its confluence with the Arkansas in 1673. In 1682, La Salle traveled down the Mississippi all the way to the Gulf of Mexico and claimed the entire region on both sides of the Mississippi and its tributaries for France, naming the territory Louisiana in honor of Louis XIV. The stage was then set for French control and settlement of the region that became Missouri. The French developed an active trade in furs and hides with the Indians and built settlements, first at Ste. Genevieve and a few years later at St. Louis. In addition to fur trade, French settlers also engaged in agriculture and mining.

At the conclusion of the French and Indian War in 1763, France ceded its North American territory east of the Mississippi River to England. In a separate treaty, France allowed Spain to take possession of all of its holdings west of the Mississippi River. This prompted many French settlers east of the Mississippi to relocate to the west side, believing that conditions for them would be better under Spanish rule than English. Even under Spanish control, the culture of what was to become Missouri remained decidedly French. The Spanish exerted minimal cultural influence on the region since Spain did not seek to settle the area with colonists from Spain, and most Spanish residents were in service of their government for a given period of time, after which they returned to Spain. To administer its new territory, Spain created five districts: St. Charles, St. Louis, Ste. Genevieve, Cape Girardeau, and New Madrid.

French-Canadian trappers and traders Francois and Joseph Lesieur, employees of Gabriel Cerrè of St. Louis, made the first European settlement in the southeast Missouri lowlands when they built a trading post a few miles north of present day New Madrid near the mouth of Chepoosa River which later became known as St. John's Bayou at a location known as "L'Anse a la Graisse" which translates "Greasy Cove" or " Greasy Bend."[1] The location was so-named because it was a favorite spot for Indian hunting parties to boil down bear and bison grease for cooking.[2] While 1783 has been the traditional date given of the Lesieurs' settlement, it appears that it was possibly a few years later that a more permanent settlement was made. Peter LaForge in a 1796 letter written to New Madrid commandant Charles Dehault Delassus states: "Some traders in pursuit of gain came to L'Anse a la Graisse, a rendezvous or gathering place of several Indian nations.... A first year of success induced them to try a second and to this others. Some of them determined to establish their homes where they found a sure trade and unlimited advantages"[3] LaForge's wording seems to suggest that trading was carried out only seasonally at L'Anse a la Graisse initially then the traders made a more permanent settlement there.

Robert McCay (McCoy), who served the Spanish government before the Louisiana Purchase, testified before the General Land Office commissioners that he passed by the area that became New Madrid en route from Vincennes to New Orleans in December 1786 and found "there was not any person living there, it being a perfect wilderness." He continued that when he returned in the spring of 1787 "there were about twelve persons living on the spot where the village now stands, being employed in trading with the Indians; among the number was Joseph Lesieur."[4]

The Lesieurs had much success in trading with the Delaware and Shawnee Indians in the region and apparently made a good choice in the location of their trading post. Reuben Gold Thwaites adds an editorial note on page 282 of *Early Western Travels 1748–1846* stating that "New Madrid was originally the site of a Delaware Indian town."[5] About 1794 Francois Lesieur moved a few miles south of New Madrid and founded another trading post that became known as Little Prairie near the current location of Caruthersville.[6] Fortescue Cuming described Little Prairie in 1807 as "containing twenty-four low houses and cabins, scattered on a fine and pleasant plain inhabited chiefly by French Creoles from Canada and Illinois." Cuming went on to report what he learned about other inhabitants of the area: "We were informed that there were several Anglo-American farmers all round in a circle of ten miles."[7] The 1811–1812 earthquakes destroyed the small settlement of Little Prairie, after which Francois Lesieur established his trading business at Point Pleasant which is on the Mississippi River east of present day Portageville.

Real settlement of New Madrid and the surrounding area began with George Morgan's plan to establish an American colony near L'Anse a la Graisse. Morgan, at one time a Revolutionary War officer, an Indian agent in the vicinity of Fort Pitt, a trader, and a land speculator, had been involved in several land schemes. One of Morgan's early business enterprises took him to the Illinois Country as a partner of the firm of Baynton, Wharton, and Morgan to engage in the fur trade. Following their failure in this effort, the firm became part of what was known as the Indiana Project. This involved a large tract of Indian land in what became West Virginia ceded by several Native American tribes following what is referred to as Pontiac's War. Virginia also claimed this land and a long legal battle ensued in Congress. Following Virginia's cessation in 1784 of its claims to land lying west of the Ohio River, Morgan and his partners lost any hope of turning a profit from the Indiana Project. Morgan then turned his attentions toward Spanish Louisiana.[8]

Following the Revolutionary War, Spain had concerns that the United States might have aspirations to encroach on their Louisiana colony located on the west side of the Mississippi River. Their ambassador, Diego de Gardoqui had two goals: make trading concessions within its holdings elsewhere in the world to the United States in exchange for the United States' acceptance of keeping the Mississippi River closed to free trade and according to historian Max Savelle "alienate the Americans of the West from the United States."[9] To achieve the second goal, Gardoqui conveyed to Morgan that he (Gardoqui) would welcome a proposal for a land grant in Louisiana. Another factor which Spain hoped to exploit was the frustration of Kentuckians with the United States over its inability to secure access to the Mississippi River for shipment of its products to New Orleans which would be much less costly than shipping overland to the east. At the same time Gardouqi was making overtures to Morgan, James Wilkinson, a brevet brigadier general in the army during the Revolutionary War, was in contact with the Spanish governor of Louisiana, Miró, about the possibility of Kentucky leaving the United States and becoming a part of Louisiana in order to gain navigation rights to the Mississippi River. Wilkinson had moved to Kentucky following the war where he involved himself in land speculation along with politics and other businesses.[10]

Morgan quickly responded to Gardoqui by laying out his plan for a colony near the mouth of the Ohio River. Gardoqui had a favorable reply then Morgan presented his plan in detail. Morgan requested a large tract from above the mouth of the Ohio River extending southward to the confluence of St. Francois River with the Mississippi. Morgan further wanted to be in command of the colony, have a body of representatives of the settlers, freedom of religion, and a division of the land grant into 320-acre plots to be sold at one-eighth dollar per acre to any settlers who might come. Gardoqui gave Morgan permission to find a suitable location and survey the land. Morgan appears to have been ahead of his time in city planning. His original plan for New Madrid designated tree lined streets, preservation of a natural lake in the center of the town, and the laying out of a 12-acre park. He further stipulated that no trees along any of the streets should be cut or injured.[11]

Morgan went even further than directed by Gardoqui. He began soliciting settlers to his colony before the plan had Spanish royal approval. Morgan circulated pamphlets promoting his plan and apparently had little trouble finding people interested in moving to his proposed colony. Coming down the Ohio River, Morgan and his party of 60 surveyors, potential settlers, and ten Indians reached the Mississippi in February 1789. They landed opposite the mouth of the Ohio at a Delaware Indian encampment. Morgan and part of his group headed toward St. Louis to meet with the commandant Manuel Perez, while the remainder accompanied the Indians to their camp on St. John's Bayou. Upon Morgan's return, the group decided on a location near L'Anse a la Graisse which Morgan named New Madrid.[12] Perez cordially received Morgan and provided him with guides, provisions, and supplies.[13]

This group spent the remainder of the winter building cabins and surveying for the town and farms. In the spring they began planting crops while in May, Morgan traveled to New Orleans to secure Governor Miro's approval of his plan.

In New Orleans, Morgan received a less than an enthusiastic response from Governor Miró about his planned colony. Miró had been influenced by Wilkinson's scheme to convince Kentuckians to leave the United States and become a part of the Spanish territories and differed with Gardouqi over the advantages of Morgan's plan.[14] Miró agreed to allow settlers to come in but would not permit any public worship other than Roman Catholic and would require an oath of allegiance to the Spanish king. Morgan wanted no restrictions on religion since he knew many of the Anglo-American settlers he would attract were not Catholic. However, Miró did agree to honor grants already made to those who had come with Morgan and to give Morgan 1,000 acres and an equal amount for each of his sons. He also offered Morgan the position of assistant commandant of New

Madrid.[15] Miró refused to give Morgan the size of land grant he requested and forbid that any land granted to him to be sold to new settlers, instead, it was to be given gratis to newcomers.

Morgan departed New Orleans in late June for Philadelphia. Despite his plan not receiving ratification by Governor Miró, Morgan continued to promote New Madrid. Soon after arriving in Philadelphia he published a pamphlet containing questions and answers relating to the soil, climate, vegetation and other conditions at New Madrid along with a testimonial letter from settlers at New Madrid, all providing a very glowing report on conditions there.[16] Morgan also sent a letter to Gardoqui detailing his trip to locate a settlement on the west bank of the Mississippi and his meeting with Miró. At that point, Morgan seemed willing to work under the conditions that Miró outlined.

Shortly after his letter to Gardoqui, Morgan apparently lost interest in the New Madrid project. It is not clear why, but about this time, Morgan's brother, Dr. John Morgan, died and left George in charge of his estate which was to be used by Dr. Morgan's children. The estate consisted of land in western Pennsylvania. Morgan also had hopes of reviving the case of the Indiana Company against the state of Virginia to recover the disputed land.[17]

For whatever reason, Morgan never returned to New Madrid, but his efforts did interest settlers in the possibility of moving to the west side of the Mississippi River in exchange for free land. Historian Louis Houck notes that Morgan's efforts "set in motion that stream of immigration which, a few years afterwards, began to move into Louisiana."[18] Historians differ on the fate of those first coming with Morgan to New Madrid. Houck writes that "they nearly all remained, or if they returned home up the Ohio, soon came back with others."[19] Savelle on the other hand suggests that "practically all those who had come with Morgan however, returned to their homes."[20] Additional settlers did come to New Madrid, mostly French and Creoles from Illinois and Vincennes.[21] A few Americans from Kentucky and Tennessee settled in the area however, until 1804, the French made up the majority of the inhabitants.

Governor Miró appointed Pierre Foucher as commandant at New Madrid. He followed basically the instructions that had been given to Morgan and informed the newcomers that they would not have to pay for land but would be required to take an oath of allegiance to Spain. Foucher brought a detachment of 30 soldiers to build a fort which they named Fort Céleste.[22]

The French and American settlers coming to southeast Missouri differed in their lifestyles. Here as elsewhere, the French tended to live in towns with gardens located behind their houses. They also preferred to hunt, fish, and trade with the Indians who came to New Madrid rather than farm. Americans, on the other hand, located on farms outside of town and came with the express purpose of growing crops to sell. Pierre LaForge writes Lieutenant Governor Delassus from New Madrid that "the creoles will never make this a flourishing settlement. It will be the Americans, Germans, and other active people who will reap the glory of it."[23]

By 1790, a small amount of corn was being grown, but not enough to make the area self-sufficient. Residents relied on supplies from Illinois and Kentucky and from Ste. Genevieve, farther up river. Supplies became especially short after the building of Fort San Fernando at the confluence of the Wolf and Mississippi rivers where Memphis, Tennessee, is now located. As the amount of game decreased, the Indians also moved farther west. LaForge notes that "the Indians removed themselves further off and were seldom here, the traders knew very well where to find them, but the inhabitants waited for them in vain."[24] This forced even the French inhabitants to look at farming as a means of subsistence. The first year that agriculture became a major occupation in the New Madrid region was 1796. LaForge writes, "It is in reality then only since the year 1796, that we may regard the inhabitants of this post as having engaged in cultivation."[25] This marked a gradual transition from trading and trapping as the primary economic activity to farming as the principal economic force driving settlement. While the population of New Madrid grew slowly in the late 1700s, the production of corn and other crops increased dramatically. LaForge reported that the production of corn at New Madrid almost tripled between 1794 and 1796.[26]

The Spanish government opened a road in 1789 that eventually stretched between New Madrid and St. Louis which was referred to as the El Camino Real (King's Highway). However, only the stretch from New Madrid to Ste. Genevieve was much used. Above Ste. Genevieve, most overland travelers preferred to cross the Mississippi River and travel on the east side of the river. A number of settlers received land grants from the Spanish authorities along the route of this road in the New Madrid District.

Spain returned Louisiana to France in 1800 and three years later France sold the territory to the United States. However, during the time between its return to France and purchase by the United States, France never actually took possession of Louisiana. It continued to be governed by Spanish officials.

The purchase of Louisiana by the United States opened the region around New Madrid to settlement by Americans. Even so, growth of New

Madrid and the surrounding area was slow. Major Amos Stoddard who represented the United States in ceremonies at St. Louis to receive the Louisiana Territory from France noted in his report on the newly acquired land that in the lowlands below Cape Girardeau, "The population of this tract in 1804 at 1350, including 150 slaves. About two thirds of the population is composed of English Americans; the other third of French. For three years commencing in 1800, the increase was only six persons."[27] The population of Louisiana in total showed a substantial increase between 1804 and 1810. Gradually, the French villages began to take on the look of American towns as the newcomers opened stores and built with different architectural styles. In 1808, an English language newspaper, the *Missouri Gazette*, opened in St. Louis and English began to replace French as the primary language.[28]

Growth in the New Madrid District was somewhat slower because the large tracts of swampland impeded east-west travel and gave rise to a rather negative picture of the region including its reputation as an unhealthy environment in which to live. Settlement was confined to sandy ridges within a few miles of the river. The complication of verifying Spanish land grants deterred others. The New Madrid earthquakes of 1811–1812 further slowed growth and development as did settlement of land claims resulting from the earthquakes. The earthquakes and earthquake land claims are discussed in detail in Chapter 4. By 1811, most of the southeast Missouri lowlands remained unsettled and little explored and abounded in wildlife. Travel through the interior of the Bootheel could best be accomplished using canoes to navigate the small rivers and streams through the swampland and making portages around low ridges.

Travelers through the area shortly after the Louisiana Purchase recorded their observations about the New Madrid area. Fortescue Cuming traveled through the area in 1808 and described New Madrid this way:

> New Madrid contains about a hundred houses, much scattered on a fine plain of two mile square, on which however the river has so encroached during the twenty-two years since it was first settled, that the bank is now half a mile behind its old bounds, and the inhabitants have had to remove repeatedly farther back. They are a mixture of French Creoles from Illinois, United States Americans, and Germans. They have plenty of cattle, but seem in other respects to be very poor. There is some trade with the Indian hunters for furs and peltry, but of little consequence.[29]

Spanish land grants made prior to the transfer of Louisiana to France in 1800 were generally honored, provided the requirement of Spanish law had been fulfilled, which often was not the case. The requirements for completion of a Spanish land grant required several steps. A settler received a grant by first making a petition to the commandant in the district where he wished to obtain land. This could be for a particular tract or any tract of the specified size that was vacant. Once approved by the commandant the petition was sent to the lieutenant governor in St. Louis who would order a survey. However, these surveys were seldom made. After the survey, the approved request and surveyor's report was to be taken to officials in the governor's office in New Orleans for final completion. Because of the expense and difficulty of travel at that time, in the majority of the cases this step was not taken.[30] Congress provided in 1805 for a claim of one square mile of land for any person who had made improvements on the land before 1804. Some settlers devised rather ingenious methods to substantiate their claims. Edwin James relates such a method he heard about while traveling with the Stephen Long expedition 1819-1820:

> A person, somewhere in the county of Cape Girardeau, being desirous of establishing a claim of this kind of tract of land, adopted the following method: The time having expired for the establishment of a right, agreeably to the spirit of the law, he took with him two witnesses to the favourite spot, on which he wished to establish his claim, and in their presence marked two trees, standing on opposite sides of the spring; one with the figures 1803, and the other 1804, and placed a stalk of growing corn in the spring. He then brought the witnesses before the commissioners, who upon their declaration, that they had seen corn growing at the place specified, in the Spring between 1803 and 1804, admitted the claim of the applicant, and gave him title to the land.[31]

As Cuming continued down the river, he saw one settlement below New Madrid, but no more until reaching Little Prairie. By this time, exploitation the vast timber resources of the Bootheel had already begun, as Cuming records seeing "five lumber loaded boats."[32]

Christian Schultz, a German, who visited the region in 1807 and 1808, described how the town appeared to him. "This town, which formerly, under the Spanish government, was protected by a fort and garrison, contains at present no more than thirty indifferent houses, including the chapel which is fast tumbling to pieces."[33] Schultz went on to discuss the economy and lifestyle of the inhabitants.

> They begin to raise considerable crops of cotton at New Madrid, but it always bears the lowest price, as its quality is much injured by the early frosts…. They raise corn and meat for their own consumption and never have any to sell. On the contrary, we were repeatedly solicited by them to spare a part of our stores. Land is worth two dollars an acre exclusive of improvements…. What few inhabitants there are seem to have very little intercourse with each other. The men mostly follow boating, and the women, during their absence, make out to raise a little corn to keep themselves alive until the return of their husbands, when they eat, drink and dance as long as their money lasts.[34]

Transportation of goods to and from the southeast Missouri lowlands required the use of boats on the Mississippi River. Traders employed three different types of craft for plying these waters. *Pirogues* were large dugouts adapted from the way Indians fashioned boats by hallowing out the trunks of large trees. This craft was long and narrow making it relatively easy to paddle against the current but was limited in the amount of cargo it could haul. The *bateau* was a large, heavy, flat bottom boat which could carry larger loads but was more difficult to steer and was particularly difficult to move upstream. However, with their flat bottom they could navigate relatively shallow water. Oars were the usual mean of propelling these boats. One oar was generally used in the rear as a rudder. Keelboats, another type of boat used for long distance river transportation, could be rowed or sometimes equipped with sails under the right conditions but was often pulled by men with ropes on the river bank or poled in shallow water. Having a keel made this boat easier to control and faster that the flatboats.

During the first few decades of the 1800s, the Indian fur trade continued to be an important part of the economy in the region along with agriculture. Robert Goah Watson came to New Madrid in 1805 from Detroit to operate a fur trading business owned by his uncle. Shortly before his death in 1855, he penned a memoir about his experiences in that business. This memoir provides helpful insights into the fur trade of that era in the Bootheel.

Watson operated a trade network bringing Indian trade goods from London through Canada to Detroit then to Vincennes and down the Ohio to the Mississippi then to New Madrid. Watson also brought supplies which he traded or sold to the French and American settlers at New Madrid. Furs were purchased from Indians through the winter months until March then sent by boat back to Detroit. Watson would also purchase various items of local produce and ship them to New Orleans by boat. Watson notes that although their skins were shipped by boat, the traders "generally followed their shipments of skins by land."[35] The trading business was fraught with dangers and difficulties. The hazards of navigating the rivers and facing inclement weather always proved challenging but in addition, there were those who wanted to buy a trader's goods with counterfeit money and the rivers harbored robbers or pirates as well. Watson writes that "not a day from 1809 to 1815 but some innocent man, the owner of some flat boat loaded with produce had been imposed on by some of this call by purchasing of them for money, which they called good, and on good solvent banks, when in fact it was nothing but the basest kind of counterfeit money."[36] Watson also relates how his boat was pursued for two days by robbers intent on taking the money he had from selling produce in New Orleans. Fortunately, the pursuers were never able to over take Watson.[37]

Flatboats were the primary means of moving supplies and trade goods up and down the Mississippi River before the steamboat era. They were sometimes subject to attacks by river pirates (*One Hundred Years of Progress of the United States*, Hartford, CT: L. Stebbins, 1872).

Sometimes the outlaws were apprehended. New Madrid was the site of the trial of the leader one of the most notorious river pirate gangs of this era, Samuel Mason. Mason and his gang stayed at Cave-In-Rock, Illinois, on the Ohio River for a time and then committed robberies up and down the Mississippi River. Mason, his family, and other gang members rented a house at Little Prairie and were captured there by Robert McCoy (McCay) in January 1803 who was commander of the Spanish boats patrolling the Mississippi around New Madrid. Mason and fellow gang members were taken to New Madrid where they were tried by the commandant then sent to the governor in New Orleans. The Spanish governor ordered the gang to be turned over to American authorities. While on their way to Jackson, Mississippi, the Mason gang escaped from McCoy. They were later captured after Mason's gang members had killed him for the reward offered. Two gang members were tried and hung in Mississippi.[38]

By 1811, the southeast Missouri lowlands had been under governance of the United States less than a decade. While it possessed valuable timber, good farmland, and abundant wildlife, its growth was slow primarily because the vast areas of swampland made travel to its interior difficult. Geography dictated the location of most settlements. Settlers were scattered on farms received through Spanish land grants along or within a few miles of the Mississippi River. Settlers chose sites on the higher sandy ridges for their homes and farms because these areas were less prone to flooding. Some settlements such as New Madrid and Point Pleasant were placed too near the banks of the Mississippi River and those had to constantly be moved back to escape the bank eroding forces of the river.

Extending from New Madrid southward to Little Prairie, four other settlements existed in what would become Pemiscot County. One of these, Gayoso, became the county seat of Pemiscot County for a time. Others were located on Little River, Big Lake, and Portage Bay. North of New Madrid, settlements were located on what was referred to as Big Prairie, a part of the Sikeston Ridge, which extends to about the present location of Sikeston. Settlers also located on the west bank of the Mississippi opposite its confluence with the Ohio at what is now referred to as Bird's Point. This portion of the lowlands from Bird's Point to Commerce at the edge of Crowley's Ridge was called Tywappity Bottoms. Settlers may have been in this area as early as 1789.[39] A settlement existed in the 1790s near the present location of Portageville. This was the farthest inland a settlement existed at that time. The settlement was on Portage Bay which Houck describes. "Here canoes and pirogues, came up the St. Francois and Little Rivers through Portage Bay, and cargoes, were carried across the land to waters connecting with the Mississippi."[40] Settlement and development were to be further interrupted as a series of devastating earthquakes loomed in the near future which would severely damage many of the settlements and cause significant changes to the land and waterways.

CHAPTER 4

The New Madrid Earthquakes

The complex subsurface geological structures of southeast Missouri have produced numerous earthquakes, both historic and prehistoric. The most notable historically were the New Madrid earthquakes occurring in the winter of 1811 and the spring of 1812. This series of earthquakes not only brought important changes to the landscape of the southeast Missouri lowlands but their effects reached more distant areas. Church bells rang in Charleston, South Carolina, and Boston, Massachusetts. Cracked pavement and plaster occurred in other distant areas such as Richmond, Virginia, Washington, D.C., and Norfolk, Virginia. The shaking stopped clocks and rattled crockery in New Orleans.[1] It has been estimated that the earthquakes were felt over an area of 1,000,000 square miles.[2]

On December 6, 1811, at approximately 2 a.m., the first of a series of severe earthquakes began which continued shaking southeast Missouri until February 1812. Arch Johnston and Eugene Schweig of the Center for Earthquake Research and information at the University of Memphis, Schweig now with the United States Geological Survey, state that "the sequence included at least six and (possibly nine) events of estimated moment magnitude M ≥ 7 and two of M ≈ 8." They further state that "the two largest probably exceeded the size of any continental western US earthquake."[3] Since there were no instruments in the area and the Richter scale for measuring earthquake magnitudes was many years in the future, estimates of the strength have been determined from descriptions of observers present in the region and effects on the landscape studied later.

Numerous accounts of observers in the area at the time of the quakes and others visiting the area shortly afterwards attest to their severity and damage. A few quotes from some of the eyewitnesses help to illustrate the destructiveness of these earthquakes. Eliza Bryan, a resident of New Madrid, wrote an account of her experiences to Methodist minister Lorenzo Dow in 1816. This is perhaps the most quoted of the first-hand accounts of the earthquakes. She describes the confusion caused by the earthquakes this way:

> On the 16th of December 1811, about two o'clock, A.M. we were visited by a violent shock of an earthquake, accompanied by a very awful noise resembling loud but distant thunder, but more hoarse and vibrating, which was followed in a few minutes by the complete saturation of the atmosphere, with sulphurious vapor, causing total darkness. The screams of the affrighted inhabitants running to and fro, not knowing where to go, or what to do—the cries of the fowls and beasts of every species—the cracking of trees falling, and the roaring of the Mississippi—the current of which was retrograde for a few minutes, owing as is supposed, to an irruption in its bed formed a scene truly horrible.[4]

Bryan also provides a chronology of the events. The first occurring about 2 a.m. followed by lighter shocks "until about sunrise ... at which time one still more violent than the first took place." She notes that several lighter shocks were felt but on "the 23rd of January, 1812 ... one occurred as violent as the severest of the former ones, accompanied by the same phenomena as the former." She observes that from then "until the 4th of February the earth was in continual agitation, visibly waving as a gentle sea." On February 4 "there was another shock, nearly as hard as the preceding ones. Next day four such, and on the 7th about 4 o'clock, A.M., a concussion took place so much more violent than those which had preceded it, that it was denominated the hard shock."[5]

Bryan goes on to describe the effects of the shocks on the land. "In all the hard shocks mentioned, the earth was horribly torn to pieces—the surface of hundreds of acres, was, from time to time, covered over, of various depths, by the sand which issued from the fissures, which were made in great numbers all over this country, some of which closed up immediately after they had vomited forth their sand and water, which it must be remarked, was the matter generally thrown up. In some places, however, there was a substance somewhat resembling coal, or impure stone coal, thrown up with the sand."[6]

John Bradbury, a British scientist, published an earthquake account in his *Travels in the Interior of America in the years 1809, 1810, and 1811*. Bradbury was traveling down the Mississippi near New Madrid in December 1811 when the first of the quakes struck. He described one of the shocks experienced on the river this way: "The trees on both sides of the river were most violently agitated and the banks fell in, in several places, within our view, carrying with them innumerable trees, the crash of which falling into the river, mixed with the terrible sound attending the shock, and the screaming of the geese, and other wild-fowl, produced an idea that all nature was in the state of dissolution."[7]

Colonel John Shaw from Wisconsin was staying 30 miles north of New Madrid on the night of the first shock. He chronicled changes in the landscape: "The timber land around New Madrid sunk five or six feet, so that the lakes and lagoons, which seemed to have their bed pushed up, discharged their waters over the sunken lands. Through the fissures caused by the earthquake, were forced up vast quantities of hard, jet black substance, which appeared very smooth, as though worn by friction. It seemed a very different substance from either anthracite or bituminous coal."[8]

The earthquakes so frightened residents of the area that they quickly fled their immediate vicinity although this gave little protection since the earthquakes affected such a large area. Shaw recounts, "a young woman about seventeen years of age named Betsey Masters had been left by her parents and family, her leg having been broken below the knee by the falling of the weight-poles of the roof of the cabin." Shaw located Masters and "cooked up some food for her, and made her condition as comfortable as circumstance would allow." Shaw further noted that "in abandoning homes, on this emergency, the people only stopped long enough to get their teams, and hurry in their families and some provisions. It was a matter of doubt among them, whether water or fire would be most likely to burst forth, and cover all the country."[9]

Zadok Cramer, author of *The Navigator*, which provided information about the navigation of numerous rivers in the United States including the Mississippi, notes in the 1817 edition changes to the Mississippi River brought about by the earthquakes: "The island [island number 10] and the right bank opposite it, shew the first evident marks of the effects of the earthquake which commenced December 16, 1811. The right bank for several miles above and below the island, appears to be several feet, about three or four, as near as I could judge from the adjoining land, lower than it formerly was. Many of the trees standing in all directions on the island, and particularly the willows on the willow point opposite it, clearly evince the concussion of the earth."[10]

Mathias Speed was in charge of two flatboats carrying cargo down the Mississippi River in February and experienced the earthquakes occurring then including waterfalls in the river. His account was published in the *Bardstown Repository* newspaper in March of 1812. Mathias and his crew were awakened at 3 a.m. on the seventh to "the violent agitation of the boat, attended with a noise more tremendous and terrific than I can describe or any one conceive." The group discovered that the island (Island No. 9) where they were tied up was sinking. They rowed to the middle of the river "to be out of danger from the trees, which were falling in from the banks—the swells in the river were so great as to threaten the sinking of the boat every moment."[11]

Speed and his crew experienced difficulty in covering any distance on the river because of its retrograde current. Eventually they reached Island No. 10 and "took the right hand channel of the river ... and reached within about half a mile of the lower end of the town [New Madrid] we were affrighted with the appearance of a dreadful rapid or falls in the river just below us, we were so far in the suck that it was impossible now to land." Speed and his crew navigated over the falls then tied up at New Madrid. Speed learned from other boatmen that other falls were present in the river below New Madrid. He found New Madrid deserted with most of the buildings in ruins and that the town had sunk. Speed returned northward by land and described what he saw: "I found the surface of the earth for 10 or 12 miles cracked in numberless places, running in different directions—some of which were bridged and some filled up with logs to make them passable; others were so wide that they were obliged to be surrounded; in some of those cracks the earth sunk on one side from the level to the distance of five feet, and from one to three feet there was water in most of them." Speed also noted that "the inhabitants had generally left their dwellings and gone to the higher grounds."[12]

The eyewitnesses describe a horrific scene during the earthquakes which frightened most residents into fleeing their homes. Below New Madrid total destruction befell the small settlement of Little Prairie. James Fletcher, a resident of Little Prairie, wrote a letter January 21, 1812, from Nashville to the *Pittsburgh Gazette*. In this letter he writes that "on the 16th of December last, about 2 o'clock, A.M., we felt a severe concussion of the earth ... about sunrise another severe one came on, attended with a perpendicular bouncing that caused the earth to open in many places—some eight to ten feet wide." Fletcher also noted that in some areas "a beautiful white sand" had been blown out of openings in the earth.[13] Daniel Bedinger and a Dr. Foster were passengers on the barge *Louisville*. Excerpts from Bedinger's journal were published in the Washington, D.C., *National Intelligencer*, March 14, 1812. They experienced a powerful shock around 2 a.m. on December 16, another at 8 and a third at 10. Desiring to know what happened at Little Prairie, Bedinger and Dr. Foster took a smaller boat and attempted to land but "found it altogether unsafe to attempt a landing as the banks were all broken to pieces and huge masses were, at short intervals tumbling into the river."

"They however called aloud and were answered by a black man, who shewed himself at some distance off. From him they understood that all the inhabitants but himself had that morning, in the utmost consternation, fled into the country to the westward of the village."[14] Ultimately, Little Prairie was destroyed and the site is now under the Mississippi River.

The information contained in the eyewitness accounts quoted here along with others, indicates that the 1811–1812 earthquakes brought significant changes to the landscape of the Bootheel. The first organized study of these earthquakes did not occur until 1912 when Myron L. Fuller published his report of field investigations in the form of U.S. Geological Survey Bulletin 494. Several distinct features produced by the earthquakes were identified by Fuller and later investigators. These include landslides, uplifts, sunk lands, sand blows, and fissures. Johnston and Schweig note that "the most extensive and dramatic present-day evidence that survives from the 1811–1812 ruptures is not the current seismicity but the sandblow and fissure liquefaction features preserved in the alluvial soils of the upper Mississippi Embayment."[15]

Liquefaction caused by the 1811–1812 New Madrid earthquakes was the major cause of damage at that time in the southeast Missouri lowlands. The same would be true of potential future earthquakes. During liquefaction, energy from the earthquake increases the pressure on water in the pore spaces of unconsolidated sediments saturated with water, particularly sands and silts. This pressure forces the particles apart so they are no longer in contact with one another and thus lose their ability to support the weight of structures and causing the sediments to behave as a liquid. Liquefaction requires soils saturated with water, making the southeast lowlands with its thick alluvial soils and relatively high water table extremely susceptible to this process. Liquefaction produces extrusive sand features in the form of elongated sand fissures and circular sand boils. In these features, liquefied sand is forced upward and onto the surface. Extrusive sand features can vary in size from a few feet to ones covering several acres. Such features are sometimes referred to as sand volcanoes. At times, liquefied sand and air can be forced upward with explosive force to a height of several feet accompanied by a loud sound. Seismologist David Stewart and geomorphologist Ray Knox documented what they consider to be the world's largest seismically induced sand boil approximately eight miles west of Hayti, Missouri. This sand boil, nicknamed "The Beach," is about 1.4 miles long and covers 136 acres.[16] Crop production is negatively affected in areas around

Linear sand blows between Caruthersville and Blytheville, Arkansas. The Light areas are where coarse sand was forced to the surface. Such areas of sand produce poor crops (photograph by Myron L. Fuller, 1912, United States Geological Survey).

sand boils. The extruded sand has few nutrients and a low water holding capacity thus crops grow poorly in areas of extensive sand boils. Sand boils are readily evident in many places in the southeast lowlands from aerial photography, particularly during times of the year when crops aren't growing in fields.

As the liquefied sand makes its way to the surface, it cuts across existing layers of sediment, forming sand filled fissures known as sand dikes. Such dikes can present engineering challenges in certain types of construction. A good example of this is the lake constructed in 1996 by the Missouri Conservation Department in the Little River Conservation Area just east of Kennett, Missouri, in Dunklin and Pemiscot counties. Pumps started filling the above ground lake in late summer 1996. An inspection in January 1997 revealed that the lake was not filling as expected. In fact, it was losing water at the rate of one inch per day or 2,500 gallons per minute.[17] Studies to determine the cause of the leakage revealed that the six to ten feet of clay on the lake bed was cut with numerous sand filled fissures connecting to the hundreds of feet of permeable sand underlying the surface clay. These sand dikes provided a conduit to the permeable underlying sands allowing the lake water to drain off. Consequently, repair required expensive thorough reworking of the lakebed which involved removing the sand fissures and recompacting the clay. By fall of 1999, engineers determined that the lake was now holding water, but the repairs cost nearly one-third as much as the original cost of the project.[18]

The earthquakes also produced large areas of sunk lands. Fuller identified three types of sunk lands: sand sloughs, river swamps, and lakes with standing water. Sand sloughs are depressed areas between two parallel fissures which have extruded sand forming low ridges. Fuller describes river swamps as depressed areas along streams but the water is not deep enough to prevent timber growth. Lakes are described as "essentially permanent bodies of water occurring in depressions of the bottom lands near the Mississippi and other streams or along the depressed channels of streams like the St. Francis." They result from a greater amount of subsidence than river swamps.[19]

Fissure caused by 1811–1812 earthquakes filled with sand in Mississippi County. Lakes and ponds built over such sand fissures will not retain water (photograph by Myron L. Fuller, 1912, United States Geological Survey).

The sunk lands are primarily restricted to areas along the Mississippi, St. Francis, and Little rivers. A.N. Dillard, who lived in the New Madrid area during the earthquakes, describes the sunk lands: "The region of the St. Francis is peculiar. I have trapped there for thirty years. There is a great deal of sunken land, caused by the earthquakes of 1811. There are large trees of walnut, white oak, and mulberry, such as grow on high land, which are now seen submerged ten and twenty feet beneath the water. In some of the lakes, I have seen cypresses so far beneath the surface, that, with a canoe, I have paddled among the branches."[20]

Swampy area along the Varney River near Kennett caused by earthquake induced subsidence. Trees in foreground killed by subsidence, new growth seen in the background. Many such swampy areas have now been drained and converted to farmland (United States Geological Survey; photograph by Myron L. Fuller, 1908).

An extensive area of subsidence extends from Marked Tree, Arkansas, northward to the Missouri state line along the St. Francis River. Much of this area of sunk land is now included in the St. Francis Sunk Land Wildlife Management Area. A second major sunk land area lies near Manila, Arkansas. It extends from south of Manila to the Missouri state line. This area contains Big Lake, one of the numerous lakes formed by the earthquakes and is of particular interest since it serves as terminus of the floodway ditches constructed by the Little River Drainage District to drain farmland in the southeast Missouri lowlands. Researchers have determined that uplift of a structure referred to as the Manila high and subsidence of the Little River channel resulted in the formation of Big Lake. They state that "Little River was ponded twice, apparently in response to deformation in 1811–1812 and between 90 B.C. and A.D. 1640."[21] Other sunk lands are present along Varney River northwest of Kennett. Stewart and Knox note that "at least ten earthquake lakes were formed."[22] Lakes and areas of subsidence occurred throughout the southeast lowlands. One particularly large area of subsidence forming along Little River was Lake Nicormy lying between Kennett and Hayti.[23] Drainage of this area was not accomplished until construction of the Little River Drainage District. Most of these earthquake lakes were shallow, usually six to ten feet. The largest and most well-known of the lakes formed by the New Madrid earthquakes is Reelfoot Lake. While not in the southeast Missouri lowlands, it lies just across the Mississippi River in Obion County Tennessee. Reelfoot Lake formed as a result of the uplift of the Tiptonville Dome which dammed Reelfoot Creek followed by subsidence of the creek up stream from the uplift. Drainage has now eliminated all of the lakes with the exception of Reelfoot and Big Lake.

Using extant eyewitness accounts and field studies, scientists have now been able to summarize the sequence of shocks that took place in the New Madrid seismic zone between December 1811 and February 1812. The first shock occurred about 2:15 a.m., December 16, 1811. It was centered near Blytheville, Arkansas, at the intersection of a subsurface structure known as the Blytheville Arch and a fault known as the Bootheel Lineament which runs northeastward near the center of the Reelfoot Rift. At 8:15 a.m. on the same day and at around noon on December 17, two additional shocks along the same fault system caused the abandonment of the town of Little Prairie. The first shock is estimated to have a moment magnitude of 8.1 and the two succeeding shocks are estimated at 7.2 and 7.1, respectively. Strong aftershocks continued as some observers noted that he ground was in almost continuous motion. January 23, 1812, at 9:00 a.m. another major shock was felt. This earthquake was centered closer to New Madrid along what seismologists call the New Madrid North fault. The estimated moment magnitude for this quake is 7.8. Again severe aftershocks were felt, all of which today would be considered major earthquakes. On February 7, 1812, at 3:45 a.m. what many residents described as the most severe shock occurred near New Madrid. This event, with a moment magnitude estimated at 8, resulted in the destruction of New Madrid by the Mississippi River and the formation of Reelfoot Lake through both uplift and subsidence. It is estimated that during the whole sequence more than 200 shocks with a moment magnitude of 5 or greater occurred.[24]

What happened to the southeast Missouri lowlands and its residents as a result of this series of earthquakes? Johnston and Schweig make the following observation: "Had the New Madrid earthquakes occurred a century or so earlier they would have been included in the realm of paleoseismology; had they occurred a century or more later, millions of people would have been at risk and abundant instrumental macroseismic data would be available. However, they occurred in the transition, the crease in history, when the Mississippi River was for a brief period the western frontier of a new nation."[25]

The region was sparsely populated at the time and the existing structures were mostly log or wood frame construction. The few masonry structures, mostly chimneys, fell with the first shocks. The wood construction proved more durable although near the epicentral areas little was left standing. Eyewitness accounts indicate that people quickly fled their dwellings soon after the earthquakes began thus lessening the chance of injury from falling structures. In modern earthquakes most deaths and injuries come from collapsing buildings. The entire region including northeastern Arkansas had a population of 1350 whites and 150 slaves in 1804.[26] While the number of Indians living in the region was unknown some have estimated the population including Indians at 15,000.[27] Whatever the actual number, it was small compared to today. The sparse population combined with small wooden buildings helped reduce the number of casualties although the exact number is not known. Boatmen on the Mississippi River faced the perils of caving banks, temporary falls, strong waves, and retrograde current at times. Eyewitnesses mention debris from broken boats floating in the water but it remains unknown how many may have lost their lives on the river.

The earthquakes affected the region in ways other than the destruction of structures. One important impact was the changes the earthquakes made to the rivers and streams draining the area. The earthquakes certainly did not create the swampland. Ample testimony from early travelers in the area attests to the swampy nature of the region before their occurrence. However, the combination of uplift in some areas and subsidence in others disrupted drainage and choked some channels with fallen trees. Changes to streams also compounded transportation difficulties.

Spanish Mill serves as a good example of such changes. The present location of Boekerton in New Madrid County was the site of Spanish Mill in the 1700s. The flow of Little River at that time was strong enough to operate a mill. Keel boats could travel up and down Little River and via distributary channels reach the St. Francis River to the west. Little River also had a connection to the Mississippi River through Bayou Portage and Portage Open Bay. The earthquakes cut off this connection to the Mississippi and caused the channels that allowed travel to the St. Francis River to become too congested to navigate eliminating any chance of easy travel east and west across the Bootheel. The Spanish Mill settlement was thus abandoned.[28] Similarly, the channel of the St. Francis River east of Crowley's

Ridge became swampy and clogged with logs, making navigation difficult. Historian Conevery Bolton Valencius notes that "before the earthquakes, the St. Francis was no swampy backwater, but a riverine highway."[29]

Many settlers in the New Madrid area left out of fear of other quakes and in some cases because of damage to their farmland. It caused others to have second thoughts about settling there. Sinking caused some tracts to become too wet for farming while sand blows resulted in a blanket of sand over the surface making the land unproductive. Fear of future shocks and damage to land resulted in decreased land values. Between 1810 and 1820 the population of New Madrid County dropped by 27 percent. From 1820 until 1830 there was a population increase of only 54. It was 1840 before the population exceeded that of pre-earthquake levels.[30] Merchant and trader Robert Goah Watson describes the effects of the earthquakes on the residents and his business: "Plantations, stock of all kinds, cribs of corn, smoke houses full of meat, were offered for horses to leave on. At that time I was carrying on the Indian trade pretty extensively. The whole white population, or all that could leave as well as the Indians, left largely in my debt, leaving me considerably indebted to persons here and in other places and little or no means to pay with. We had a trying time, our population having all left, no business doing and no capital to do business."[31]

In order to provide some relief for those living in the earthquake area, Congress passed legislation in February 1815 entitled "An Act for the relief of the inhabitants of the late county of New Madrid, in the Missouri Territory, who suffered by earthquake." This act marks the first time the United States government passed a measure to aid victims of a natural disaster. The first section of the law permitted the exchange of damaged lands for up to 160 acres. It was possible for someone owning only a small lot to exchange it for a 160-acre farm although the law did limit the amount that could be exchanged to 640 acres. A second section of the law required the territorial recorder of land titles to issue earthquake certificates to any one having a claim. While the measure was well-intended and meant to help individual farmers, speculators benefited the most. Because of the slow communications of the day, speculators in St. Louis learned of the program before New Madrid residents. They hastened to New Madrid and bought land from residents who did not know about the new law in order to exchange it for highly desirable farmland in central Missouri.[32] However, some New Madrid residents took advantage of the situation by selling the same tract of land several times to different speculators.[33] The process became so fraught with fraud that the United States Attorney General William Wirt ruled in 1820 that land could only be transferred from the owner at the time of the earthquakes or his direct heirs.³⁴ All of this created a nightmarish problem sorting land titles and finding who had legitimate claims. In total, 516 certificates for new land were issued.³⁵

Descriptions of the region by visitors in the years following the earthquakes provide a picture of the slow recovery and progress. Timothy Flint, a Presbyterian minister and missionary in the Mississippi Valley, spent the winter of 1819 at New Madrid with his family in the home of Mrs. Dinah Gray who came to New Madrid because of Morgan's colonization scheme. Flint describes the area this way:

> This district, formerly so level, rich, and beautiful, had the most melancholy of all aspects of decay, the tokens of former cultivation and habitancy, which were now mementos of desolation and desertion. Large and beautiful orchards left unenclosed, houses uninhabited, deep chasms in the earth, obvious at frequent intervals—such was the face of the country, although the people had for years become so accustomed to frequent and small shocks, which did no essential injury, that the lands were gradually rising again in value, and New Madrid was slowly rebuilding, with frail buildings, adapted to the apprehensions of the people.³⁶

By 1837, conditions seem to have improved for the region according to Alphonso Wetmore's 1837 *Gazetteer of the State of Missouri* where he gives this description of the New Madrid region and its economic activities:

> There is an immense shipping business done there in stock and lumber for the southern markets. The steam saw-mills within this county furnish considerable quantities of railroad timber for the states of Mississippi and Louisiana. The timber thus furnished is cypress only. In the county of New Madrid there are two prairies, each about five miles square, and these are by far the most fertile and highly cultivated parts of it. In one of these prairies there are two cotton gins; and from these about 150 bales of cotton are annually sent to market. The other prairie is almost an entire corn-field. There is shipped annually from New Madrid about 75,000 bushels of corn; this is the principal staple of the county. Nothing seems to prevent New Madrid from being among the largest towns in Missouri.³⁷

While the region did slowly recover from the affects of the earthquakes and eventually saw large numbers of settlers moving there to exploit timber and find farmland, New Madrid never grew to the level of Wetmore's prediction.

The New Madrid earthquakes affected residents of the region in ways other than just fear of additional shocks, the destruction of property, and changes in streams and farmland, it also affected the religious environment of the region. Historian Tom Kanon notes that "the psychological impact on the region's population was profound. The earthquakes affected the frontier community's religious climate, resulting in an initial surge of pietistic passion, then, once the earthquakes had subsided, a subsequent decline in devout fervor."³⁸ The earthquakes occurred on the heels of what has been termed the Great Revival or Second Great Awakening. This surge in religions fervor on the American frontier took place in the first decade of the nineteenth century at camp meetings where attendance sometimes climbed to the thousands. Meetings lasted several days with nearly continuous preaching often involving preachers from various denominations. The meetings were characterized by fervent sermons about God's coming judgment and emotional responses by hearers. Most evident were physical movements or exercises as they were called at the time. Some individuals exhibited their whole body jerking, others fell to the ground motionless while yet others would dance, laugh or even bark like a dog. One of the most notable meetings took place at Cane Ridge Meeting House in Kentucky where Barton W. Stone, a Presbyterian at the time, preached. In August 1801, a camp meeting was held there lasting six or seven days. Stone provides a description of the meeting: "It was judged by military men on the ground, that there were between twenty and thirty thousand collected. Four or five preachers were frequently speaking at the same time, in different parts of the encampment, without confusion. The Methodist and Baptist preachers aided in the work, and all appeared cordially united in it—of one mind and one soul and the salvation of sinners seemed to be the great object of all." Stone went on to state that "this meeting continued six or seven days and nights."[39]

Several things added to residents feeling that judgment may be near. In addition to the earthquakes, a comet, officially now designated C/1811 F1, was visible much of 1811 in addition, rumors of war loomed as the eve of the War of 1812 approached. Comets have historically been seen to portend disasters and the reference to wars and rumors of war in the New Testament book of Revelation brought reflections of end times and God's judgment to their minds. The story is told of Kentucky preacher, Valentine Cook, who upon feeling the first earthquake, ran into the night in his bedclothes shouting, "My Jesus is coming!" His wife ran after him, begging him to wait for her to whom he replied, "When the Lord comes, I wait for nobody."[40] Those fleeing the earthquakes often united in prayer. John Shaw describes the actions of nearly 2,000 people fleeing New Madrid. Upon reaching higher ground 30 miles north of New Madrid and seven miles inland from the Mississippi River. "It was proposed that all should kneel, and engage in supplicating God's mercy, and all simultaneously, Catholics and Protestants, knelt and offered solemn prayer to their Creator."[41]

Membership numbers for the Methodist Western Conference show a 50 percent increase between 1811 and 1812 while growth for the rest of the country was less than half that number. Tom Kanon notes that while "conversion estimates for the various Protestant denominations are scarce ... by all written accounts, one can easily surmise the New Madrid earthquakes caused a surge in church membership throughout the West."[42] Kanon notes that the church, rather than "trying to calm the apprehensions ... played into their fears."[43] Penick observes that "preachers flocked to the affected region" to take advantage of people's fears.[44] In the 1812 minutes of the Presbyterian Synod of Kentucky, the church appears grateful for the earthquakes because "many additions have been made to the Church last year."[45] Those turning to religion during the earthquakes were sometimes referred to as "Earthquake Christians" since many tended to become backsliders after the earthquakes subsided, relieving their fears.[46]

Research within the last three decades has produced evidence that the 1811–1812 earthquakes were not the first major disturbances to strike southeast Missouri. Studies of earthquakes occurring within the past 10,000 years using dendrochronology (tree ring dating), sedimentology, and archaeology reveal that several large earthquakes have occurred within the New Madrid Seismic Zone during that time. Johnston and Schweig conclude that "the data all are consistent with as few as two and as many as four earthquakes in the 2000 years prior to 1811."[47] A detailed study of liquefaction by seismologists Li, Schweig, Tuttle, and Ellis revealed that two strong earthquakes occurred within a hundred years of A.D. 900 and 1350. They conclude that these earthquakes would have had a moment magnitude of at least 6.8 in order to produce the widespread liquefaction observed.[48]

A somewhat newer study of liquefaction features located at more than 250 sites suggests that the average recurrence rate for 1811–1812 size events is 500 years for the past 1200 years. This is based on an earthquake in A.D. 900 plus or minus 100 years; another in 1450 plus or minus 150 years; and finally the 1811–1812 sequence. This means that the recurrence range is between 200 and 800 years.[49] Seismologists estimate the 900 and 1450 events to be similar in strength to the 1811–1812 earthquakes.

The strongest earthquake since the 1811–1812 series occurred October 31, 1895, near Charleston, Missouri, and is believed to have had a magnitude of 6.7. The shock caused sand blows and extensive structural damage. Charleston, Puxico, and Taylor, Missouri; Alton and Cairo, Illinois; Princeton, Indiana; and Paducah, Kentucky, sustained the most damage which included downed chimneys, cracked walls, shattered windows, and broken plaster in schools, churches, private homes, and commercial buildings.[50]

While earthquakes can't be predicted, seismologists have looked at the recurrence rates of earthquakes along the New Madrid Seismic Zone in order to assist with planning for the possibility of a future large earthquake.

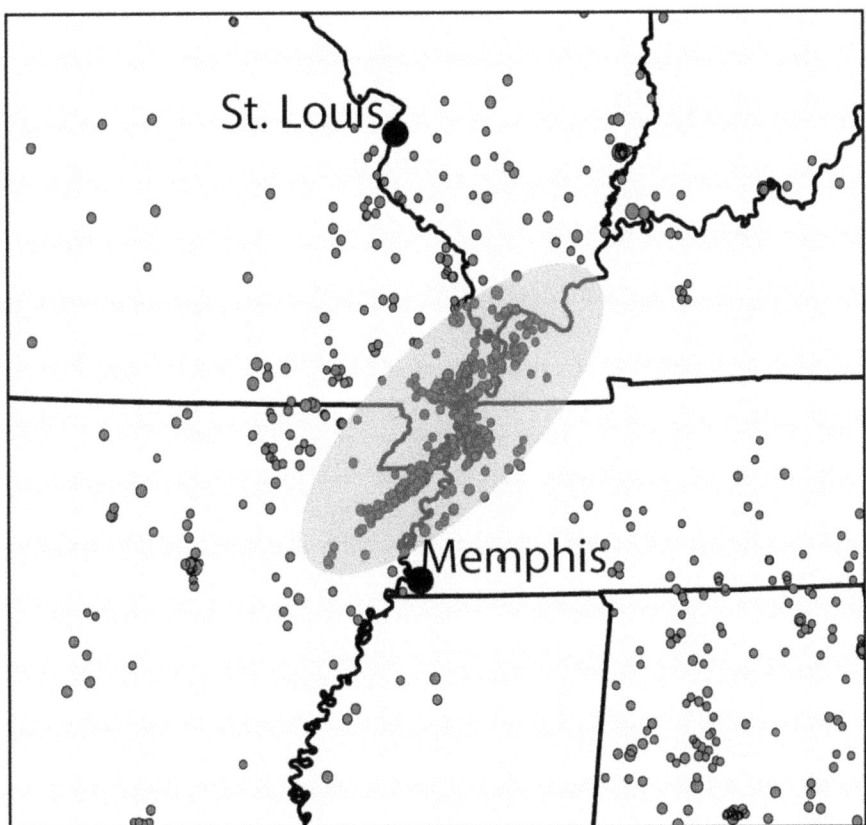

Map showing recent earthquakes in the New Madrid Seismic Zone. The pattern of recent earthquakes helps delineate the fault systems making up this seismic zone (United States Geological Survey).

An event similar in size to the 1811–1812 earthquakes would drastically affect the entire area between St. Louis and Memphis. With the large population in this area and the modern infrastructure, the damage would be several orders of magnitude greater than in 1811–1812 including loss of life. Estimates of damage range into the tens of billions of dollars. Such an earthquake would severely disrupt and damage power plants, power distribution systems, communication systems, levees, roads, bridges, buildings, gas lines, and water lines. The large number of unreinforced masonry buildings would be especially vulnerable. Medical facilities could not handle all of the injuries, and thousands would likely be left without food or water for several days. Even a smaller earthquake in the range of 6.5 magnitude would cause extensive damage especially from liquefaction induced ground failure.

There is no overall preparedness plan for the entire region however, some cities have revised building codes, and some buildings, especially those containing communication equipment such as telephone switching facilities have been retrofitted with steel support structures. Most emergency response units have developed and practiced evacuation and response plans. Individuals are encouraged to put together their own personal emergency preparedness kits which include such items as food, water, blankets, flashlights, and first aid supplies.

Seismologists have used various models for trying to determine the probability of future earthquakes. One major difficulty in this effort is that there is no certainty that a fault system will behave exactly the same in the future as it has in the past. These are complex structures covering a large geographic area and it is often unclear how intersecting faults interact with one another. Currently, the United States Geological Survey places the probability of a magnitude 7 or greater earthquake in the next 50 years at 7 to 10 percent and a 28 to 50 percent probability of a magnitude 6 or greater earthquake in the next 50 years. The probability of smaller earthquakes is greater. Even earthquakes with a magnitude of 4 or 5 can cause structural damage. In fact, earthquakes of magnitude 2 or less occur weekly in the New Madrid Seismic Zone. However earthquakes of this magnitude are usually detected only by instruments and do not cause any damage. The region is currently monitored by about 270 seismograph stations in a cooperative network involving several universities and the United States Geological Survey.

Another significant historical event took place on the Mississippi River at the same time as the earthquakes. The first steamboat to travel western inland waterways churned its way down the Ohio and Mississippi rivers to New Orleans during the time the New Madrid earthquakes were occurring. The steamboat, named the *New Orleans*, came from the collaboration of Robert Fulton, Robert Livingston, and Nicholas Roosevelt. Fulton and Livingston began using steamboats commercially on the Hudson River in 1807. Roosevelt, an experienced mechanic and iron founder, spent six months in 1810 on a flatboat with his wife, Lydia Latrobe Roosevelt, studying the Ohio and Mississippi rivers. He talked with boatmen and studied the actions of the rivers in various seasons. This proved to be time well spent as Roosevelt was able to successfully complete his voyage to New Orleans at the time of one of greatest natural disasters to ever hit the central United States. Roosevelt reported the results of his study of the river to Fulton and Livingston. The three concluded that a steamboat could operate in these waters and a project was begun to build such a boat. Roosevelt supervised the building of the craft which began its trip in late September 1811 carrying Roosevelt, his wife Lydia, and their three-year-old daughter Rosetta; an engineer; a pilot, six hands; two female servants; a male waiter; a cook; and a Newfoundland dog named Tiger.

The *New Orleans* first stopped at Cincinnati where it was greeted by a large crowd. The trip continued to Louisville where they made another stop for fuel and supplies and to greet crowds. The voyage was delayed at Louisville several days until the Ohio River rose enough for the *New Orleans* to navigate past the Falls of the Ohio. Also while at Louisville, Mrs. Roosevelt gave birth to their second child, a son. Their first earthquake encounter occurred while at anchor below the Falls of the Ohio. Those on board described what they felt was as if "the vessel had been in motion and had suddenly grounded."[51] Each afternoon the *New Orleans* would stop so that the crew could cut wood for the next day's run. At these times, the crew often experienced the earth shaking. Upon reaching New Madrid, the party found the town severely damaged and the inhabitants "terror stricken" and begging "to be taken on board." Because of insufficient provisions, the crew had to deny passage to them.[52] On one occasion, the pilot believed that he was lost because the earthquake had changed the banks of the river so much. Trees from caving banks and other debris made navigation hazardous and all familiar landmarks had disappeared. On another occasion, the entire island to which they were moored for the night disappeared. The *New Orleans* however successfully completed its journey and was placed in service hauling freight between Natchez, Mississippi, and New Orleans. Completion of this voyage ushered in the age of the steamboat on the western rivers.

Chapter 5

Settlement, Early Agriculture and Civil War

On June 4, 1812, President James Madison signed legislation making Missouri a territory. The intended southern boundary of the new territory was to be 36° 30' north latitude. However, as time passed and it became apparent that Missouri was going to become a state sooner than the Arkansas territory to the south, some residents, especially large landholders of the Bootheel, felt that their property would become more valuable if it were included in Missouri. In 1817, the first petitions reached Congress requesting statehood for Missouri but in these requests, the southern boundary was at 36° 30' which corresponds to the northern boundary of Tennessee. One of the largest landowners in the region was John Hardeman Walker who settled with his father in the area around Little Prairie in 1810. Walker established a large cattle plantation, using the swampland for grazing and came to be known as "Czar of the Valley." While many people left the area following the 1811–1812 earthquakes, Walker remained, becoming one of the most influential men in the region. He wanted his land to be a part of Missouri and began lobbying state legislators and even representatives in Washington to include the Bootheel in Missouri. Walker was aided in his efforts by Dr. Robert D. Dawson of New Madrid, his brother-in-law; Senator James Evans; John Scott, congressional representative from the territory; and Judge Richard J. Thomas from Jackson.[1]

The territorial legislature adopted a petition to Congress asking that the southern boundary for the southeastern part of the state be extended to 36° north latitude. It also called for additional land on the western and northern borders to be included within the state. After much debate, the proposed northern and western boundaries were reduced but the extension of the southern boundary in the southeast was retained. The Missouri Enabling Act signed by President James Monroe March 6, 1820, which granted permission for the Missouri Territory to write a constitution and form a state government described the southern boundary this way: "Beginning in the middle of the Mississippi River, on the parallel of thirty-six degrees of north latitude; thence west, along that parallel of latitude, to the St. Francois River; thence up, and following the course of that river, in the middle of the main channel thereof, to the parallel of latitude of thirty-six degrees and thirty minutes; thence west, along the same, to a point where said parallel is intersected by a meridian line passing through the middle of the mouth of the Kansas River."[2] This jog in the southern boundary of Missouri assured that Walker's land holdings would be included in the new state and gave Missouri its "bootheel."

John Hardeman Walker played a major role in changing the boundary lines in southeast Missouri to ensure that his land was included in Missouri rather than Arkansas thus giving Missouri its "Bootheel" (Houck, *A History of Missouri*, vol. 1, 1908).

The admission of Missouri into the union caused contentious debate in Congress and became a national issue because of the question of slavery. Speaker of the House Henry Clay from Kentucky devised a compromise. What became know as the Missouri Compromise admitted Missouri as a slave state and Maine as a free state, maintaining the balance between the two. The agreement also contained a provision prohibiting slavery in the remaining territory obtained in the Louisiana Purchase above 36° 30', the southern border of Missouri except in the Bootheel.

The end of the War of 1812 brought a large influx of new settlers into Missouri, but few came to the southeast lowland region. This migration focused on areas along the Mississippi north of its confluence with the Ohio and especially westward along the Missouri River from St. Louis. The Boonslick region in central Missouri became a favorite destination.

While the majority of the newcomers headed for Boonslick, a few settlers did slowly begin filtering to the interior of the southeast Missouri lowlands after the end of the War of 1812 to find farmland in spite of its reputation as an insalubrious place to live. Settlement occurred later here than most of the remainder of the state except perhaps some of the interior regions of the Ozarks. By the end of 1820, no public land in the New Madrid region was being offered for sale because it had not yet been surveyed. Settlers simply chose land hoping the right of preemption would be extended to them when the United States began public land sales. Such settlers were sometimes referred to as squatters. Preemption gave settlers the first right to purchase land on which they had settled and made improvements whenever land was offered for sale. Congress addressed the issue by enacting 16 bills between 1804 and 1830. Most of these laws applied to specific states or territories. Congress passed a law in 1830 granting preemption for up to 160 acres on which a settler had made improvements the previous year. This law was to be in effect for only one year although it was renewed in 1832 and in 1834.[3] In 1841, Congress passed a law making permanent the right of preemption.

Geography dictated where newcomers established farms and settlements. Until the 1820s, settlers restricted their location to areas along or within a few miles inland from the Mississippi River. Only Indian traders, hunters, and trappers had penetrated the swampland of the Little River and St. Francis river valleys earlier. Settlers who eventually established farms in various parts of the interior of the region confined themselves to the high sandy ridges, particularly the Sikeston Ridge beginning just north of New Madrid and the Kennett-Malden Prairie extending in a north-south direction through Dunklin County. Travel could be made along the Sikeston Ridge to reach New Madrid to the south or northward to the Benton Hills and then to Cape Girardeau without crossing long stretches of swampland. Likewise travel northward following the Kennett-Malden Prairie which intersects the upland of Crowley's Ridge. Crowley's Ridge could then be followed to reach Cape Girardeau thus again avoiding crossing extensive areas of swampland. Travel across the swampland required using a canoe to weave through narrow channels. In Dunklin County, residents could travel to Hornersville then by boat up Little River as far as Portage Bayou near what is now Boekerton and overland to reach the Mississippi River.

As settlers began to establish themselves, the state legislature formed new counties out of New Madrid County which at the time of statehood encompassed the entire lowland region. First formed in 1821 was Scott County. Its location across from the confluence of the Ohio and Mississippi rivers received more settlers than other lowland counties since the Ohio River provided one of the most accessible routes for entering Missouri. Next organized was Stoddard County in 1835 followed by both Dunklin and Mississippi counties in 1845 and Butler County in 1849. In 1851, the final Bootheel county, Pemiscot, was formed.

The settlers entering the southeast lowlands before the Civil War came primarily from Kentucky and Tennessee. Tennessee settlers made up the majority of the settlers in all of the counties except Scott, Stoddard, and Mississippi where settlers from Kentucky were most numerous. These settlers were predominately what Geographer Russel L. Gerlach describes as "Old-Stock American," meaning that they were several generations removed from their immigrant ancestors. He further describes them as being descended from Scotch-Irish immigrants.[4] The term Scotch-Irish refers to settlers originally from Scotland who settled in Ulster, the northern most province of Ireland, during the late Middle Ages. When immigrants from this region came to America they adopted the term Scotch-Irish to distinguish themselves from other Irish immigrants. The Ulstermen were mostly protestant Presbyterians whereas other Irish immigrants were Catholic.[5]

Only those farms located along the Mississippi River had access to shipping points to sell commodities they produced. More interior farms tended to be primarily subsistence farms or selling only to a local market. Selling to commercial markets required transportation to Cape Girardeau, the primary supply center for the region, not an easy task before improved roads or rail transportation. In general, the crops found growing throughout the region included corn, oats, wheat, and cotton. Small amounts of hemp and tobacco were also grown.

Wetmore's *Gazetteer of Missouri* published in 1837 provides some description of early agriculture in the southeast lowlands. For Scott County Wetmore lists "corn, oats, tobacco, and grass" as the crops being grown and "horses, cattle, and hogs" as the livestock there.[6] In addition to corn and oats, Wetmore adds cotton to the list of crops grown in New Madrid County along with horses, mules, cattle, and hogs. He also notes the fur trade as being an important part of the region's economy.[7] In contrast to Scott and New Madrid counties which have access to river transportation, Wetmore observes that Stoddard County, because it is "surrounded by almost impassable swamps" raises "nothing for exportation except cattle and hogs."[8] Wetmore further elaborates on how transportation from the interior of the southeast lowlands to the Mississippi River is accomplished: "The most usual communication between the counties of Stoddard and New Madrid is in canoes, through the lakes and swamps that are spread out over the sunken lands in the vicinity of the channel of the east branch of Castor River. The distance from the principal settlements of Stoddard by this devious woter-route [sic] is about one hundred miles, and only twenty by land."[9]

The Bootheel has long been associated with cotton production however, before the Civil War cotton was grown sporadically in small amounts. Farmers in the interior of the region would have to transport their crop by wagon to Cape Girardeau for ginning and sales. The 1840 census shows Scott and New Madrid counties with cotton production, while the 1850 census reports no cotton for any Bootheel county. The 1860 census shows cotton produced only in Stoddard and Dunklin counties.[10]

Report Number 130, February 28, 1849, accompanying the House of Representatives Bill 810 which eventually led to passage of the Swampland Act of 1850, further characterized the problem of transportation in the Bootheel by describing what a traveler would have to do to journey from New Madrid to West Prairie in northern Dunklin County. This description highlights why development of the interior of the lowlands lagged behind the remainder of the state: "To go from one point to the other, they must either go around the head of the delta or swamp, or else go south nearly to the Arkansas line to a place where the swamp can be waded, by ferrying the channel of Little River, and then can only be passed on horseback, not with any vehicle."[11]

Most livestock was produced under the free-range system in which producers allowed stock to roam freely to graze rather than confining them to pastures. Thomas Beckwith whose grandfather came to southeast Missouri in 1812 explains how stock was kept tame enough to catch when raised under the free range system: "The horses and cattle would come up to get salt, and this would keep them gentle, and hogs were kept domesticated by feeding them a few ears of corn, but if neglected, they would become as wild as deer of the forest, and much harder to tame and would stray far away from home."[12]

While settlers continued moving into the southeast lowlands and establishing farms, relatively few towns sprang up, and little other development took place through the mid–1800s. Most of the early settlers came for farmland and began establishing farms on their chosen land. Beckwith states that the first task facing new settlers was providing shelter. Usually a family lived in a tent until their first cabin, constructed of logs, could be built. Initially the floors were dirt but later log joists would be covered with split logs smoothed on one side referred to as puncheons. Beckwith also discusses the gardens grown by these early settlers since they had to supply most of their own food. "The early settlers had cabbage, beans, Irish potatoes and turnips in great abundance. They also had orchards and some settlers raised great quantities of apples and peaches."[13]

Life was difficult for these early settlers since land had to cleared before planting a crop. They had to deal with stumps, weather extremes, and floods. Poor drainage and a lack of levees made floods especially devastating. Beckwith describes the losses from a flood in 1858: "The corn is silking and tasseling, giving promise of a yield of fifty or more bushels per acre. Much of the wheat is already cut and in the shock. The gardens are filled with a variety of vegetables ready for use. And then imagine the river rising higher and higher, every day and every hour."[14]

In such conditions, livestock had to be moved to higher ridges, but in doing so there was a risk of loosing the stock. Beckwith describes what happened to one farmer "when driving his hogs and cattle to some mounds on James' Bayou, crossing one of the swift sloughs lost all of his hogs and cattle by their being sucked under a drift by the current."[15]

Robert Goah Watson writes in 1855 about changes he has seen in weather patterns that had affected the kind of crops grown: "The staple of this country from 1805 to 1812 was cotton. The average yield of an acre was 1000 to 1200 pounds of seed cotton. Since 1812 there has been a great change in our climate; the winters have grown colder and the other seasons more changeable. The raising of cotton has been entirely abandoned for last thirty-five years, our staple now has been corn."[16]

As settlers, mostly from southern states, moved into the Bootheel, slavery arrived with them. Like the remainder of the state, most slaveholders owned only a few slaves who generally worked alongside their owners in the fields. New Madrid and Mississippi County farmers used slaves more extensively than any of the other counties in the southeast lowlands. Census data for 1850 record 160 slave owners and a total of 1,010 slaves in Mississippi County and one owner having between 70 and 100 slaves. New Madrid County's 236 slave owners held 1,777 slaves. The largest slaveholder owned between 100 and 200 slaves. These numbers can be contrasted with Dunklin County, which had only 44 slave owners with 171 total slaves and no one had more than 15. Pemiscot County had 208 slaves and 71 slaveholders. The number of slaves was directly related to the size of the farms in a county. Mississippi and New Madrid counties had the largest farms in the region because their location fronting the Mississippi River made larger, commercial farms feasible. Settlement of the interior lowland counties lagged much behind those bordering the Mississippi River because of a lack of transportation, while in all lowland counties, most farms were between 20 and 50 acres in 1860, Mississippi County had 108 farms over 100 acres. Four were between 500 and 1,000 acres and one was 1,000 acres or more. New Madrid County had 116 farms of 100 acres or more. Five consisted of between 500 and 1,000 and five were over 1,000 acres.[17]

In 1860, 21 percent of Mississippi County's population was slave, while the slave population reached 31 percent in New Madrid County. All other Bootheel counties had 10 percent or fewer slaves. In the counties of Boone, Callaway, Clay, Cooper, Howard, Lafayette, and Saline in central Missouri's Little Dixie region, the slave numbers as a percentage of the population resembled those of Mississippi and New Madrid counties.

By the mid–1800s, nearly all of the southeast lowland was public land for which there had been little interest in purchasing. Congress believed if it gave this land to the states, then local drainage projects could bring the land into cultivation. On September 28, 1850, Congress passed the Swampland Act which gave to the states all public land designated as swamp and overflow land. Missouri in turn gave its swampland to the respective counties. This land had relatively little value even though it held vast timber resources. In fact, early settlers seeking land to farm often viewed the timber as an obstacle rather than as a resource and sought to clear the land as quickly as possible, but inadequate transportation across the swampland limited both utilization of timber and widespread agricultural development.

No large towns existed in the lowlands, but by 1860 the following were the largest settlements: Clarkton, Kennett, and Hornersville in Dunklin County; New Madrid in New Madrid County; Commerce and Benton in Scott County; Charleston in Mississippi County; Bloomfield in Stoddard County; Poplar Bluff in Butler County; and Caruthersville and Gayoso in Pemiscot County.

The Civil War further disrupted the already slow development of the southeast lowlands. With most settlers coming from Tennessee and Kentucky, residents of the region obviously had southern sympathies. In the presidential election of 1860, Lincoln did not receive a single vote in Dunklin, Pemiscot, New Madrid, or Stoddard counties. But, the sentiment was apparently not for immediate secession since the Constitutional Union candidate, John Bell, whose platform was neutral on slavery but supported

5. Settlement, Early Agriculture and Civil War 63

the preservation of the Union carried all of the southeast lowland counties except Butler where Douglass out polled the other candidates.

Historian Floyd Shoemaker notes that in 1862 in Dunklin County "Southern sympathizers met at Clarkton and adopted a resolution calling for the secession of what came to be called the 'Independent State of Dunklin.'"[18] Local residents in various communities organized units to serve with the Missouri State Guard, which the State Militia had been renamed by Governor Claiborne Jackson at the outbreak of the war. While some residents enlisted in the regular Confederate army, most served with the Missouri State Guard commanded in southeast Missouri by the colorful Jeff Thompson. Thompson earned the nickname "Swamp Fox" because of his ability to use the swamplands to his advantage in evading pursuing Union forces and to move into position undetected in order to launch an attack. Most regimental units for the Union supporting Home Guard and Missouri State Militia were recruited outside of the lowlands however one company for the Missouri State Militia was formed in Stoddard County.[19]

The southeast lowlands saw numerous skirmishes and small engagements during the Civil War. Much of the action was the result of guerrilla units in the area. While some were legitimate supporters of either the Confederate or Union forces, others simply seized the opportunity for lawlessness. Such groups raided farms taking horses, mules, and other supplies. They also invaded towns, robbing stores and burning buildings. Even uniformed troops of both sides took whatever supplies they wanted from local residents without payment.

The largest battles occurred in the New Madrid area in the fall of 1861 and spring of 1862. In early November 1861, Grant, in his first combat action of the war, landed at Belmont, Missouri, opposite Confederate fortifications at Columbus, Kentucky. An engagement ensued with little advantage being gained by either side, Grant retreated back to Cairo, Illinois. With fortifications at New Madrid and on Island No. 10, just north of New Madrid, the Confederates controlled the Mississippi River below Cairo. In March 1862, Union forces besieged New Madrid which Confederate forces evacuated on March 13, moving some forces to Island No. 10 and others to Tiptonville, Tennessee. Island No. 10 was then attacked and Confederate forces there surrendered April 8, 1862. This placed the middle Mississippi River under Union control.

Another significant battle took place in late April and early May 1863 when Confederate General Marmaduke entered Missouri from Arkansas hoping to capture Union forces at Bloomfield. These forces retreated to Cape Girardeau with Marmaduke following. Marmaduke's troops encountered

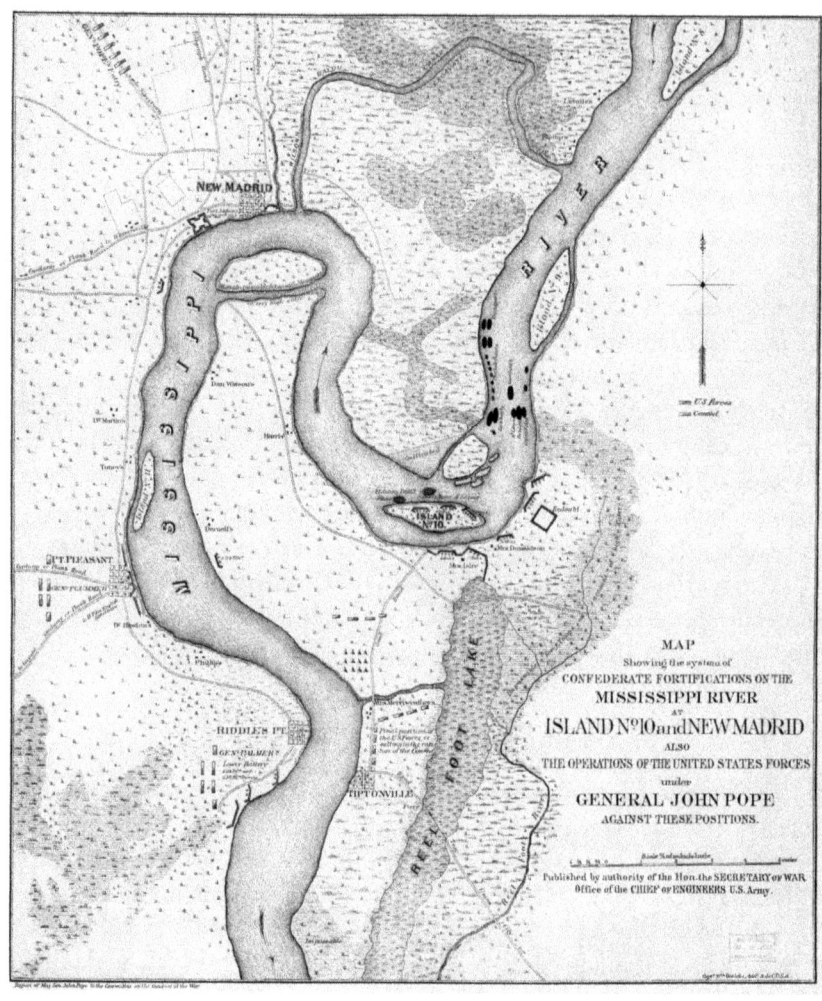

Map showing Confederate fortifications in the vicinity of New Madrid (Wm. Hoeicke, *Map showing the system of Confederate fortifications on the Mississippi River at Island No. 10 and New Madrid also the operations of the United States forces under General John Pope against these positions*, Philadelphia: Bowen & Co. Lith, 1862; retrieved from the Library of Congress, https://www.loc.govitem2007 633934 (accessed February 24, 2016).

stiff resistance there and were forced to retreat back toward Bloomfield fighting as they traveled down the military road atop Crowley's Ridge trying to reach Arkansas. At Chalk Bluff the St. Francis River cuts through Crowley's Ridge. At that location on May 1, the Confederate forces repulsed the pursuing Union forces while building a floating bridge that allowed

Top: St. Francis River near Campbell, Missouri. Fleeing Confederate troops escaped pursuing Union troops by crossing the river here to reach Arkansas. *Bottom:* Bluffs of white sand and clay along the St. Francis River between Missouri and Arkansas from which the Battle of Chalk Bluff derived its name (photographs by the author).

them to escape across the St. Francis River into Arkansas. The Battle of Chalk Bluff left Union forces largely in control of southeast Missouri.

Historian Robert Sidney Douglass describes the conditions in southeast Missouri following the Civil War by noting that "many flourishing towns were practically depopulated during the war. The inhabitants were either killed in war or in the raids of the bands from either side, or else they were driven away and found shelter in other places." He then describes some of the material losses as well: "Houses were destroyed and burned and even whole villages were practically wiped out of existence by the torch, fields were destroyed, in many cases all the fencing disappeared. The stock that existed at the time of the war was either killed or driven away by the soldiers and robber bands."[20]

As the southeast lowlands emerged from the devastation of war the residents were about to embark on a period of major changes in both the physical geography of the landscape and the social structure of the region.

Chapter 6

Transportation

The decade before the Civil War brought frenzied efforts toward transportation improvements in Missouri. Efforts focused on building railroads and plank roads. Missouri had 49 plank road companies chartered and the Bootheel was not left out of the plank road movement.[1] Builders constructed roads by using planks and logs along sections of roads crossing streams and low lying areas to make them easier to travel. The legislature chartered five plank road companies in the Bootheel, but only two actually built plank roads.[2] One such road was constructed from Point Pleasant, located ten miles south of New Madrid, to Clarkton in Dunklin County. This road was built by Point Pleasant and Dunklin County Road Company, chartered by the General Assembly in 1855. The contractor for the project was Henry E. Clark from whom the town of Clarkton derives its name.[3] Completion of the project required building several plank bridges, including one over Little River. Travelers paid a toll of 75 cents for a two-horse carriage and 25 cents per bale of cotton hauled.[4] A toll gate was located eight and a half miles east of Clarkton on the bridge crossing New River.[5]

While this road existed for a relatively short time, it provided an important link for the interior of the Bootheel to the Mississippi river. Troops of both sides during the Civil War considered the plank road to be of strategic importance. A January 1862 letter from Confederate General Jeff Thompson, while headquartered at New Madrid, to Colonel Solomon G. Kitchen at Clarkton, alerted Kitchen to the importance of the plank road: "I am alive to the importance of defending the plank road. And hope you will give them hell if they come before I get there; and if you have to retreat come over the plank road, as I will hold this end against the devil."[6] This plank road was partially destroyed during the war and never properly repaired or maintained. The few repairs made used poles instead of planks giving rise to the term, pole road. It was also referred to as the washboard road and was so rough that travelers preferred to journey several times farther instead of using this route.

The Missouri General Assembly chartered other roads in southeast Missouri as well. A charter was issued to the New Madrid & Stoddard Plank Road Company which built a road from the Hickman, Kentucky, ferry 20 miles north of New Madrid to Crowley's Ridge in Stoddard County.[7] The Dunklin and Pemiscot Plank Road Company was chartered in 1855 to build a road from Kennett to the Mississippi River, but the road was never built. The legislature chartered the New Madrid Plank Road Company in 1851 to construct a road from New Madrid northward through Big Prairie to the Scott and New Madrid County lines. It appears that this road was also not built. Another plank road company, the New Madrid and West Prairie Road Company, was chartered in 1855.[8] The company planned to construct a road west from New Madrid across the Little River swamps to the higher land in Dunklin County at West Prairie. West Prairie was near the present location of Malden. Contractors Francis Biggins and W.N. O'Bannon sold part of the land granted to them by the counties involved to pay indebtedness but stopped construction before the Civil War.[9]

Despite the plank roads that were built, really effective transportation to link the interior of the Bootheel with river ports and to allow utilization of timber resources awaited the building of a network of railroads. Serious interest in railroad building in Missouri began in the 1830s and 1840s. In 1851, the state first began providing aid for the construction of railroads, and in 1852, gave aid to the St. Louis and Iron Mountain Railroad for the construction of tracks from St. Louis to Pilot Knob to carry iron from the mines there to St. Louis.[10] At a railroad convention held in Benton in November 1853, attendees agreed that the St. Louis and Iron Mountain should be extended to intersect with the proposed Cairo and Fulton.[11] Railroad building in the Bootheel, as elsewhere in the state, while initially motivated by good intentions eventually became marred by poor planning and design and corruption. The Cairo and Fulton, the first railroad across the swamplands, is a prime example. The proposal was for a route running from Bird's Point at the confluence of the Ohio and Mississippi rivers to Fulton, Arkansas.

The Cairo and Fulton was organized in December 1853 in Stoddard County. After previously being incorporated in Arkansas, the railroad received incorporation under Missouri laws in February 1855. Congress had earlier (February 1853) deeded federal land to Arkansas and Missouri which could be used to help finance the proposed railroad. The state received a right-of-way through all federal land plus every even numbered section for six miles on each side of the track. The Cairo and Fulton then received this land as a grant from the state. The counties in the Bootheel also had at their disposal land turned over to them which the state received from the Swampland Act of 1850, giving the counties a significant amount of capital in the form of land with which to aid railroads. The counties of Stoddard, Butler, Dunklin, Scott, and Ripley subscribed 16,780 shares of stock amounting to $429,500.[12] This stock was paid for by the conveyance to the Cairo and Fulton of land valued at per acre. Ownership of some of this land, particularly in Dunklin County, became the subject of extensive litigation as much as 40 years later.

A prerequisite for receiving state bonds required a railroad to raise private money. Because of the low land prices, the railroad did not yet want to sell the land deeded to it by the counties. Instead, it issued corporate bonds and was then able to begin selling its state bonds. Construction finally started in 1857, and on April 1, 1859, the first train reached Charleston.

Things degenerated for the Cairo and Fulton in the ensuing years as the Civil War began. Poor construction and design in its roadbed and bridges made the tracks unsuitable for heavy trains and higher speeds. Newspapers questioned the intentions and practices of the Cairo and Fulton.[13] By 1866, with only 30 miles of track constructed, holders of Cairo and Fulton bonds forced a sale of the railroad because of a failure to meet interest payments. Commissioners for the state purchased the railroad and then resold it to Joseph C. Read, A.J. McKay, John C. Vogel, and Samuel Simmons, receiving $350,000. This group then resold the Cairo and Fulton to Thomas Allen who had also purchased the St. Louis and Iron Mountain Railroad.

Allen began rebuilding track and extended it to Poplar Bluff under the name Cairo, Arkansas, and Texas. He also brought the Iron Mountain line from Pilot Knob to Belmont. Between 1870 and 1874, a line was constructed from Bismarck to the Arkansas state line and finally through Arkansas to the Texas state line at Fulton, Arkansas. In 1874, Allen consolidated both lines as the St. Louis, Iron Mountain, and Southern Railroad Company.[14] This marked the beginnings of transportation improvements in the Bootheel, although it would take another two decades for a complete rail system to be in place for the region. The St. Louis, Iron Mountain and Southern Railroad Company became a part of the Missouri Pacific in 1881, controlled by railroad baron Jay Gould.

Controversy over ownership of Cairo and Fulton land that had been granted by the counties continued for several years. Charles P. Chouteau and others who purchased the company's bonds secured by land filed suit to have the land sold to satisfy the bonds. The case was eventually decided by the Missouri Supreme Court, which sided with the bondholders. A sale was held November 2, 1882, in Kennett, and Chouteau purchased the land. The situation became even more complicated. Dunklin County still claimed the land within that county and had also sold some of it to individuals before the foreclosure sale. A compromise was reached in which Chouteau gave up claim to the land sold to individuals and the county gave up claim to the rest of the land. To further complicate the matter, in 1890, the Dunklin County Court filed a petition to regain title to the land even though Chouteau had been paying the required taxes on the land. Resolution came in 1894, when the state supreme court gave a judgment favoring Chouteau.[15]

The next Bootheel railroad enterprise began in 1875 when Oscar Kochtitzky (father of Otto Kochtitzky, the first engineer of the Little River Drainage District) along with State Auditor George B. Clark, and A.M. Shead obtained the New Madrid and West Prairie charter with the intention of completing it as a plank road. Instead they constructed a narrow-gauge railroad between New Madrid and Malden.[16]

After obtaining the New Madrid and West Prairie Road Company charter, Kochtitzky, Clark, and Shead needed capital to build their railroad. Shead brought a fellow Ohioan, Charles L. Luce, a wholesale dry goods businessman from Toledo into the enterprise as a full partner. After deciding to build a railroad instead of a plank road, the company was renamed Little River Valley and Arkansas Railroad, with construction beginning in 1877. Luce supplied clothing, groceries, and tobacco to the workers instead of cash for their labor. The line went into operation in 1878 but proved unprofitable. Following three years of unprofitable operation, the Little River line was sold to St. Louis investors that included J.W. Paramore for $243,000.

Paramore, originally from Ohio, served with distinction in the Union army during the Civil War. He began his railroad career after the war with the Tennessee and Pacific Railroad but became interested in the cotton business so he moved to St. Louis and with some other investors started the St. Louis Compress Company. His goal was to make St. Louis the receiving point for cotton from the southwest from which it could then be shipped to eastern states. Paramore wanted to have an interest in a railroad over which to ship Texas cotton to St. Louis. His opportunity came in 1879 when he was contacted by James P. Douglass who operated the Tyler Tap Railroad in Texas. Douglass needed additional funding which

6. Transportation

Steamboats on the Mississippi River provided a vital link between southeast Missouri and outside markets. However, areas of the Bootheel located inland from the Mississippi lacked adequate transportation until the building of railroads (*One Hundred Years of Progress of the United States*, Hartford, CT: L. Stebbins, 1872).

Paramore arranged with some eastern investors. On May 17, 1879, the Texas and St. Louis Railway Company was organized. Eventually, Paramore left the cotton business to devote full time to railroad building. This company, through acquisitions, evolved into the St. Louis Southwestern Railroad, popularly known as the Cotton Belt. Paramore built narrow-gauge railroads—those with rails three feet apart instead of the standard four feet, eight and a half inches, earning him the moniker "Narrow-Gauge King."

Paramore's railroad ventures made him a nemesis of railroad baron Jay Gould who hoped to have a monopoly on midwestern and western railroads.[17] Ironically, the settlement in Arkansas that developed where Paramore's Texas and St. Louis Railway intersected with Gould's St. Louis, Iron Mountain and Southern Railroad came to be named for both men—Paragould, an honor that Jay Gould in particular was not pleased about—his name was second after all. For a time he refused to list Paragould on his line's schedule. Gould eventually gained control of the Cotton Belt in 1891 after the expense of upgrading the line to standard gauge tracks and equipment

First train to reach Kennett, 1890. Receiving rail service was important for the growth and development of towns throughout southeast Missouri (courtesy Tony Byrd, Kennett, Missouri).

pushed it into bankruptcy. In the region of the southeast Missouri lowlands and the lowlands of northeast Arkansas which were new frontiers in the late 1800s, entrepreneurs with big visions of railroads, timber, land drainage, and agriculture sometimes had even bigger egos, often clashing in bitter disputes.

Railroad pioneer Louis Houck of Cape Girardeau deserves the most credit for knitting together a system of railroads to service the Bootheel. The formidable terrain of much of region before significant drainage discouraged interest in building roads and railways, but without adequate transportation there was no way to utilize the vast timber resources existing there. Otto Kochtitzky, writing about the Bootheel before the completion of Houck's network of railroads, said: "There was little present value in the timber as there were no transportation facilities for lumbering except at a few points and, therefore, more than half the acreage of Southeast Missouri was considered of no value."[18] Houck built his network of railroads by purchasing some existing lines, completing and expanding them, and establishing new lines where none existed. His need to have outlets for his roads several times brought him into conflict with Jay Gould.

Houck's first foray into railroad building was his 1880 contract to complete 15 miles of the defunct Cape Girardeau and State Line Railroad track from Cape Girardeau to connect with the Iron Mountain at Delta. What Houck lacked in experience and training as a railroad man, he made up in determination. He often came into conflict with workers as Houck biographer Joel Rhodes notes, "Never known for prompt payment of debt anyway and perpetually strapped for cash, Houck faced frequent work stoppages and confrontations due to late compensation."[19] Houck not only completed the railroad on schedule, albeit by using a few tricks such as using less than the required number of ties and even removing a completed section of rail behind and using the material to build forward.[20] By 1889, he had extended his railroad to the Current River at Hunter, picking up major business from William Brown's stave mill at Brownwood and T.J. Moss, one of largest tie producers in the country, headquartered at Puxico. He also added the business of numerous sawmills located along the route. Despite his successes, by 1890 Houck was having trouble paying interest on outstanding bonds. In March of 1893, after Houck refused an earlier offer from Jay Gould to buy his Cape Girardeau Railway Company, Gould lawyers filed a petition to place the Cape Girardeau line in receivership, setting in motion a tenacious three-year legal battle.[21]

Houck's legal battle with Gould didn't deter his forging ahead with his plan for a railroad system in the Bootheel. The system he put together there proved to be his most successful railroad venture and is responsible for making possible utilization of the region's timber resources. In 1891, he began the process by purchasing the St. Louis, Kennett and Southern Railroad which had been built in 1890 by A.J. Kerfoot and Eugene S. McCarty.[22] The line was poorly constructed and Houck made few improvements. Tracks were laid without a graded roadbed, half the appropriate numbers of ties were used, and the tracks simply forded sloughs with no bridges being built. In some places, tracks curved around stumps.[23] The poor conditions of the tracks forced the trains to travel slowly. C.C. Redman of Kennett relates his experience of traveling on this line in 1891, which illustrates just how slow travel was on many Bootheel lines:

> You could walk off and leave it [the train] when it was on high ground and the best of the road, but when it was crossing the sloughs, where the water was a foot or two over the rails, it barely crept. There was no drinking water in the coach. There was no need for it. They kept a tin cup in the coach and you would get out on the step, or on a stump and dip up good running water and drink. On this trip of mine, I got thirsty and took the cup and got out on a stump, got a drink and then dipped up and handed it at the windows and watered every passenger on the coach and got back on as the rear steps came creeping by.[24]

By 1895, Houck had extended the St. Louis, Kennett and Southern from Kennett to Caruthersville. Houck organized a new company the

Pemiscot Railroad Company, to build this important leg of his network. His contract required building a levee for the tracks to be laid on and a ditch along side to divert water. Pemiscot County offered Houck 40,000 acres of land to build the railroad. Houck actually purchased the land for $1.25 per acre. Because the land was considered worthless, Houck had difficulty finding an investor. Finally, J.E. Franklin of Jackson put up half the money in return for half the land and railroad stock. The county was to return the note when Houck completed the road. Houck then used the land to secure investors in the project. Houck had to build this line under the most challenging conditions. It was started from both ends, Kennett and Caruthersville, and had to cross Lake Nicormy an almost impenetrable swamp beginning just east of Kennett. In his memoirs, Houck noted that his engineer lost his way one day while making observations in the area. Houck stated that "before this road was constructed between Kennett and Caruthersville, no more communication existed across this overflow district during a large part of the year than between Africa and South America."[25]

Between 1897 and 1901, Houck built four more railroads as part of his Bootheel network, mostly in response to the timber interests of specific landowners who invested in his companies. The Kennett and Osceola Railroad is an example. It ran initially from Kennett to Arbyrd and was then extended to Leachville, Arkansas. A.R. Byrd, who owned significant acreage below Senath, and C.A. Boynton, a large landowner in Arkansas who planned to establish sawmills there, both subscribed stock in Houck's company to entice him to build these extensions.

Houck built the St. Francois Valley Railroad from Campbell to Caligoa in 1898, followed by the Pemiscot Southern from Pascola to Deering in 1901. The Clarkton Branch Railroad, organized in 1901, began at Gibson on the Campbell to Kennett line ran to Clarkton. However, owners of the Gideon-Anderson Lumber Company enticed him to extend the line to Gideon. Malden residents then persuaded Houck to bring a line to their town, which provided his network with another connection to the Cotton Belt. This network gave the Bootheel multiple connections with the Cotton Belt, Frisco, and the St. Louis and Iron Mountain railroads all of which had skirted the major portion of the Bootheel, particularly the swampy areas holding significant timber resources. In addition, Houck's railroads had a connection to the Mississippi River at Caruthersville.[26]

Houck built two other short line railroads to serve the timber industry, the Missouri and Arkansas Railroad and the St. Louis, Morehouse and Southern. These roads eventually made a connection from Cape Girardeau through Commerce to Morley and Morehouse and finally to Pascola. At

Morley, the railroad made a connection with the Iron Mountain. The extension to Morehouse was due to the timber interests of the Himmelberger-Luce Lumber Company which sought more favorable freight rates than those offered by the Iron Mountain. The Himmelberger-Luce and later the Himmelberger-Harrison Lumber Company became the largest hardwood sawmill in the United States.[27] By mid-year 1900, Houck connected his St. Louis, Morehouse and Southern to his Clarkton Branch at Tallapoosa. This completed a rail route from Cape Girardeau throughout the Bootheel.

Houck first discussed the sale of his network of railroads with Frisco executives B.F. Yoakum and B. L Winchell in 1901. The trio came to an agreement to arrange the transfer in several phases. First, in April 1902 a new company, the St. Louis and Gulf, was organized with Houck as president and financed by the St. Louis Trust Company. This new company then purchased Houck's individual lines in the Bootheel for a total $1,333,000 ($558,000 in cash and assumption of $775,000 bonded indebtedness). Houck resigned as president in September 1902. The St. Louis and Gulf was sold to the St. Louis, Memphis and Southeastern June 1, 1904. This company then sold to the St. Louis and San Francisco (Frisco) July 19, 1907.[28] Houck's achievement made transportation available for both large-scale exploitation of timber resources in the lowlands and the movement of agricultural products, when land became cleared for farming. Personal and business travel also became much easier. The esteem in which Houck was held in southeast Missouri is reflected in this statement in the *Dunklin Democrat* at the time of his resignation from the St. Louis and Gulf Railroad: "It seems strange to think of the Houck railroads of South East Missouri being out from under the hands of this active man. He has certainly done more for South East Missouri than any fifty men, and if he has prospered, we have prospered with him."[29]

The trend of consolidation in the operation of the Bootheel railroads began as the period of major railroad building ended. When timber resources were depleted, some lines were discontinued. A few additional short-line railroads were built in the twentieth century by individual lumber companies to aid in the removal of timber from tracts of land they controlled. W.D. Lasswell organized the St. Louis, Kennett and Southeastern Railroad to haul logs harvested from land he owned near Campbell. Frisco purchased this line in 1927.[30] In 1903, the Gideon-Anderson Lumber and Mercantile Company headquartered in Gideon organized the Gideon and North Island Railroad Company to haul logs to its mills in Gideon and Malden from the 18,000 acres of timberland they eventually controlled. They operated the 29 miles of this railroad until 1929, when it became part of the Cotton Belt lines.[31]

In 1903, the Wisconsin Lumber Company, a subsidiary of International Harvester and supplier of wood for manufacturing Harvester's farm equipment, started the Deering Southwestern Railroad. This road initially ran from the mill and center of the companies operations at Deering to Hickory Landing on Little River near Hornersville where it made a connection with the Cotton Belt. The Deering Southwestern almost exclusively hauled lumber. Local residents sometimes ascribed a different meaning to the initials, D.S.W. Railroad—Dern Slow Wiggling Railroad—suggesting that the condition of the tracks were similar to many other lowland railroads.[32] Between 1910 and 1911, the road was completed to Caruthersville and then sold to the Cotton Belt in 1929.[33]

Seth Barnes of Marston, owner of large tracts of land in New Madrid County, organized the St. Louis and Memphis Railroad in 1898. This railroad ran from Paw Paw Junction (now Lilbourn) to Portageville. Barnes contemplated other railroad ventures but could not generate enough support. With consolidation of the local short lines into larger systems, the opportunities for small railroad entrepreneurs diminished rapidly early in the twentieth century.[34] By 1914, the Frisco, Cotton Belt, and Iron Mountain controlled virtually all of the rail lines in southeast Missouri with a combined total of 775 miles of track with one mile of track for every 2,636 acres, a much more favorable ratio than the state as a whole or many other states. Local land promoters used the presence of this network of railways in their advertising, stating that "there is not an acre of land in Southeast Missouri farther than six and one-half miles from a railroad."[35]

The construction of railroads throughout southeast Missouri brought the attention of the region's vast resource of wildlife and fish to sportsmen. Hunting clubs that sprang up across the area could be accessed by rail. This prime hunting and fishing area was now within an overnight train ride from urban centers such as St. Louis. St. Louis sports writers published columns in the city's newspapers about this hunting and fishing paradise. Railroads encouraged sportsmen, hoping to increase traffic. They even offered refrigerated cars in which to bring back the game they harvested. St. Louis map publisher, Arista C. Shewy published a guide to the region in 1892 titled *Shewey's Guide and Map to the Happy Hunting Grounds of Missouri and Arkansas The Paradise of the Hunter and Fisherman*. Shewey lists the locations that can be accessed along each railroad line in southeast Missouri. Also included are tables listing the special "hunters' rates." For example, hunters could travel on the Cotton Belt Line from St. Louis to Malden for $8.10 which included guns, dogs, and camping equipment up to 200 pounds. He also notes that guides and teams can be secured at Malden. Hotel accommodations could be found for as little as one dollar a day.[36] Shewey described some of the hunting found in the lowlands: "Between Cairo and Malden are what is know as the sunk lands, vast marshy tracks, with ridges of dry lands swarming with duck, geese, swan, brant and all varieties of water fowl. These lands can be reached from LaForge, Ristine, Paw Paw junction or New Madrid. Good hotel accommodation can be had at New Madrid, also guides and boats."[37] Groups wanting to make a hunting or fishing trip could charter on the Iron Mountain Route special hunting cars with sleeping accommodations for 30 with a cook, cooking utensils, dishes, and full equipment provided. The car could "be side-tracked at any point desired."[38] However, such extensive hunting caused depletion of the region's wildlife and required stronger state regulation of hunting and fishing to protect resources.

Road construction proceeded slowly in the lowlands as did railroad building. Most road building responsibility rested with the counties until the mid–1920s. Missouri passed what was called the Centennial Road Law in 1921. With a $60 million bond issue, the law promised to "get Missouri out of the mud." The law also established the Missouri Highway Department overseen by a State Highway Commission. This began the establishment of a modern state highway system. With future passages of gasoline taxes, the first in 1924, funding for highway projects was assured. As highways expanded, railroads came under increasing competition from trucks for hauling freight and automobiles for personal travel. By the late twentieth century, railroads, suffering financial losses, reduced the number trains and eliminated many miles of tracks. Numerous towns that owe their existence to the coming of the railroads in the Bootheel now no longer have rail service and landmark depots have disappeared or been transformed into other uses.

Settlement in the lowlands began along the Mississippi River in order to have access to markets. That outlet is still vital to the movement of southeast Missouri agricultural products. Agricultural products once transported by rail to these ports are now moved primarily by truck.

Chapter 7

Timber

The building of a railroad network ushered in a new era for the Bootheel. Land that had as Otto Kochtizky stated, "no value" suddenly became sought after for its timber. As timber supplies became depleted in eastern and northern areas, timber men eyed the vast forests of the lowlands and its exploitation began. James F. Brooks, chief engineer for the St. Louis, Kennett and Southern Railroad described southeast Missouri timber in a letter to Louis Houck, president of the railroad:

> There are immense bodies of oak of every variety, gum, locust, ash, and great cypress brakes. The cypress is sound of the red variety. It runs from one to three feet in diameter and is very tall and straight and ought to run 10,000 feet of lumber to the acre. There are dense forests of red and white oak, gum, soft maple, honey locust, ash, hickory, and cottonwood. The red oak is magnificent and three, four, and five feet in diameter and free from knots. The white oak is scattered but of great size. The locust runs from 1,000 to 1500 feet to the tree and there is more of it than I ever saw elsewhere. It is in great demand for wagon hubs. The ash, gum and other timber are equally good and grow in abundance.[1]

Correspondence of Otto Kochtitzky indicates the great amount of interest in southeast Missouri timber at the end of the nineteenth and early twentieth centuries. Kochtitzky received letters from business interests and individuals seeking information about the availability and price of good timberland. He and his brother along with other partners frequently bought and resold large tracts of land for timber while some of the land they purchased they held and they sold the timber themselves.[2] Land given to the counties by the state as a result of the Swampland Act of 1850 sold slowly for many years. The minimum price was set at $1.25 per acre and no person could buy more than 2,000 acres. The legislature revised the law in 1868,

A logging operation in Dunklin County at Kern's Mill around 1900. Oxen were used more frequently than horses or mules in hauling logs (Dunklin Democrat Photos [P0826] 023795; The State Historical Society of Missouri Photograph Collection).

removing the acreage limit but the minimum price remained at $1.25 per acre. With a railroad network in place, interest in these lands quickly increased and sales became brisk.

The southeast lowlands' economy became dominated by big timber operations. There were dozens of sawmill operations throughout the Bootheel which varied in size from small mills buying stumpage rights on a limited acreage to large operations controlling tens of thousands of acres of land. The four largest were Himmelberger-Luce, later Himmelberger-Harrison, centered at Morehouse; Wisconsin Lumber Co., a subsidiary of International Harvester, with headquarters at Deering; Gideon-Anderson at Gideon; and Brooklyn Cooperage, a subsidiary of American Sugar Refining, located at Poplar Bluff.[3] Other large sawmills were owned by T.J. Moss, C.A. Boynton, A.R. Byrd, Lindus Lumber Company, W.D. Lasswell, and J.A. Hemphill.

The timber industry was the primary economic force in the Bootheel at this time. In 1899, Dunklin, Mississippi, New Madrid, Pemiscot, Scott, and Stoddard counties together shipped 160,461,618 board feet of lumber of all types. In addition, Bootheel counties also shipped logs, pilings, walnut logs, railroad ties, fence and mine posts, and lumber for cooperage. These items are not included in the figure above.[4] Dunklin County hosted 15 sawmills, while Pemiscot County was home to thirty-eight sawmills. The Bootheel region led the entire state in forest products.

The lumber industry in the Bootheel reached its peak from 1890 to around 1915. Pemiscot County shipped 74,819,789 board feet in 1899, after which its production dropped. Dunklin County shipped 44,104,000 feet of lumber in 1910, while New Madrid and Pemiscot shipped 83,392,000 and 17,620,000, respectively.[5] Production after this time appears to diminish although large amounts of lumber continued to be produced into the late 1920s with some logging continuing into the 1930s. Numbers for 1917 show 19,020,000, 51,540,000, and 12,270,000 board feet for Dunklin, New Madrid, and Pemiscot counties. While these numbers represent a large volume of lumber production, they also show a gradual decline in the region's forests.[6]

During this period, lumber created wealth for those holding large tracts of timberland and brought growth to towns. J.A. Hemphill, for example, operated a mill at Kennett from 1915 to 1929, with an annual capacity of nearly 20 million board feet and employed 300 to 400 people, making it Kennett's largest employer at the time. Timber was hauled from the swampland east of Kennett to the mill, over their own railroad.[7] C.A. Boynton owned 60,000 acres in Missouri and Arkansas, and operated mills utilizing lumber from this land.[8] By 1930, Gideon-Anderson controlled more than 18,000 acres of timber and its mill had a capacity of 10,000 board feet per day.[9] Gideon-Anderson Lumber and Mercantile Company moved to New Madrid County in 1900 after being organized in Indiana. Its officers included William P. Anderson, M.S. Anderson, Charles F. Meentemeyer, M.V. Mumma, and Frank E. Gideon for whom its headquarters town, Gideon, was named. The company also included three cooperage firms, Gideon Cooperage, Senath Cooperage, and Anderson-Poorman Cooperage. They operated mills at Gideon, Marston, and Caruthersville with a combined daily output of 180,000 board feet of lumber, specializing in high quality hardwoods. Late into the twentieth century the company operated a wooden box factory at Gideon. The company also operated other businesses in Gideon such as a large department store, hardware store, and farm equipment dealership.

The largest company, Himmelberger-Harrison Lumber Company

A large log being hauled through Holcomb, Missouri, by an ox team. Timber of immense size was harvested in the southeast Missouri in the late 1800s and early 1900s (Dunklin Democrat Photos [P0826] 026997; The State Historical Society of Missouri Photograph Collection).

controlled over 200,000 acres of land in southeast Missouri and operated the largest hardwood sawmill in the United States.[10] An inventory of 12 to 15 million board feet of lumber on their Morehouse yard was not uncommon.[11] The Isaac Himmelberger family operated sawmills in Logansport, Indiana, during the 1860s. About 1880 they started a mill at Buffington in Stoddard County then in 1890, they purchased a mill at Morehouse. The Luce family joined with the Himmelbergers in 1895 to form the Himmelberger-Luce Lumber Company. The Luce family owned several hundred thousand acres of land in New Madrid County. W. Harrison acquired the Luce interest in 1902 and the company was reorganized as the Himmelberger-Harrison Lumber Company.[12]

The Wisconsin Lumber Company had its beginnings when William Deering, developer of the successful Deering Harvester, started buying land in Dunklin and Pemiscot counties to obtain lumber for building his harvesters. Deering's company merged with McCormick Harvesting Machine Company and three other competitors in 1902 to form International

J.A. Hemphill Lumber Company mill in Kennett. Large lumber mills were common in the southeast Missouri lowlands during the peak of the timber industry in the late 1800s and early 1900s (courtesy Tony Byrd, Kennett, Missouri).

Harvester. International Harvester then formed a subsidiary organization, Wisconsin Lumber Company to utilize Deering's southeast Missouri timberlands. By 1905, International harvester was using 20 million board feet of lumber annually in its production of farm machinery.[13] The site for their mill was chosen according to local folklore because it is where six yoke of oxen hauling by mud boat the boiler for the mill from Hickory Landing on Little River became bogged down and could not be moved any further. Deering was chosen as the name of the location of the mill. The community also had a store, barbershop, recreation building with a bowling alley, pool hall, dance floor, and theater. There were schools, one for whites and another for blacks, also a ball field and playground.[14]

The Wisconsin Lumber Company's mill at Deering had a daily average capacity of 60,000 board feet, making it the second largest hardwood lumber mill in the United States. Annually they cut timber from 2,500 acres of land.[15] They owned 60,000 acres of timber land in southeast Missouri and leased an additional 22,000 acres in Arkansas.[16] Species harvested included oak, ash, cypress, elm, cottonwood, sycamore, maple, gum, tupelo, and hickory. In addition to needs of International Harvester, the company shipped lumber to all parts of the United States and exported lumber to England, Scotland, Germany, France, Italy, Holland, Spain, and other countries.[17] The town Wisconsin Lumber Company built around its mill featured houses built for workers to rent and a hotel, primarily offering a place for company officials to stay when visiting Deering.

One of the most widespread uses of Bootheel lumber was in cooperage or the manufacture of barrels. A variety of food and non-food items were packed in barrels for shipping. Barrels were made in two types: slack stave

A logging camp in southeast Missouri about 1910. Often wives and children lived with the timber cutters in camps. This camp was probably cutting timber for the Himmelberger-Harrison Lumber Co. headquartered in Morehouse (Himmelberger-Harrison Lumber Company Records, Special Collections and Archives, Southeast Missouri State University).

and tight stave. The slack stave barrels were suitable for non-liquid material such as flour, grain, or sugar, while tight stave barrels were used for transportation of liquids. Nearly all lumber companies in the lowlands supplied material for staves and numerous cooperage manufacturers were scattered over the region. The largest barrel maker, Brooklyn Cooperage Company purchased more than 60,000 acres of land in Butler County to make barrels for its parent company, American Sugar Refining Company. It located its plant in Poplar Bluff and at the peak of its operations there between 1900 and 1927 employed 1200 people. As timber supplies dwindled, the plant closed in 1927.[18]

Harvesting timber in the lowlands of southeast Missouri was challenging to say the least. It also brought an influx of new people into the region. Edward C. Matthews III, writing about the Matthews family in Scott County, describes the life of those working as timber cutters: "Many of the timber cutters in those days [1890s and early 1900s] were hoboes recruited form passing trains. The logging camps where the lumberjacks lived were canvas cities, with a huge circus tent serving as a mess hall surrounded by much smaller lodging tents. As the timber was harvested ... the logging camps were periodically moved to a new location. The usual wages were from twenty to twenty-four cents an hour, plus food and lodging. The workdays were said to be ten hours, but in reality went from dawn to dusk."[19]

Those coming to work in the timber of the southeast lowlands for the most part were white hill people from Kentucky and Tennessee.[20] Thad Snow, an early 1900s land owner in Mississippi County, described the timber worker or "woods workers" as Snow refers to them in a story he wrote for the *St. Louis Post Dispatch*: "Many thousands of workers have come to us for logging and land clearing from the poor and over populated hills of Kentucky and Tennessee.... Some of them are upright and proud, and I have been proud to have them as co-workers. But they have been accustomed to a low scale of living, and they are not always prepossessing in appearance and habits."[21]

Snow further explains the land clearing process: "they worked in family groups taking it a strip or medium-sized plot at a time."[22] Snow states that workers were usually paid $8 to $12 per acre for clearing land.[23] Even in the early twentieth century the southeast Missouri lowlands was still a place where those seeking to escape from the law sometimes came. Law enforcement officials from east of the Mississippi River seldom pursued wrong doers across the river. Snow notes, "The country was then so uninviting that every newcomer was presumed to have left his former abode under a cloud and pursued by a sheriff."[24] Some lumber mills also hired African American workers such as Wisconsin Lumber Company at their Deering mill. However they lived in separate parts of the town built by the company for its workers.

In many areas, the timber was flooded and had to be from boats, leaving stumps from six to 15 feet tall. In some areas, logs were cut during the drier months and then floated out through sloughs during high water periods. Timber men employed both mules and oxen in hauling logs, although oxen usually proved superior in pulling logs through the muddy swamps. With their cloven hooves, oxen get better traction when working in mud. Loggers hitched them in teams of four, six, or eight. The logs were either drug or loaded onto wagons. Because of the deep mud, it was necessary to cover the wagon wheels to keep mud out of the spokes.[25] Some loggers made wagon wheels from round slabs cut from logs. Life-long Wardell resident Bill Crabtree describes another method of hauling logs, the "mud boat": "One of the vehicles that the loggers used when the mud got too deep for the wagons to haul the logs out of the swamp was a mud boat. It was shaped like a boat on the bottom, even with a shallow keel shaped like a V so it would slide through the mud easily."[26] Crabtree indicates that these mud boats were pulled by either oxen or mules.

Larger logging operations built railroad spurs also know as "dummy lines" into the woods about every mile. Logs were loaded on tramcars, often pulled by oxen or mules as well as locomotives, and hauled over these tracks to the mill. Lumber companies eventually used steam-powered cable skidders to pull logs from the area where they were cut to rail spurs for loading.[27]

Not only was the work of harvesting timber and land clearing physically demanding work, there was also the risk of becoming ill. The southeast Missouri lowlands had long bore the reputation for being an unhealthy place in which to live because of diseases associated with the swampland, particularly malaria, referred to as "chills and fevers." Many attributed it to bad air from the swampland or decaying vegetation. In fact, the term malaria comes from the Italian word meaning "bad air." For example, Mary Smith-Davis's discussion of malarial diseases in her *History of Dunklin County* written in 1896 illustrates this understanding: "The malarial season in Dunklin County is from the middle of July to the middle of October; this presumably caused by the decaying of rank vegetation grown in the spring and early summer. During dry seasons malarial diseases are much less prevalent than during wet ones."[28] The presence of malaria in the southeast Missouri lowlands as well as all of the southern bottom lands of the United States became a more serious health issue as large numbers of people moved to these areas and worked in the lowlands because of timber harvesting, land clearing, and drainage projects. Life in these lowland areas exposed thousands to the disease.

As far back as 2700 B.C. Chinese medical writings described the symptoms of malaria. In the second century B.C. they used preparations from the plant, *Artemisia annua* or annual wormwood, to treat fevers. In 1971, Chinese scientists isolated the active ingredient, known as artemisinin, from this plant which has been developed into highly effective antimalarial drugs. In the sixteenth century, indigenous South American tribes in Peru showed Spanish Jesuit missionaries how to use the bark of a tree to treat fevers. The tree was first referred to as Peruvian bark and later named by the Spanish, Cinchona. The active ingredient in this bark is what we now know as quinine, one of the most effective antimalarial drugs.[29] As early as 1823, Dr. John Sappington of Arrow Rock, Missouri, began using quinine to treat fevers and chills. Sappington questioned the standard medical treatment of the day which included bloodletting, purging, and use of mercury compounds. However, his methods were questioned and some physicians had concerns about the side effects of quinine while at the same time freely using calomel which can lead to mercury poisoning. Because of his promotion of quinine, Sappington was denied admission to the St. Louis Medical Society. Not deterred, Sappington manufactured and sold millions of his "Dr. Sappington's Anti-Fever Pills," which became one of the best known patent medicines of nineteenth century. In 1844, he also authored a book on the subject, *The Theory and Treatment of Fever*. His use of quinine represented a significant medical advance that eventually became a standard treatment for malaria.[30] Two of the most widely used drugs for the treatment of malaria remain artemisinin and quinine although synthetic antimalarial drugs that work in a manner similar to quinine have been available since World War II.[31]

It was 1880 before scientists understood that parasites in the blood caused malaria. French army surgeon Charles Laveran made the discovery and received a Nobel Prize for his work in 1907. In the 1890s, Italian researchers Giovanni Grassi and Raimondo Filetti named the specific parasites causing malaria. A British medical officer, Ronald Ross, proved in 1897 that mosquitoes transmitted malaria parasites. He received a Nobel Prize for his work in 1902. Finally, in 1899 Italian scientists including Giovanni Grassi and Amico Bastianelli allowed *Anopheles* mosquitoes to feed on malarial patients in Rome then sent the mosquitoes to London where they infected two volunteers with malaria. Today, it is well understood that the parasites that cause malaria are four species of *Plasmodium* and that it is transmitted only by the female *Anopheles* mosquito. Scientists have also learned that two species of *Plasmodium, vivax* and *ovale* can enter a dormant stage in the liver and become active again after two to four years. By the early 1950s, because of effective treatments, insect control, tighter screens on houses, and improved drainage malaria had been eliminated from the United States. However, the three species of *Anopheles* mosquito that transmitted the disease in the United States before it was eliminated are still very much present thus there is always a risk of reintroduction.[32] Malaria remains a serious health problem in many parts of the world, particularly in tropical regions. The World Health Organization estimates that 627,000 deaths resulted world wide in 2012 from malaria. The most affected areas are Africa south of the Sahara and in tropical Pacific Islands such as New Guinea.

Control of malaria along with yellow fever played a crucial role in construction of the Panama Canal which was completed just prior to the beginning of the work on the Little River Drainage District in southeast Missouri. In 1906, 21,000 of the 26,000 employees working on the canal project were hospitalized at some point for malaria. By 1912, the number hospitalized had been reduced to 5,600 through insect control and treatment for malaria.[33]

The effectiveness of quinine had been known in the United States since Dr. Sappington marketed his tonic and was an ingredient in a variety of patent medicines marketed as chill and fever tonics in the early 1900s. Grove's Chill Tonic and Mendenhall's Chill and Fever Tonic were among the most popular of that era. Even with the availability of such medicines, malaria remained a serious problem in the southeast Missouri lowlands through the 1920s. Those who sought medical treatment from physicians and received the correct dosage of quinine recovered. However, the poor, such as the timber workers and tenant farmers who could not afford the services of a physician, often relied on the so-called chill and fever tonics sold in most general stores. Unfortunately, these chill tonics contained an inadequate amount of quinine. Physician and historian Margaret Humphreys writes, "The amount of quinine in chill tonics was rarely sufficient to make a dent in the disease. One physician found a young boy swarming with parasites—yet the boy had consumed three bottles of Grove's Chill Tonic in the previous three weeks."[34] In June of 1929, the eastern district of Missouri federal court ordered that 60 dozen bottles of Mendenhall's Chill and Fever Tonic warehoused in St. Louis be seized and destroyed by United States Marshals charging the J.C. Mendenhall Medicine Co. with adulteration of the product and misbranding. Testing by the United States Agriculture Department revealed that the bottles contained only the equivalent of 6.32 grains of quinine instead of the 8 grains specified on the label.[35] The standard treatment usually meant giving 30 grains of quinine daily for three days then ten grains daily for eight weeks.

Thad Snow had a lot of experience seeing malaria ravage timber workers and others in southeast Missouri or "Swampeast" Missouri as Snow termed it. He described what it was like to suffer from malaria:

> A few days after the human victim has been bit and infected he comes up with a chill, after which he has a few hours of fever. The first chill isn't so bad, usually. That is, his bones don't ache too badly and his teeth don't chatter. If he has his first chill, let us say, on Monday at noon, then the next one will come on Wednesday at about eleven in the morning and it will be about fifty per cent worse. The next one on Friday will be worse still. The chill will go on and on, striking every other day. The chills get harder and the fever that follows last longer. The poor devil losses weight drags his feet and his cheeks sink in and get "yaller" like a pumpkin.[36]

Snow was passionate about the fact that chill tonics lacked the sufficient amount of quinine to treat malaria yet that is how they were advertised and most of the poor had little alternative. He writes: "All the manufacturer of 'tonic' had to do, if his idea was to stop chills, was to put enough quinine in his solution, and put proper directions for taking on his bottle. Did he do this? Not on your life! Instead he designed his formula and directions to string out the malaria for about six weeks so that the poor devil would buy bottle after bottle till he wore the malaria out, or possibly till he finally got enough to kill the malaria germs in his blood, like a 'standard' dose of quinine would so in twelve hours' time."[37]

The malaria problem in southeast Missouri had been recognized by public health officials for several years. The seven lowland counties, Butler, Dunklin, Mississippi, New Madrid, Pemiscot, Scott, and Stoddard had a mean death rate from 1919 to 1921 of five per 10,000. For the Mississippi Delta region as whole for the same period the rate was nine per 10,000. In 1919, Dunklin County's death rate from malaria reached 12 per 10,000, which was higher than the highest county in Alabama. In 1921, a cooperative effort was made between the United States Public Health Service, the International Health Board, and the Missouri State Board of Health to make a malaria survey in southeast Missouri. The program extended beyond Missouri to include ten southern states in the study.[38] The malaria problem became more pronounced because of the rapid population growth of the lowlands in the first two decades of twentieth century. The following chart shows population growth during this period.[39]

County	Percent increases in population			Population per square mile, 1920
	1890–1900	1900–1910	1910–1920	
Butler	65	23	17	25
Dunklin	44	40	8	62
Mississippi	17	23	12	31
New Madrid	21	73	29	39
Pemiscot	103	61	36	58
Scott	17	71	5	56
Stoddard	42	13	27	37

While malaria continued to be a problem through the 1920s, data show there was a gradual decline as a result of drainage improvements. The following table shows the death rate from 1913 to 1921 from malaria per 10,000 population in the seven Bootheel counties.[40]

County	1913	1914	1915	1916	1917	1918	1919	1920	1921
Butler	26.5	18.5	5.3	16.2	13.8	7.2	6.7	8.3	5.8
Dunklin	33.3	36.0	22.6	23.2	16.5	21.2	10.5	8.3	11.8
Mississippi	12.0	6.5	4.4	4.4	6.0	2.3	3.1	7.1	2.3
New Madrid	17.4	16.1	7.5	8.6	7.6	3.7	2.0	2.8	2.4
Pemiscot	22.8	19.1	14.6	12.6	16.6	11.4	4.1	3.0	4.5
Scott	13.1	15.0	5.7	7.8	3.9	2.1	2.6	.4	1.7
Stoddard	22.3	13.6	11.1	9.0	14.0	7.5	5.7	2.7	5.7

An area in the vicinity of Sikeston was selected for the study where researchers visited 407 houses, recording the clinical history of malaria attacks and also took a blood smear which was examined by the Missouri State Board of Health. The study established that 14.7 out of every 100 individuals had a history of malaria in 1921. Also noted in the study was the condition of the screening on houses.[41] The study found that efforts should be concentrated on the individual home and the school. Education about how the disease is transmitted and how to properly screen homes needed to be emphasized. The study further concluded, "Quinine must be popularized in place of the inadequate 'chill tonics' and the 'standard treatment' should be introduced in order to diminish the percentage of 'carriers.'"[42]

As the decade of the 1920s waned, the best of the lowland timber had been harvested and owners of large tracts of swampland wondered what they would do with this land which now held little value with the timber gone. Agriculture was now the heir-apparent to replace lumber as the dominant economic force in the Bootheel. In spite of the great timber resources, most people realized that the true value of the land lay with agriculture. Virgin timber seldom brought more than $50 per acre.[43] A good cotton crop in the early 1900s could easily produce double that amount each year. With the recognition of the inherent fertility of these soils, agriculture became the obvious answer, but before this could occur, major drainage and reclamation lay ahead, opening a new chapter in the Bootheel's trek from swampland to farmland.

CHAPTER 8

Beginning Reclamation

A study of the first interest in drainage of the lowlands requires us to go back chronologically to the time of early settlement in the region. Some of the earliest explorers of the southeast lowlands recognized that in order for this region to become suitable for agriculture, significant drainage would be required. Amos Stoddard, who represented the United States in the transfer of the Louisiana Purchase from France, in his *Sketches of Louisiana* discussed the need for drainage:

> The flat country on the Mississippi extends from the mouth of the Arkansas to the head of what is called Tiwappaty bottom, a distance of nearly four hundred and fifty miles. The river St. Francis runs nearly parallel to the Mississippi, and from thirty to forty miles (in some places less) to the west ward of it, for the distance of about four hundred and sixty miles, and mostly through the flat country already mentioned. Nearly half of the lands between these two rivers are covered with swamps and ponds, and periodically inundated. These swamps filled with cypress are mostly dry in the summer, though unless they be drained at great expense, or banks constructed to keep the water from them, they will never be of any service to agriculturalists, other than as ranges for cattle.[1]

Opinions varied on the efficacy of draining the large swampy areas. In fact, some early visitors did not think it would ever be practical to drain and develop the area. Estwick Evans, who visited the area in 1818, commented, "These swamps are very extensive, being incapable of cultivation, will ever render the climate of this part of the country insalubrious." He even ventured to give his assessment of the value of the Louisiana Purchase: "Much of the Louisiana Purchase is not worth a cent."[2]

Many landowners and county officials believed that with the right plan, the swampland could be drained and made into productive farmland. As early as 1826, Senator Thomas Hart Benton introduced legislation which directed the General Land Office to report on lands unfit for cultivation in Missouri and Illinois. Their report provided scant information and concluded that there was little to be gained by reclamation of the swampland.[3] An 1834 study by the Secretary of the Treasury surveyed land registrars in the area who agreed that it was feasible to construct both levees and drainage systems.[4] A report to the House of Representatives in 1836 presented plans by John Rodney for reclamation of the southeast lowlands. This plan advocated building a levee between the Scott County Hills south of Cape Girardeau and the Ozark uplands, removing drifts from the St. Francis River, building a channel to divert water from Little River south of New Madrid to the Mississippi River, and finally to improve the Little River channel through the lowlands. The cost of these improvements was estimated in the report to be $167,500.[5] While the general sentiment was that the lowlands could be reclaimed, the political climate in Washington opposed massive expenditures on internal improvements. Between 1840 and 1849, the Missouri legislature sent repeated petitions to Congress requesting the federal government to either proceed with a plan to reclaim the swampland or turn that land over to the state. In 1846, the House Committee on Public Lands, to which petitions from the Missouri General Assembly had been referred, made a report which discussed the slow rate of public land sales in southeast Missouri, "in 1824, less than one fifth had been sold." The report also noted the same results for those lands brought to market in 1835, "less than one tenth have been sold."[6] This report painted a dismal picture of the land and climate because of a lack of drainage: "but such is the insalubrity of the climate from the noisome exhalations escaping from the extensive surface of the surrounding marsh lands, in a climate where malaria is rapidly engendered, that no human being can dwell in them with safety, and that they yet remain the habitation of the buffalo, the elk, and the bear." The report also expressed concerns over the negative effects the conditions there have on settlement in surrounding areas: "The malign influence arising from those swamps on the health of the more distant surrounding country is severely felt and shown by the sparseness of the population on the public lands in several surrounding counties in Missouri and Arkansas which have long since been surveyed and brought into market."[7] The recommendation of the report was to transfer swamplands to the state so that they could be sold and drained.

The Missouri General Assembly enacted legislation in February 1847 appointing five southeast Missouri citizens, three from New Madrid County and two from Stoddard County, to a special commission tasked with surveying a route for a Mississippi river levee from New Madrid to the Arkansas state line and a route for a canal from near Bloomfield to the Mississippi River in the vicinity of New Madrid.[8] This group of commissioners conducted the surveys and issued their report in September 1848. They recommended a route for the levee following the "highest land." The commissioners also recommended construction of a canal from the junction of Castor and Little River to the Mississippi River, a distance of eight and a half miles. The surveyors found it was "impracticable to proceed further than about six miles, in the direction of Bloomfield." They encountered what was described as an "ocean of water" and found "it impossible to work our way through with light canoes—after three days hard labor."The commissioners presented a cost estimate for the levee of $47,282 and for the canal $41,032.[9] Possibly because of the commissioners' recommendations, the legislature chartered the New Madrid and Stoddard Canal Company in March of 1849. The company was authorized after $100,000 in stock had been subscribed to build a canal from near Point Pleasant on the Mississippi River to near Bloomfield. The General Assembly even sent petitions to Congress asking for land grants to aid the New Madrid and Stoddard Canal Company. However, no aid was forthcoming and no canal as described was built.

In 1847, the 166 delegates meeting at Bloomfield in a swampland convention urged representatives and senators to press for legislation granting the swamplands to the states.[10] Shortly thereafter, the Swampland Act of 1850, signed by the president on September 28, 1850, turned over what had been designated as swamp and overflow land to the respective states. The federal government had no taste for funding reclamation of these lands thus "sought to free itself of them entirely." Missouri, on March 3, 1851, passed legislation which ceded the swamplands to the counties except the swampland in the Bootheel counties which the state retained.[11] The state legislature appointed a Board of Swampland Commissioners which was to plan the drainage and reclamation of the retained swamplands and appropriated $50,000 for operations of the board which organized at a meeting at Benton in May 1851. The board appointed John Rodney whose drainage plan had been a part of a report to the U.S. House of Representatives in 1836 as topographical engineer. Unfortunately, Rodney died a short time later. The only other meeting the Board of Swampland Commissioners held was in September 1851. The board approved surveys to be made and construction contracts. However, the board never developed a comprehensive plan for the area and by the end of the next year had spent its entire budget of $50,000. With no more source of funding, the state legislature early in 1853 dissolved the board and seemed to follow the federal government's sentiments in not wanting responsibility for reclamation of the lowlands by ceding all of the swamp and overflow lands held by the state including those in the Bootheel to the respective counties, authorizing them to sell the land to finance reclamation projects. The legislature set the minimum selling price for these lands at $1.25 per acre and also permitted counties to join together to work on reclamation projects.[12] The state even went one step further in demonstrating that it did not want any responsibility for theses lands by ordering counties to refund the portion of the $50,000 the swampland commission spent in the respective counties.[13]

In its next session, the legislature designated the county clerks to receive public land and handle sales. It also authorized the selection of a superintendent of public works to oversee reclamation projects and added greater restrictions on selling land such as limiting purchasers to a maximum of 1,000 acres and permitting those claiming land by preemption to purchase up to 160 acres at $1 per acre.[14] County control of the swamplands increased in 1868 when the Missouri General Assembly made the swampland "absolute property" of the counties.[15] Counties often sold the swampland at sheriff's sales for only a few cents per acre. John Nolen reports one case in Stoddard County where 80,000 acres sold for $663.95 in 1868 at public sale. This brought accusations that county courts showed favoritism to certain purchasers. To prevent partiality and perhaps to generate more money for the benefit of county residents, the legislature in 1874 set the minimum price at $1.25 per acre. At this price, swampland was priced the same as or in some cases higher than better drained public land requiring less work to place it into cultivation, making swampland even more unattractive and slowed sales.[16]

The Swampland Act of 1850 proved to be a much greater land grant than originally anticipated because of the broad interpretation of what constituted swamp and overflow land by state agents appointed to choose land for this designation and the General Land Office. In all, Missouri received 3,346,936 acres under this act, about 1,850,000 acres of this was in the southeast lowlands.[17] Nathan Parker notes in his 1867 gazetteer of Missouri, "Complaint has been made by the people of Southeastern Missouri especially, that the surveys were incorrect—that a great proportion of land that had been returned as swamp or overflow land is really dry or arable land."[18] The goal of draining the swamps of the southeast lowlands was still on many people's minds. For example, Parker in his gazetteer outlined a three point drainage plan. First, Parker proposed constructing a levee just south of Cape Girardeau to prevent Mississippi River overflow from entering the lowlands. Second he believed an embankment across the St. Francis Valley just below

Mingo Swamp over to the Bloomfield Ridge (Crowley's Ridge), a distance of two and one-quarter miles would force water back through Mingo and into Castor River. Third, locating a dike where White River (Whitewater River) enters the lowlands. Parker admitted he lacked direct knowledge about the portion of the lowlands south of New Madrid and didn't offer a plan for the Little River Valley but estimated the cost of his proposals to be $474,600.[19] The problem of draining this swampland was not only a financial one; it was also a lack of engineering knowledge and lack of power equipment. Until near the end of the 1800s no power machinery existed to excavate large ditches. Only when the steam powered dipper dredge came into use was equipment available that could chew through the timber, stumps, and undergrowth covering the lowlands. The best that could be accomplished earlier would be low levees and small ditches built using wheeled dirt slips pulled by mules.

Engineers began to recognize that reclamation of the southeast Missouri lowlands really had four fronts. First, streams such as the St. Francois were choked with fallen timber forming drifts or rafts which impeded both the steamboat traffic and drainage. Secondly, flooding from overflow of the Mississippi and St. Francois rivers needed to be addressed with levees. Third, a drainage plan needed to be developed to remove water from the low-lying areas of the Little River Valley. Finally, any drainage plan had to address the large volume of runoff from Ozark streams that entered the lowlands west of Cape Girardeau. Between 1883 and 1895, Missouri made several attempts to devise a drainage scheme but by the end of the 1800s it was apparent that, regarding at least initial drainage and reclamation, financing was going to be left to the landowners. In essence, the task of draining the swampland and protecting overflow lands kept being passed down to smaller and smaller governmental units and ultimately it was drainage and levee districts organized by land owners who accomplished the task.

By 1858, the counties fronting the Mississippi River had constructed a low line of levees from Crowley's Ridge in Scott County to the Arkansas line. The first levees were, as S.P. Reynolds explains, built by individual planters "here and yonder putting up a small levee to protect himself."[20] Work on construction of a longer levee was mostly done by local residents.[21] In some instances, swampland was used as payment for work. For example, Pemiscot County paid for levee work in script which entitled the holder to one acre of land at $1.25 per acre. The county based payment on 20 cents per cubic yard. Unfortunately, a large flood in the spring of 1858 destroyed these low levees and made it apparent that much larger levees would be necessary to contain he mighty river.

A period of eight disastrous floods that ensued between 1882 and 1893 again highlighted the need for flood control before significant reclamation could occur. The Missouri legislature organized the St. Francis Levee District in 1893 to construct a levee from Point Pleasant to the Arkansas line. Because local levee districts would not be able to totally fund construction of the size of levees needed to contain the Mississippi River, Congress created the Mississippi River Commission in 1879. Through a combination of a tax on local landowners, appropriations from the state, and Mississippi River Commission funding from the federal government, a new levee was completed to the Arkansas line by spring of 1896. The Commission continued in partnership with local districts until 1927. The devastating flood of 1927 brought more Federal involvement into levee construction through the 1928 Flood Control Act approved May 15, 1928.[22] This act authorized "the project for the flood control of the Mississippi River in its alluvial valley ... and placed the cost burden on the federal government, ... no local contribution to the project herein adopted is required."[23]

Toward the end of the nineteenth century it had become apparent that the financing of drainage projects in the Bootheel was going to fall to the landowners. At this point, drainage had a two-fold purpose: to provide timber companies better access to timber on land they controlled and to convert land from which timber had been removed to farming so that these same companies could sell their former timber land at a profit. Missouri drainage laws passed before the twentieth century provided a convenient means for landowners to organize drainage districts, which in effect are public corporations with the power to levy taxes. S.P. Reynolds explains that in the early twentieth century, drainage laws received refinements making them more efficient. "By 1905 and 1906 workable county court and circuit court law had been evolved, made by noting the defiences [*sic*] of earlier efforts."[24]

Drainage law allowed the formation of districts in one of two ways. Districts which were entirely within one county were organized under county courts, now usually referred to as county commissions. Those districts, including land in more than one county, were organized under circuit courts. Under the county court law, the county court hires an engineer and attorney, and the county clerk and treasurer maintain all records and handle all clerical work. In contrast, under the circuit court law, a board of supervisors is selected and is responsible for operation of the district including hiring an engineer, attorney, and maintaining records. Under both methods, the process begins with a petition from land owners within the proposed district.

The first drainage district in southeast Missouri was composed of 41,000 acres and was organized in 1898.[25] Districts rather quickly began to be formed at the beginning of the twentieth century. S.P. Reynolds states, "From 1899 to 1907 many districts covering small acreage from five to fifty thousand each were organized and drainage works completed." Reynolds further states that upon completion, these districts drained "their water into the trough of the [Little River] basin."[26] By 1920, plans existed to drain virtually all of the lowlands.[27] Landowners continued organizing drainage districts. Today, slightly less than two million acres in the lowlands are included in drainage districts.[28] Several technological and economic factors merged to make the drainage of the lowlands at the beginning of the twentieth century feasible and desirable. To most of the early settlers, the forests were simply and obstacle to farming. Before 1870, "the main objective of cutting was to clear land for cultivation." The land could produce more income from growing crops than the value of the timber which "seldom was worth more than fifty dollars per acre."[29] Railroad construction in the 1890s added value to the timber. It meant that the large amount available for harvest could be moved to markets. Still, drainage was needed in some cases to make the timber stands accessible and after timber removal, drainage was necessary to clear and convert the land to agriculture. However this task required substantial power equipment that had only recently become available. The steam-powered dipper dredge which came into use around 1883 became the equipment of choice for swampland drainage. This machine was basically a steam-powered shovel mounted to platform that floated as digging progressed rather than having to move over soft, water-logged soils. Arthur F. King explains this machine's advantages.

> There have been attempts to dig drainage ditches with the steam shovel or the hydraulic dredge or the scraper bucket excavator, but only in a few cases, and under the most favorable circumstance, have they proven successful. The character of swamp land, in that it is either partially covered by water or extremely soft, generally precludes the use of any machine not mounted on a Barge or boat. Then again, the fact that there is usually a heavy growth of underbrush and timber, make the dipper dredge most desirable, because of its power and ability to handle such material.[30]

The major work of drainage of the southeast Missouri lowlands including the Little River Drainage District is set in the context of what Gary McDowell, in his dissertation exploring the economics of drainage in southeast Missouri, calls the "national drainage movement from 1900 to 1920." During this period there was increasing concern about "reclaiming wet lands" in many states.[31] He further states, "The people of the United States were more conscious of the problems of resource conservation and use in the first two decades of this century [twentieth] than they ever had been previously."[32] The idea of draining the swampland in southeast Mis-

The introduction of the steam powered dipper dredge made it possible the clear the vast areas of swampland in southeast Missouri. Such equipment was not available until the late 1800s (Little River Drainage District Collection, Missouri State Archives).

souri did not occur in isolation or just as a local concept away from national trends. It fits into the national narrative of the time that not only was conservation important but development of resources unusable in their present condition was an equally important part of conservation.

Theodore Roosevelt helped focus national attention on conservation issues as President and in speeches and political activity after leaving office. During Roosevelt's time in office, he established four national game preserves, five national parks, 18 national monuments, 51 Federal bird reservations, 150 national forests, and started 24 reclamation projects. The reclamation projects involved building dams and reservoirs in western states to provide water for irrigation of arid land. This ushered in the period from the 1920s until the mid–1960s that has been termed the era of big dam construction. Authors David P. Billington, Donald C. Jackson, and Martin V. Melosi write that Progressive Era water policy focused on the "efficient use of a vital natural resource."[33] The benefits derived from dam construction included flood control, irrigation, reduced soil erosion, improved navigation, and generation of electricity. By the late 1960s however, those concerned with environmental impacts began to see dams and drainage in a different light. Billington, et. al note that dams "were now being critiqued more closely in terms of erosion of downstream channels, changes in fish population and riparian vegetation, water evaporation loss, displacement of native peoples, dwindling scenic wonders, and urban sprawl."[34] Added to that list was the destruction of historic and archaeological site. Many of the same arguments were applied to drainage: straightening channels affected aquatic flora and fauna and drainage of wetlands destroyed a vital ecosystem.

In a speech on "The New Nationalism" given at Osawatomie, Kansas, on August 31, 1910, for the dedication of the John Brown Memorial Park, Roosevelt said, "Conservation means development as much as it does protection." This concept fit well with plans for the drainage and development of swampland in various parts of the country by drainage districts and local governments. The remainder of his speech dealt with his belief that special interest groups should not be allowed to influence the political process and the need for an increased role of the federal government in the regulation of businesses. The address was met with mixed responses. Some believed it was among the best American speeches while others termed it as "communistic" or "socialistic."

Roosevelt convened a governors' conference on conservation and natural resources at the White House in May 1908. The following June he appointed the National Conservation Commission. This commission issued a report to Congress in February 1909 containing an inventory of the nation's natural resources, the first time such a detailed study had been made on a national level. The report dealt with forest, mineral, land, and water resources. The majority of the report viewed conservation much in the same way as we see conservation today: controlled and efficient usage, reducing waste, and replanting renewable resources such as forests. It also mirrored the view of President Roosevelt, one of the most conservation minded presidents. However, the perspective of the report on swampland differs markedly from today's emphasis by many conservation groups on the preservation and restoration of wetlands. The report reflects Roosevelt's view that development is also important stating, "Reprehensible ... is the waste arising from nonuse. It becomes reprehensible when it affects the common welfare and entails future injury. Then it should be rectified in the general interest."[35] The report goes on to assert that the cost of drainage would be made up in the increased value of the land and that the 75,000,000 acres of overflow and swampland estimated to be present in the United States if drained "would furnish homes for 10,000,000 people."[36] One other connection of the drainage and development of the southeast Missouri lowlands to this national trend in the early twentieth century is that Isham Randolph, who served as a consulting engineer to the Little River Drainage District during the development of the plan for drainage, also is mentioned in the *Report of the National Conservation Commission*. Randolph served as chairman of the Illinois Conservation Commission and attended a joint conservation conference in Washington, D.C. in December 1908 of representatives from each state. This joint conference issued a report stating, "We hereby indorse the said report [report of the National Conservation Commission] as a wise, just, and patriotic statement of the resources of the nation."[37] Randolph's role will be discussed in more detail in later chapters.

The interest in drainage and development of swampland in the eastern United States led to the organization of the National Drainage Congress to promote Federal support for drainage projects. This organization grew out of discussions among delegates to the 1911 National Irrigation Congress in Chicago who were also interested in drainage and levees. Since major Federal support had been given to the building of dams and reservoirs to irrigate and reclaim arid western land many felt that similar aid should be provided for the draining of swampland. An organizational meeting was held during the Chicago conference which elected officers and adopted a constitution. The second meeting of the National Drainage Congress was held in New Orleans in April 1912 and the third was in St. Louis in 1914. The organization also began publishing a monthly magazine, *National Reclamation Magazine*, in December of 1921 in Kansas City, Missouri.

David R. Francis, former governor of Missouri and former Secretary of the Interior and president of the 1904 St. Louis World's Fair, addressed the National Drainage Congress in New Orleans making a plea for Federal government involvement in swampland reclamation projects:

> It is a crime to longer neglect the reclamation of these lands [swamp and overflow]. Do you ask why government aid should be necessary for the successful prosecution of the work? I answer there is a multitude and variety of reasons. Because the Federal Government is the only power or authority that can unify the many and often conflicting interests involved. Missouri has enacted a statute under which some of our overflowed lands have been drained, but our Arkansas neighbors fear the water when it has found its way to their swamps. Furthermore, a plan sufficiently comprehensive to be effective must cross not only private ownership and county boundaries but state lines a well. If the General Government can irrigate arid lands, why can it not drain overflowed lands...?[38]

Guy Elliott Mitchell of the United States Geological Survey echoed the sentiments of Francis in an article entitled "To Farm America's Swamps," published in the April 1908 issue of the progressive magazine *The American Review of Reviews*. In his article, Mitchell advocated for the federal government to fund swampland drainage projects in much the same way it did irrigation projects in the western United States. Mitchell cited cost estimates of $10 per acre or less for drainage. He argued as others had that "the federal government alone is capable of adjusting conflicting elements, securing the co-operation of individual land-owners, districts, and states, and building the great works, many of them of an interstate character."[39]

The issue of federal support for drainage projects came up repeatedly in Congress supported by members of the National Drainage Congress as well as the Department of Agriculture and Department of the Interior. Since much of the swampland had already passed into private ownership Congress was wary of the constitutional authority to fund such projects even though the argument was made repeatedly that drainage in many cases crossed state lines and federal support had already been provided for the building of levees. In contrast, the western irrigations projects were carried out on public land. A secondary argument was the improved public health that would result from reducing the mosquito population. Ultimately Congress decided against taking on swampland drainage. McDowell suggests that "by 1915 Federal efforts were not needed to develop the nation's wet lands." Rather, "it was the activities of thousands of local agencies in local promotion, organization, and construction of drainage works" that ultimately accomplished the transformation of swampland.[40]

Statistics from the 1930 United States census in the following table help to demonstrate the affect of the national drainage movement and the organization of local drainage projects on drainage activity from the late 1800s to 1930. About 62 percent of the Missouri drainage enterprises were located in the southeast. Between 1920 and 1930 Missouri showed a little over 21 percent increase in drainage organizations resulting in a more than 56 percent increase in improved acres.

Year	Acres of Land Placed in Drainage Enterprises United States	Acres of Land Placed in Drainage Enterprises Missouri
Before 1870	919,117	0
1870–1879	2,516,942	0
1880–1889	6,052,807	0
1890–1899	5,957,503	63,150
1900–1904	7,665,823	423,226
1905–1909	18,328,017	1,183,462
1910–1914	16,448,377	655,261
1915–1919	15,802,902	350,562
1920–1924	7,428,179	419,451
1925–1929	3,288,426	54,460
Total to 1930	84,408,093	3,150,022

As shown by the table, the national drainage movement affected other states as well. According to the 1930 census, thirty-five states had drainage enterprises.

Some notable drainage projects constructed during this period of the national drainage movement include the draining of the Black Swamp area in northwestern Ohio and northeastern Indiana, prairie wetlands in central Illinois, north central Iowa, and Minnesota, lowlands in the Great Lakes region, bottomlands of the lower Mississippi Valley in Arkansas, Louisiana, and Mississippi, and lowlands along the Texas Gulf Coastal Plain and the Florida Everglades. The Chicago Sanitary and Ship Canal was another monumental drainage achievement of this era. Completed in 1900, it reversed the flow of the Chicago River and prevented sewage from flowing into Lake Michigan. The canal connected Lake Michigan to the Mississippi River by reversing the flow of the Chicago River from Lake Michigan to the Des Plaines River which flows into the Illinois River. The chief engineer for this project was Isham Randolph. Of course the Panama Canal stands as one of the premier accomplishments of this period of drainage projects and canal building. Randolph was appointed to the board of consulting engineers for the Panama Canal in 1908.

One of the earliest efforts at drainage improvement in the southeast lowlands was the straightening of a section the Little River channel in New Madrid County beginning in 1885. Charles Luce who first came to southeast Missouri to partner with Oscar Kochtitzky, George B. Clark, and A.M. Shead to build the Little River Valley and Arkansas Railroad, acquired several thousand acres of swampland when the railroad sold its business to J.W. Paramore, S.W. Fordyce, and others. Luce wanted a more secure title to these lands, so he contracted with New Madrid County for work on clearing and straightening the Little River channel from the St. Louis, Iron Mountain Railroad to the south county line, accepting title to these and some additional swamplands as payment at $1.25 per acre. Luce was to be compensated 14½ cents per cubic yard for excavation work. State law at the time did not specifically allow counties to use land obtained under the Swampland Act for any purpose other than reclamation and drainage. Luce's primary purpose was to secure permanent title to these land holdings and increase the value of the land by providing better access to some of its timber. He organized a company, the Luce Dredging Company, hiring Otto Kochtitzky to oversee the operation of the dredge Luce procured for $10,000. Kochtitzky was paid $100 per month for his work which began in 1886 and continued until the dredge burned in 1889.[41]

Although Luce died in 1886 just as the dredging was getting started, his heirs continued the work until the dredge burned in 1889. Kochtitzky apparently could not convince Clarence Brown, manager of the Luce properties, to purchase another dredge and continue the work.[42] Since the work was not completed in accordance with Luce's contract with New Madrid County, the county sued to obtain title to 100,000 acres Luce and his partners received for railroad construction. Attorneys for the Luce estate countered that the county had no claim on the land since they had been accepting tax payments on the property thus substantiating that Luce was owner of the property. New Madrid County then made a new dredging contract, extending the deadline to January 1, 1899.[43] James M. Pollard contracted to complete the work with Kochtitzky again supervising. The New Madrid County Court accepted the work as completed May 25, 1899, and granted title to the Himmelberger-Luce Land and Lumber Company for 150,000 acres which Kochtitzky notes that "all except about 20,000 acres was covered with medium growth red gum, oak, elm, and ash timber."[44]

After receiving title to the land from New Madrid County, the Himmelberger-Luce Company had to deal with settlers living on some of the tracts under preemption. These settlers were allowed to buy their land at $1.25 per acre which most of them chose to do. Kochtitzky was tasked with locating these claims. He advised the Himmelberger-Luce Company to buy out these settlers to keep their tracts of land in tact but the company decided not to do that. According to Kochtitzky, these claims amounted to about 2,000 acres in 40- to 80-acre tracts.[45] While Luce's effort to straighten a portion of the Little River did little to significantly improve drainage over a large area, according to Kochtitzky, it "demonstrated the benefit of ditching and immediately started the effort of draining large separate areas."[46] The Himmelberger-Luce Land and Lumber Company, along with others who owned large tracts of timberland, petitioned to organize the first drainage district in the Bootheel in 1898. This project was located in northern New Madrid County and was called the Otter Slough Drainage District.[47] Kochtitzky noted problems with the Missouri drainage laws at that time: "This statute required that each landowner should assume the construction of his portion of the ditch." He further noted that "this law depended too largely on mutual cooperation of landowners, which is seldom possible."[48]

Kochtitzky arranged landowner meetings in New Madrid County seeking support and suggestions for revisions to the law. With the help of several lawyers, he drafted a bill which was presented to the state legislature and enacted into law in 1900.[49] The state legislature made minor amendments in 1909 and 1911. The law had pronounced influence on the organization of drainage districts not only in Missouri but nationally as well. Charles Kettleborough, author of *Drainage and Reclamation of Swamp and Overflowed Lands*, notes that the National Drainage Congress called for states to enact more effective drainage laws and meeting in New Orleans in April 1912 approved a model drainage law. This model was based on the 1900 Missouri law promoted by Kochtitzky. Several states adopted versions of this model law.[50] Kettleborough goes on to praise Missouri's efforts to enact workable drainage laws: "Probably no state in the Union has done more to develop consistent, scientific, comprehensive, and practicable drainage laws than Missouri, and a study of the progress of drainage legislation in that state is inspiring."[51] The organization of other districts throughout the area soon followed. Kochtitzky pointed out in his autobiography that local districts at the time often "increase the overflow condition at the outlet point."[52]

Otto Kochtitzky was a leader in promoting drainage in southeast Missouri and was the first chief engineer of the Little River Drainage District (John Nolen, *Missouri's Swamp and Overflowed Lands and Their Reclamation*, report to the 47th Missouri General Assembly, 1913).

Without an overall plan to remove water from the entire area, water was simply moved from the higher, better drained areas and dumped into the lower lying areas, making conditions there worse. According to Kochtitzky, the lack of experienced and trained engineers meant that many ditches "would require reconstruction within a few years."[53] Kochtitzky himself was a self-taught engineer, never completing formal training. He learned to survey and spent an extensive amount of time examining the swamplands, which gave him a keen understanding of their nature and what would be required for their drainage. Kochtitzky was born May 4, 1855, in South Bend, Indiana. His father, Oscar von Kochtitzky was born into, as Otto described it, "an old Silesian or Polish aristocratic family" in Hungary.[54] The elder Kochtitzky came to the United States about 1850. He served with an Ohio unit during the Civil War and farmed in Indiana and Illinois, moving his family to Lebanon, Missouri, in 1867.[55] In 1870, Oscar was elected state representative for Laclede County and the family moved to Jefferson City. Later, Oscar became the chief clerk in the office of the Missouri registrar of lands.[56] Otto came to southeast Missouri with his brother John to do some surveying for the registrar of lands office. It is then that Otto learned about the abandoned plank road company which his father and other investors obtained, building instead of a plank road, the Little River Valley and Arkansas Railroad which operated for three years. His father continued living in New Madrid after sale of the railroad and held a variety of city and county offices as well as serving as labor commissioner under Governor Marmaduke. After failing in a zinc mining venture in southwest Missouri, Oscar died in Jefferson City in 1891.[57]

Kochtitzky made a couple of failed attempts at farming in the Bootheel. After his marriage in 1883 he and his wife moved to Malden where he worked in his brother's grain business which was destroyed by fire. He then managed to operate a grain business with two other partners.[58] In 1886, Kochtitzky began surveying and supervising the dredge under Charles Luce's contract with New Madrid County. When the dredge burned, he no longer had a job so he moved first to Virginia and then North Carolina doing survey work. Kochtitzky seems to have been smitten with swampland reclamation work however. He returned to southeast Missouri in 1894 when the Himmelberger-Luce Land and Lumber Company resumed work on the Little River channel with Kochtitzky again supervising the work.[59]

From this point, it seems that Kochtitzky's destiny was in swampland reclamation. He purchased a dredge about 1900 and won the bid on a contract with a newly formed drainage district in New Madrid County. Kochtitzky allied himself with the largest landowners and most influential families in the region such as the Himmelbergers, the Matthews, and the Hunters, sometimes partnering with them in making land purchases and sales.

All of his working life in the twentieth century was devoted to either carrying out contract work on drainage projects or in the promotion and planning of drainage districts. Kochtitzky's intimate knowledge of dredging equipment led him to apply for and receive a patent for an improvement to the floating dipper dredge. These machines consist of a platform to which is mounted an "A" frame with cables running to the boom. Also attached to this "A" frame are two braces called spuds which extend to the ground on each side of the dredge to hold it in place while it is operating. The spuds were raised and lowered by a system of cables. His patent, received in 1924, related to providing a better method of attaching the spuds. Kochtitzky's design provided a flexible mounting of the spuds, which would allow the dredge to pull itself forward while the spuds are on the ground. This was especially useful when the dredge was operating in conditions where there was not sufficient water to completely float the platform. However, his most notable achievement was in the promotion and development of a drainage plan for the Little River Drainage District and serving as its first chief engineer before returning to contract operations of his dredges.

At the beginning of the twentieth century, the stage was set for large scale drainage of the southeast Missouri lowlands. Technology was in place to make possible construction under difficult conditions, experience with small projects provided an understanding of how drainage districts should operate and demonstrated their economic benefits to landowners, and updated laws provided the mechanism for their organization.

The feasibility and prospects of drainage, demonstrated by the success of small drainage districts in all Bootheel counties, also spurred interest in land trades. Land there was often bought and sold in large parcels, placing control of drainage decisions in the hands of a relatively few, powerful landowners. These landowners also saw the potential of large profits in their hands as well when land values escalated as drainage developed and railroads moved timber to markets and the productivity of the Bootheel was recognized.

Land trades described by Otto Kochtitzky in his autobiography serve to illustrate the kind of speculation and land transactions taking place during the first decade of the twentieth century. Businessmen with money to invest often bought land for just the amount of taxes owed on it. Kochtitzky, Jack Matthews, and Joseph Hunter purchased 1,600 acres of timberland for 50 cents per acre, which they resold for $1.75 per acre. Kochtitzky and another partner purchased an 800-acre tract of swampland at $3 per acre and within two months sold the timber for $5 per acre, as Kochtitzky explains, "over several glasses of good beer at the 'Last Chance Saloon.'"[60] At the time, Kochtitzky made a notation that the land would increase in value $5 per acre per year over the next 20 years. His partner sold his portion 16 years later at $80 per acre. Kochtitzky describes the purchase of 10,000 acres for $50,000 by a non-resident purchaser. This purchaser sold the land two years later for $150,000.[61]

Land traders and others made concerted efforts at promoting southeast Missouri and its land, and encouraging farmers to move to the area to farm.

They extolled its virtues and advantages, and down-played its problems such as poor roads and drainage. One early effort was directed by the Missouri Immigration Society, publishers in 1880 of the *Handbook of Missouri*, which included articles on each section of the state and other features such as railroads, manufacturing, mining, and the various crops grown. Each section was written by a prominent business man or professor. The section on the southeast lowlands was prepared by Louis Houck. Houck wrote in the publication, "overflows are far less frequent than is generally thought. Nor is the area of this overflow extensive." At the same time, the book emphasized that cheap land was available and the productivity of the region's soils and its favorable climate, "The soil is of unsurpassing fertility.... A total failure of crops is unknown."[62] With some large blocks of land in the hands of visionary, determined, and profit-minded landowners who were determined to make their investment in Bootheel land more lucrative, the stage was set for the development of a drainage project on much grander scale than had been attempted before, which could remove water from the entire Little River Valley.

CHAPTER 9

Little River Drainage District: Organization and Opposition

In 1905, business activity was moving at a rapid pace in the Bootheel. The region now had rail services, increasing the value of timberlands. In areas with improved drainage, more land was being prepared for farming. New businesses such as banks, retail establishments, grain milling facilities, and lumber mills were being started in most towns of the area. As the timber harvest increased, the problem of what to do with cut-over land became a more pressing issue. The lumber companies that held large blocks of land wanted to sell their cut-over timberland for agricultural usage. The Himmelberger-Harrison Lumber Company opened a separate division, the Himmelberger-Harrison Land Selling Company, to do just that. The Wisconsin Lumber Company set up a program to finance the sale of its cut-over land to farmers. Their plan allowed a farmer to have 17 years to pay and required no payment the first two years. Unless converted to agricultural use, land ceased to be an asset for owners. While counties still required property taxes to be paid on cut-over land, it did not produce any revenue. Wisconsin Lumber Company even tried farming some of the land itself, but the effort proved to be unprofitable. This brought into sharp focus the need to develop a large-scale plan for the overall drainage of the Bootheel. Without adequate drainage, the land was not attractive to potential buyers. The success of numerous small drainage districts in individual counties encouraged landowners to consider the possibility of an overall plan for the removal of excess water from the region.

Before 1907, a total of 46 drainage districts had been organized, all by county courts. By 1910, these drainage districts had constructed over 900

Much of the southeast lowlands resembled this photograph once timber had been removed. Converting fields of stumps into farmland presented a major challenge. Such land held little value for the lumber companies thus they wanted to dispose of it (Little River Drainage District Collection, Missouri State Archives.)

miles of drainage ditches throughout the Bootheel. The drained area covered nearly 400,000 acres. At the end of the first two decades of the twentieth century, all of the lowlands in southeast Missouri in need of drainage were included in one or more drainage districts.[1] Drainage also increased land values. For example, average land prices in Dunklin County before any drainage projects ranged from $12 to $20 per acre. After drainage, the range was $40 to $80. Figures for other counties in the area are similar.[2]

The major obstacle that remained for complete drainage was ditches to carry the water out of the Little River Valley. Prior to the valley's drainage, Otto Kochtitzky described it as a "level depression or trough lying between the Skeston Ridge and Crowley's Ridge or St. Francis Terrace."[3] Runoff from the Ozarks fronting the southeast lowlands and water from individual drainage districts in the area all accumulated in the Little River Valley where it eventually flowed into Big Lake in Arkansas.[4]

Kochtitzky, employed by the Himmelberger-Harrison Lumber Company to oversee their 180,000 acres of timberland in New Madrid and Stoddard counties, became one of the strongest voices advocating an overall plan to drain the lowlands. This involvement with Himmelberger-Harrison

Lumber Company allowed Kochtitzky to become well acquainted with most of the major landowners in the region. He left Himmelberger-Harrison in 1902 to further study the drainage issues and continue his land trading business.[5] Kochtitzky spent much of his time putting together a detailed topographic map of the lowlands. He printed 1,000 copies of this map, which he sold. The map became quite popular with land dealers and landowners who were interested in improving drainage. According to Kochtitzky, the map helped galvanize interest in a large drainage district because it enabled all interested parties to see "the problem alike."[6]

In December 1904, a dozen of the major landowners in the Bootheel area met in Cape Girardeau to discuss what steps needed to be taken in order to establish a drainage district with the capability of draining all of the Little River Valley. Otto Kochtitzky at the request of the Himmelberger-Harrison Lumber Company invited landowners to attend the meeting. Emerging from this initial meeting were plans to establish what became the largest drainage district in the United States. The successful drainage of the lowlands not only brought a change in the physical but also the social landscape of the southeast Missouri lowlands forever. It also ushered in important changes in the kinds of crops grown.

This initial meeting included primarily landowners who controlled several thousand acres each and held close ties to the lumber industry. Among those in attendance at the initial organizational meeting were John H. Himmelberger, S.P. Reynolds, J.M. Blazer, R.B. Oliver, and Otto Kochtitzky. These and others who promoted the district's formation displayed great vision and could see beyond the tangled, overgrown, waterlogged cut-over timber land to productive agricultural fields producing bumper crops of cotton, corn, wheat, alfalfa, and other crops. They were tough and determined pioneers who were not afraid of challenges and risks but who also remained focused on making a profit from this difficult yet rich land.

The first hurdle to over come in forming a drainage district of this size was to have proper legal authority. The Missouri statutes in 1905 did not provide for a drainage district which encompassed more than one county. All previous districts had been organized under the jurisdictions of county courts. Senator R.B. Oliver of Cape Girardeau drafted and introduced the necessary legislation which passed both houses of the General Assembly and was signed April 8, 1905, by Governor Joseph Wingate Folk.[7]

A petition with the majority of the landowners' signatures was the next step. The process was made somewhat less difficult because so much of the land in the proposed district was held in large blocks by timber

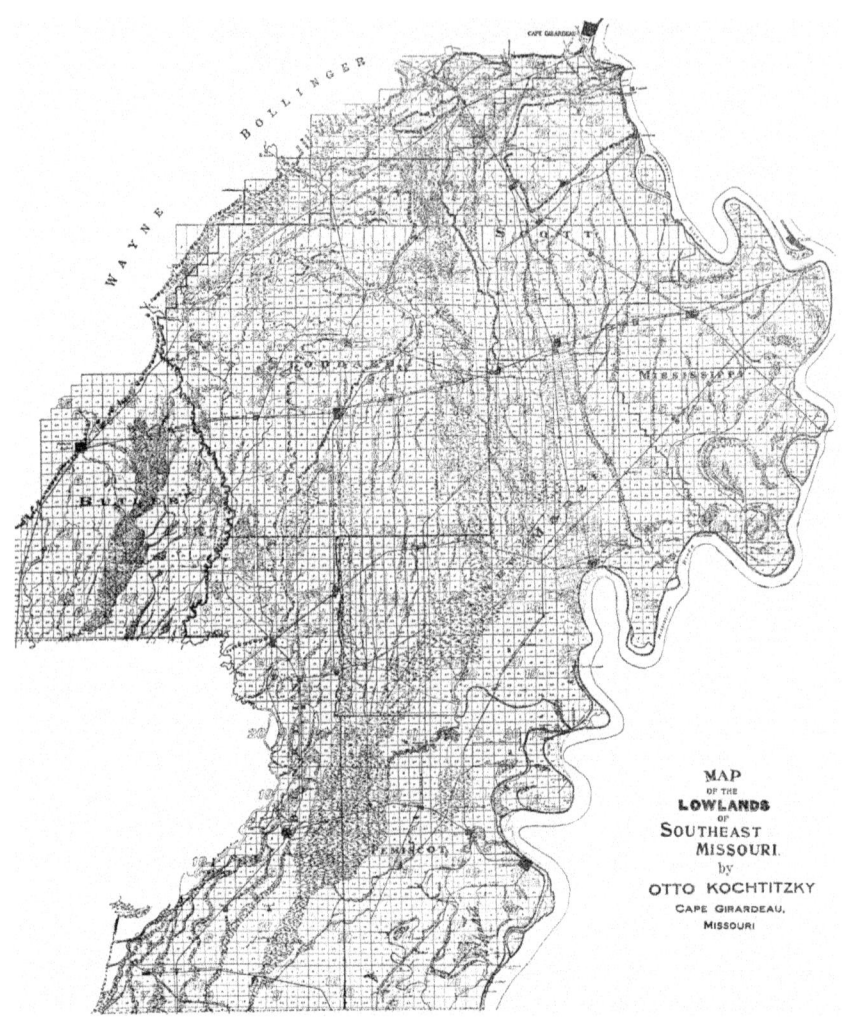

Otto Kochtitzky's original map of the southeast Missouri lowlands he made in 1902 to help with drainage planning (John Nolen, *Missouri's Swamp and Overflowed Lands and Their Reclamation*, report to the 47th Missouri General Assembly, 1913).

interests and insurance companies. In New Madrid County, for example, the 81 signatures on the petition represented 100,078 acres. Some of these were families and partnerships which were listed more than once. Himmelberger-Harrison Lumber Company alone owned 73,243 acres. They also owned 25,252 acres in Stoddard County, and 1,472 acres in Pemiscot County. Of the 36,078 acres from Dunklin County included in the petition, 34,450 acres were controlled by just three entities: Wisconsin Lumber Company, St. Louis Union Trust Company, and Mercer D. Wilson, a land agent.[8]

In September 1905, the Oliver law firm of Cape Girardeau filed a petition in the New Madrid County Circuit Court. The petition represented nearly 500,000 acres of land and was signed by 64 percent of the landowners. The proposed district had an estimated cost of $400,000.[9] At the time it was filed the 285-page petition was the longest ever filed in a Missouri court for a civil proceeding.[10] The petition outlined the area to be included in the district using Kochtitzky's map and the general plan by which drainage would be accomplished. The petition further requested a tax for the construction and maintenance of the drainage structures. The tax would be based on the benefit assessed to each parcel of land. Not unexpectedly for a project of this magnitude, opposition developed.

Opposition came quickly from the three railroads who owned property in the district boundaries. The St. Louis, Iron Mountain and Southern Railroad; the St. Louis and San Francisco (Frisco); and the St. Louis Southwestern (Cotton Belt) all voiced opposition because they had significant land holdings in the area and did not want these to be subject to additional tax. Additionally, ditches meant that the railroads would have to build new bridges to cross them.

The St. Louis, Memphis and Southeastern Railroad and the St. Louis and Gulf Railway Company, both of which became a part of the St. Louis and San Francisco, along with John V. Filley, the trustee for several railroad mortgages, filed objections to the Little River Drainage District incorporation in the New Madrid Circuit Court. At this time, a change of venue was requested by the objectors, sending the petition to the circuit court of Butler County, a county not included in the proposed drainage district. The objectors' first argument was that the petition for incorporation did not include a specific plan of drainage and did not outline the location and number of ditches. The court held that this was not a necessary part of the petition for incorporation according to state law. Objectors also argued that their lands should not be included in the district because high water affected them only occasionally. The court responded that this would be a matter of assessed benefits and had no bearing on the incorporation itself. The court rejected the argument that their land should not be included because it is already in another drainage district and went on to state that it was within "the right of the state, in exercise of its police power, to drain lands for the purposed of protecting the health of the people … it may also be invoked to make lands fit for use."[11] Those objecting further complained

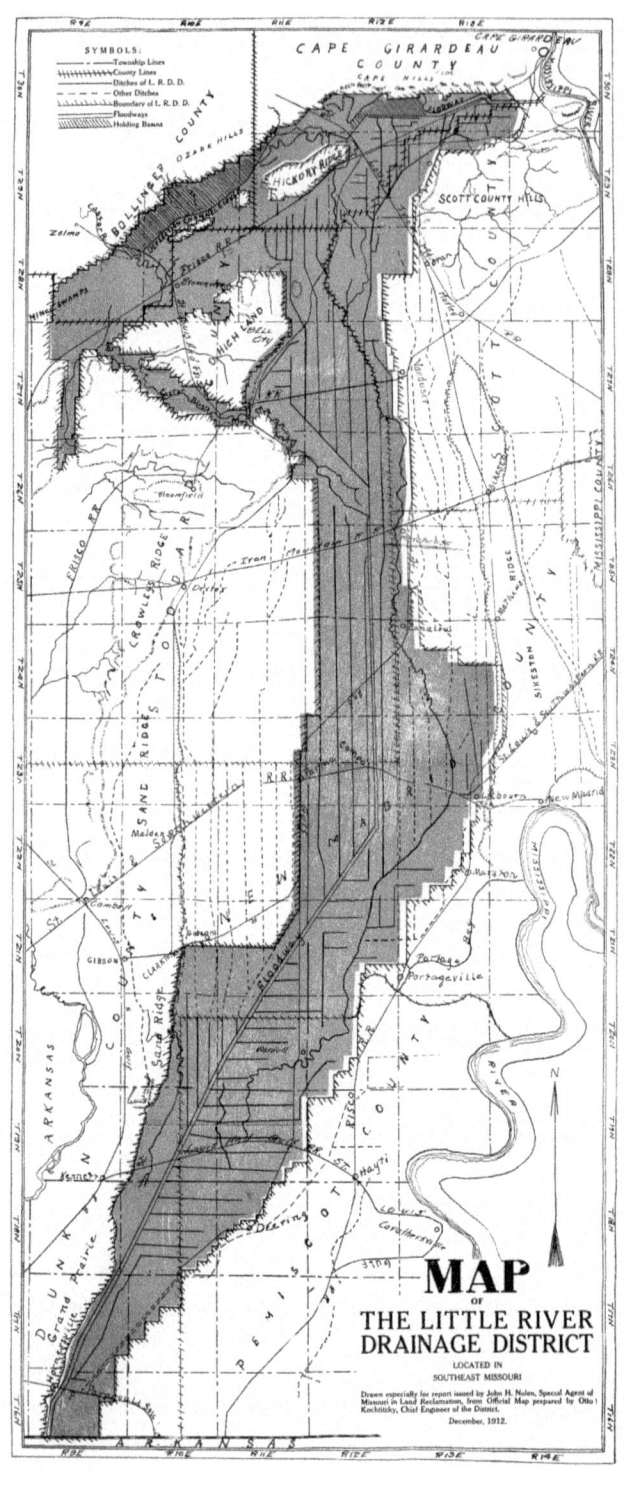

that they did not have sufficient opportunity to present reasons why the incorporation should not take place; however, the court ruled that they actually filed no evidence explaining why it should not be incorporated other than arguing the constitutionality of the law under which incorporation was to take place. The final objection was that they were not allowed to amend their written testimony. The court denied this request because it was not made until the time the case was ready to be heard. The circuit court then decreed the incorporation of the Little River Drainage District November 30, 1907. Railroad objectors appealed and made their way to the Missouri Supreme Court. However, on July 3, 1911, this court reviewed all the arguments made in objection to the incorporation and upheld the legality of the incorporation.[12]

The most ardent opponent of the Little River Drainage District was Louis Houck although he was not alone. Numerous other southeast Missouri landowners also opposed this massive undertaking. Most opposition came from those on the northeast and northwest fringes of the district who believed that their land would not benefit from this project and since in most cases their land was already included in other districts they would be double taxed. There were valid reasons for being skeptical. This was the largest drainage project that had ever been attempted in the United States and there was no guarantee of successful drainage of the lowlands and no assurance that the benefits would justify the enormous expenditure. Further objections were fueled by the passage on June 1, 1909, of a revision to state drainage laws that would permit the collection of a tax of 25 cents per acre to cover the expenses of organizing the district. This revision is usually referred to as Section 5538 in court cases and literature of the time.

Houck, once an active proponent of development and improvements in southeast Missouri through railroad building now found himself opposing additional development of the area that could come only through improved drainage. Houck was not necessarily opposed to drainage in principle and had even carried out some small-scale drainage work in the process of his railroad building. He apparently even assisted Otto Kochtitzky around 1900 in convincing reluctant supporters of the project's benefits and may have purchased some of the district's bonds.[13]

Houck began his campaign against the Little River Drainage District in a manner typical of his other battles, using both the printed word and

Opposite: **Map showing the outline of the Little River Drainage District after its incorporation (John Nolen,** *Missouri's Swamp and Overflowed Lands and Their Reclamation,* **report to the 47th General Assembly, 1913).**

the courts. Houck fired his first salvo against the district formation in 1909, with a letter to the *Daily Republican* newspaper in Cape Girardeau charging that construction of the diversion channel to carry runoff from the Ozark uplands directly to the Mississippi River would create more swamps.[14] He believed that the Mississippi River would back up the diversion channel and overflow, submerging his land that before was not subject to flooding from the river. The following year, Houck traveled much of southeast Missouri, making speeches in opposition to the drainage district. Attacking Kochtitzky's calculations for the channel depth and width of the diversion channel, Houck maintained that "with the first flood of the Mississippi, the water of this river would run into the back country with greater rapidity, and in a greater volume through this break in the river bank and deeper ditch. It would greatly increase the danger of an overflow of the whole southern country, and make more certain the calamity which will be sure to over take the land owners of that district if this visionary scheme is ever put into practical operation."[15]

Writing on July 12, 1911, to the *St. Louis Republic*, Houck contended that Missouri was in a "drainage craze," not unlike the 1868 craze by townships to provide aid to railroads. He contended that the promoters of this drainage craze were real estate speculators, contractors, bond houses, and bond lawyers. Houck maintained that the state legislature enacted drainage laws that took

Louis Houck brought railroads to the southeast Missouri lowlands but was one of the strongest opponents of the Little River Drainage District (Louis Houck, *History of Missouri,* **vol. 1, 1908).**

away constitutional guarantees by succumbing to the argument "that the state must be fully improved quickly, the land drained quickly, the empty places filled up quickly, the last tree cut down quickly."[16] Once development and rapid land clearing started, partially brought about by his railroads, Houck seemed to exhibit some remorse at the loss of the southeast Missouri wilderness as historian Bonnie Stepenoff notes, "The man who touted the railroads and the man who resisted the drainage project was also the same man, exhibiting inner conflicts between greed and altruism, ambition, and regret."[17]

Otto Kochtitzky rebutted Houck's arguments in the July 29, 1911, *St. Louis Republic*. Kochtitzky argued that the "local sentiment demands drainage." He further insisted that drainage costs are not looked at as an expense but rather as an investment by the landowners because of the increased value of the land.[18] Houck countered in the August 1, 1911, edition of the paper with six specific charges. First, that the drainage scheme was "pulled off" by those who owned no land in the drainage district. Second, it was destroying constitutional safeguards. Third, there were numerous earlier failed drainage projects. Fourth, Houck believed powerful interests such as the Wisconsin Lumber Company of Deering manipulated district boundaries so that some of their land would be excluded. Fifth, more flooding would result from the diversion channel: "A new swamp will be established along the foothills in a country now largely occupied by farms." Sixth, Houck expressed doubts that the assessment of benefits would equal the selling price of reclaimed land within a generation.[19]

A brief written by the Oliver law firm contained in the Little River Drainage District Collection at Southeast Missouri State University makes a point-by-point listing of Houck's objections and the drainage district's response. Houck had conceived of a wide variety of arguments in opposition to the district. His objections included such things as the way in which benefits were assessed on his land. Land farther away from the diversion channel was assessed as much as that nearby. He also believed that dirt removed to dig the diversion channel would prevent any water from his land draining into the channel and that water in the channel would back up and "force other waters to stand above the land and would cause sickness and endanger the health of the people of Bollinger, Cape Girardeau and Scott counties." He even stated that commissioners did not consider that every time a flood came from the hill country, his land was made better instead of worse; therefore, stopping those floods would actually stop this improvement.[20] Much of his land lay in the lowlands just below the Ozark escarpment.

Houck's next front for the battle involved the court system. He was a seasoned litigator from his railroad days and never shied away from filing lawsuits. Houck refused to pay the 25 cents per acre assessment on land in the district resulting from Section 5538 of the Missouri drainage statute. In 1910, he filed suit against Little River Drainage District in the Common Pleas Court of Cape Girardeau. Little River attorneys sought a change of venue which moved the case to the Cape Girardeau Circuit Court. The drainage district then filed a demurrer, which meant that even if everything stated in Houck's argument were true, there would still be no reason for the court to take any legal action. The court ruled in favor of the demurrer which meant Houck was liable for the tax.

Undeterred, Houck and his attorneys, which included his son Giboney Houck, appealed to the Missouri Supreme Court. Both parties agreed in court that "the only question in controversy is this cause is as to the constitutionality of Section 5538." The court up held the right of the state to create corporations for public benefit and their right to impose taxes. They further stated that it was up to the legislature to set the amounts of assessments that special taxing districts could impose either at a level rate or at a rate based on actual benefits. Houck had opposed the tax in Section 5538, arguing that it was not based on benefits. He also argued that the tax could not be imposed because the project might fail. The court responded that "the power to tax necessarily includes the power to raise the money in such time and manner as is necessary to accomplish the purpose for which the tax is levied." The court further pointed out that at the time the case was filed, a plan of drainage had been adopted, and the commission appointed for assessing benefits was at work. In addition, the court reminded the litigants that Section 5538 states, "Such levy may be made although the work purposed may have failed or have been found impractical." The court considered growth and prosperity of farms in the state to be as important as that of cities, stating: "So the prosperity and growth of the productive communities represented by its farms are equally matters of general concern. That concern is represented by the difference between a state composed of bogs and marshes not only unproductive but unhealthy, and a state in which the lands yield bountifully to the call of the husbandman, and breathe health instead of miasma."[21]

In customary Houck fashion, he moved from court to court in search of a victory. Having lost at the Missouri Supreme Court, Houck won the right to appeal to the United States Supreme Court in October 1915. The justices reviewed the arguments Houck attorneys Benson C. Hardesty, Giboney Houck, and Thomas D. Hines made against the constitutionality of Section 5538. However, the court's opinion delivered by Associate Justice Charles Evan Hughes affirmed all that the Missouri Supreme Court determined, leaving Houck without further legal remedy.[22]

The indefatigable Houck wasn't finished quite yet. Two Missouri Supreme Court cases, one in 1916 and another in 1917, involving Scott County and Cape Girardeau County respectively, established that the burden of building bridges across drainage ditches rested with the counties and not with the drainage districts. The court conceded that while such bridge building by the counties could "produce a situation of harsh injustice and hardship," it maintained that "the Legislature controls the remedy."[23] Houck saw an opportunity to at last inflict some setbacks for the Little River Drainage District if the law could be rewritten, placing the bridge building obligation on the drainage districts.

To achieve this, Giboney Houck ran for the Missouri House of Representatives in 1918. He won election by campaigning that he would seek legislation changing the drainage laws so that the drainage districts would be responsible for building bridges across ditches that traversed roadways instead of the county. Giboney won the election and did introduce the bill he campaigned on, however, the bill did not pass. This effectively ended Houck's battle against organization of the Little River Drainage District, although he would meet them in court from time to time into the 1920s when the district sought to place a lien against Houck's property because he did not pay the drainage tax owed. After repeated appeals, Houck lost these cases as well.

Following official incorporation, the statues required the new district to hold a landowners meeting to elect a board of supervisors and select a district engineer to begin surveys necessary to develop a plan for carrying out the proposed drainage project. At such meetings, landowners would have one vote for each acre of land they owned within the district. This first landowners meeting was held December 30, 1907, in Morehouse at the Odd Fellows Lodge. R.B. Oliver, Sr., attorney for the district, called the meeting to order and was elected chairman of the meeting. The primary purpose of the meeting was to select a board of supervisors. The minutes of the meeting do not show that nominations were made for these positions. A motion was made by Griff Glover to appoint a committee to nominate a list of candidates, but this was defeated. The landowners then voted by writing the name of their choice for supervisor on a slip of paper and the number of acres they owned which represented the number of votes they had. Each landowner cast five ballots, one for each supervisor to be elected.

A.J. Matthews, John H. Himmelberger, A.L. Harty, S.P. Reynolds,

Charles W. Henderson, and George S. Hanford all received votes. The first five received the highest number of votes and thus made up the board of supervisors. Those elected drew lots to determine the length of their term. Their respective terms were Himmelberger five years, Harty four, Matthews three, Reynolds two, and Henderson one, although all were reelected several times.[24]

R.B. Oliver, Sr., also fielded questions at this first landowners' meeting about the manner in which assessment of benefits would be made and the amount of taxes. Oliver explained to the group that the Butler County Circuit Court would appoint three commissioners to carry out this task, and if any landowner disagreed with the assessment, he could file an objection in circuit court.[25] Himmelberger was elected president of the board and served in that capacity until 1930. The board enjoyed a great deal of stability since no changes in membership occurred until 1923 when Charles Henderson retired and was replaced by W.P. Anderson of Gideon-Anderson. There were no further changes in board membership until 1930.

The board of supervisors selected Otto Kochtitzky to be the district chief engineer. Kochtitzky, who also had a business of contracting to construct drainage ditches, agreed to serve in that capacity only until a plan for drainage had been approved.[26] To assist in the engineering design, the board of supervisors also employed N.C. Frissell as assistant engineer. Frissell was the engineer in charge of the swampland survey for the state swampland commission.

The next step to be accomplished was the assessment of benefits to property owners from drainage. This however was not a direct task of the district since the commissioners appointed by the Butler County Circuit Court were to make the assessments. William Cooper Cracraft of Cape Girardeau, Hina C. Schult of Pemiscot County, and M.C. Reed of Stoddard County were the commissioners appointed to make the assessments.

Assessments of benefits made by the commissioners ranged from $4 to $40 per acre. Each landowner had the opportunity to file an exception with the Butler County Circuit Court if dissatisfied with the assessment of benefits made on the property. About 258 landowners filed exceptions to the amount of benefits assessed on their property. In some cases, the court reduced the amount of assessment. The hearings were finally concluded October 21, 1912, thus clearing the way for the district to begin collection of regular taxes in addition to the 25 cents per acre assessment permitted for organization expenses.[27] With an organization in place, this new district was ready to tackle the task of developing a means of draining the Little River Valley while at the same time facing the many legal challenges to its existence. The board of supervisors and the staff it employed embarked enthusiastically into the daunting task. Neither the supervisors nor the land owners realized the financial hurdles that the district must cross in just a few years, as the nation plunged into a severe depression.

Chapter 10

Little River Drainage District: Planning and Construction

While the general concept of how to accomplish drainage of the Little River Valley existed, the details were yet to be finalized. Otto Kochtitzky, chief engineer, and N.C. Frissell, assistant engineer, went to work gathering the needed information about the Little River Valley in order to draft a drainage plan. They began by making a detailed topographic survey. Four survey teams consisting of eight or nine men each were formed. These teams consisted of an assistant engineer (in charge of the party), levelman, rodman, head chain, rear chain, stake marker, two axmen, boatman or teamster, and cook. Surveyors selected a campsite and stayed in tents. They moved their campsite whenever work in a particular area was complete. The surveyors ran east-west lines across the district on section lines to obtain elevations needed to develop profiles. The survey teams ran 773 miles of such lines to gather the needed data.

Survey teams accomplished their work from mid–February to July 1, 1908, under some of the most difficult conditions imaginable. Kochtitzky, in his 1908 annual report to the Board of Supervisors, explains the difficulty in obtaining the survey: "most of territory was covered with water from six inches to three feet deep, it was very difficult and expensive." Kochtitzky explains that the District "provided movable quarters in tents, and transported same from place to place on wagons or boats or by railroad as we found it practicable."[1] One can imagine the discomfort of mud, wet tents, thick vegetation, and mosquitoes these survey crews endured to accomplish their work.

Kochtitzky kept in close contact with his survey crews. At each camp

10. Little River: Planning and Construction

Survey crews eating a meal in camp. Crews making surveys for the Little River Drainage District camped and worked in extremely difficult conditions (Little River Drainage District Collection, Missouri State Archives).

location, they would receive mail at the nearest post office. Kochtitzky wrote to each of the survey crews every two or three days. Often he gave them specific instructions about the best places to camp. For example, in a letter to J.E. Dunn, dated May 21, 1908, he advises that the crew would find good camping a Coker Landing, "which is a fishing station and near the high land of Dunklin County. From this point you can go by open water several miles north. At Coker Landing you will have better facilities for supplies and mail."[2] His letters also indicate the intimate knowledge Kochtitzky had of the region and those who lived there. His letter to M. McReynolds, July 14, 1908, is one such example. "From Clarkton take wagons six miles south to the old town of Moark. You will find a good camping place just across the road and east of M. Fisher's house which is at the south end of the old town."[3]

At times Kochtitzky questioned bills from the survey crews, such as in a May 14, 1908, letter to J.E. Dunn inquiring about the amount charged for "boat hire." Another letter to Dunn on May 20 informed him that the board had "criticized bill for camp supplies and boat hire."[4] The district's financial statement for 1908 reveals a total of $25,610.33 spent for engineering work. This included salaries, camp supplies and transportation. The district spent over $13,000 in 1908 just to get the district organized.[5]

With completion of the surveys, Kochtitzky, Frisell, and the draftsmen employed by the district prepared topographic maps and profiles to aid in developing a plan for drainage. The surveys revealed a somewhat uniform drop in elevation of about one foot per mile from the north end of the district to its south end making it easier for Kochtitzky and Frisell to design ditches to carry excess water. However, the board of supervisors did not rely solely on the expertise of its own staff. They sought the advice of some of the top drainage experts in the nation. Robert Moore, a prominent civil engineer from St. Louis; Daniel Meade, dean of the Engineering School of the University of Iowa; C.G. Elliott, chief of drainage investigations for the United States Department of Agriculture; and Arthur E. Morgan were four of the noted consultants. Morgan was at one time assistant to Elliott in the Department of Agriculture and later established his own firm in Memphis.

A particularly well-known consultant was Isham Randolph of Chicago, chief designer for the Chicago Sanitary and Ship Canal. Also a member of the Panama Canal board of Consulting Engineers, Randolph stood with the minority of engineers who recommended a lock-type canal be built. Ultimately this was the design chosen. In 1908, President Roosevelt sent William Howard Taft accompanied by five engineers to review work on the canal. Randolph was one of the engineers appointed by Roosevelt to accompany Taft. Randolph continued as consulting engineer for the district through the construction phase, and the Little River Drainage District listed him on the cover of its Bulletins as consulting engineer until his death.[6] Randolph is considered by some of those familiar the Little River Drainage District to be the real mind behind the drainage plan rather than Kochtitzky.[7] In the late spring of 1908, Randolph, accompanied by Frissell, made a field reconnaissance of the border between the hill country and the lowlands. A letter to Kochtitzky following his fieldwork contained several suggestions about handling the runoff from Castor River and other streams. His conclusion was that "the engineering problems are all within the scope of easy accomplishment and the real problem underlying this project is one of economics."[8] According to Kochtitzky's autobiography, C.G. Elliott prepared the estimates of the runoff for the district which greatly aided in the design of the ditches.

While Kochtitzky and the Little River Drainage District board considered several different approaches, drainage required two problems to be solved. First, some method was needed to divert the flow from the Ozark streams entering the lowlands to the Mississippi River. This would greatly reduce the amount of water moving through the Little River Valley that had to be drained away. Both Kochtitzky and Randolph did not believe that drainage could be adequately accomplished without first reducing this amount of water entering the lowlands. The second measure would be construction of ditches through the length of the valley and lateral ditches to bring water from farms to the ditches running through the valley. These would carry excess water out of the valley to the Big Lake near Manila, Arkansas.

By early 1909, Kochtitzky and the consulting engineers began to piece together a plan for drainage, calling for a diversion channel to move water from Ozark streams entering the lowlands directly to the Mississippi River and a main north-south ditch through the district along with lateral ditches. In total, the plan called for 85 ditches to be constructed in the lower district. All of the consultants with the exception of Moore approved the plan. Kochtitzky relates that Moore doubted that the proposed channel to divert runoff from the Ozarks to the Mississippi would work. He questioned whether a proposed levee on the south side of the diversion channel could contain the water from a large, quick flood from the hills. According to Kochtitzky, "Moore filed his objection and retired from consultation and responsibility."[9] Concerns about a possible back flow from the Mississippi River up the diversion channel during high water led to the construction of a weir 11 miles west of the Mississippi River at the point where Castor River, Crooked Creek, and Gizzard Creek enter the Diversion Channel. This structure also helped compensate from the elevation differences between these fast flowing Ozark streams and the Diversion Channel whose level is controlled by the Mississippi River. The weir was lined with concrete blocks to reduce erosion. Over time, force of the water flowing over the weir has eroded and hole about 450 feet wide below the weir. This pool has become known as the Block Hole and is a popular fishing spot with good populations of several native species. The Missouri Conservation Department which leases part of this area from the Little River Drainage District has now constructed a concrete boat ramp and parking lot to allow fishermen access to the Block Hole.

Kochtitzky outlined the proposed plan in his annual report published in January 1909: "This plan embraces the construction of a channel to carry all head waters from the hill streams to the Mississippi River at a point about two miles south of Cape Girardeau; a system of open dredged ditches approximately one mile apart for the whole area of the district where they do not exist and a main channel through the district as an outlet for such ditches."[10]

Also, a part of the proposed plan would be the construction of a levee

Block Hole. This structure was constructed to compensate for differences in elevation of the fast flowing upland streams and the diversion channel which is at the level of the Mississippi River. The force of the water eroded the pool below the rapids and it has become a popular local fishing spot. The Block Hole flows into the diversion channel (photograph by the author).

on the south side of the diversion channel to protect the lowlands in the event the diversion channel could not hold all of the runoff from the upland areas. With this basic concept in hand, detailed profiles for each ditch had to be drawn. Kochtitzky held repeated meetings with consulting engineers about the details of the plan for drainage. He made numerous trips to Chicago to confer with Isham Randolph and trips to Washington, D.C. to meet with C.G. Elliot and A.E. Morgan of the Department of Agriculture.

Kochtitzky presented the plan to the board of supervisors in mid-year 1909. the board asked Kochtitzky and one of the Oliver law firm attorneys to again present the plan to Randolph and Morgan. They did this, and both Randolph and Morgan endorsed the plan.[11] The plan was then reviewed by Major M.L. Walker of the Army Engineers and the Mississippi River Commission engineers, with both organizations giving approval and permission to cut through the Mississippi River levee below Cape Girardeau. Returning to the board of supervisors, Kochtitzky again presented his plan.

The plan adopted by the board of supervisors, on November 15, 1909, essentially divided the district into two parts: The upper portion through which the diversion channel and a strong levee on its south side is constructed and the lower section consisting of 85 ditches, one of which runs the entire 100-mile length of the district.

Once the plan for drainage was in place, Otto Kochtitzky resigned as chief engineer to resume full attention to his dredging business, as had been his plan when he accepted the position, a decision he later wished he had not made: "I have always regretted that I made this decision. Every enterprise is best served by one mind.... I should have dropped my business, and should have given all my time, energy, and ability to the service of this one great undertaking."[12] Kochtitzky did return to his dredging business and was a contractor for digging several of the district ditches. William A. O'Brien was hired to replace Kochtitzky in December 1909 and served until his death in October 1918. L.L. Hidinger succeeded O'Brien as chief engineer.

The next ten years proved to be especially busy ones for both the engineering and legal departments of Little river Drainage District. The district's attorneys were kept busy defending lawsuits challenging the district, purchasing right-of-way, and preparing for the sale of bonds. The engineering department sent survey crews back to the field to lay out the locations of the various ditches called for in the plan for drainage. They also checked calculations about runoff and other data to refine ditch designs to prepare for the contracting phase.

It became apparent that the district boundary on the northwest side of the district needed to be extended because of the benefits afforded to the land in that portion of Stoddard and Bollinger counties. The Butler County Circuit Courts heard such a petition from the Little River Drainage District in January 1918. The petition was granted, and the court appointed commissioners to assess benefits. The addition to the district included about 46,000 acres. By mid–September of 1921, engineers worked out a drainage plan for this area and let contracts for the work.[13] In its 1912 report, the board of supervisors informed landowners that they had let "contracts for practically the entire construction work called for in the 'Plan for Drainage.'"[14] There were initially over 20 different contractors, including former chief engineer Otto Kochtitzky. While local contractors carried some of the work, others came from as far as Rochester and Buffalo, New York.

Beginning in November 1914, the district began publishing its *Bulletin of the Little River Drainage District* quarterly to update landowners on the progress of construction. These publications contained a summary of the work done under each contract and a summary on the construction of each ditch, as well as a report on each landowners' meeting and an engineer's report. The board of supervisors also held monthly meetings to take care of routine business.

The next step undertaken by the district was the sale of bonds to pay for construction costs. The interest and principal of the bonds were to be paid with money from taxes collected. Bonds in the amount of $4.75 million bearing 5.5 percent interest were issued October 1, 1913. The district prepared a booklet titled *The Little River Drainage District of Missouri: Information Relative to Its Bond Issue*.[15] This publication provided some detailed statistics, such as the size of the district, price of land, population, and number of miles of railroads. Based on the previous land sales, the average price of district land stood at $37 per acre. The district reported that land in adjacent areas with adequate drainage sold from $87 to $125 per acre. They placed the benefit to the land at $13,202, 285. Interestingly, the railroad mileage boasted about by the district was a result of the endeavors of Louis Houck who now was so adamantly opposed to the district. The booklet also contained statements in support of the district and its bonds from Wood and Oakley, Chicago bond attorneys, engineers J.A. Ockerson of the Mississippi River Commission, Daniel W. Mead, A.E. Morgan, and Isham Randolph.

As construction started, the district employed six resident engineers to oversee the projects in specific areas of the district. Engineers resided in Whitewater, Cape Girardeau, Delta, Parma, Hayti, and Morehouse.[16] These engineers included L.D. Sheppard and Harry V. Newcomb who worked on the Diversion Channel and Blair Boyle, Howard Henderson, E.S. Blaine, and William Mulholland focusing on the lower district.

Key to successful construction of the necessary ditches and levees was proper equipment for contractors. Construction of major drainage projects such as the Panama Canal, Chicago Sanitary Canal, and the Little River Drainage District ditches coincided with significant technological changes in excavation equipment. The introduction of new machinery such as the floating steam dipper dredge discussed in Chapter 8 along with draglines made it possible to tackle excavation projects which only a few years earlier would not have been feasible. Draglines use a bucket controlled by cables attached to a long boom. John W. Page built the first dragline in 1909 to use in work on the Chicago Sanitary Canal by his contracting company, Page and Schnable, when he found other types of machinery inadequate for the work required. In 1912, Page started Page Engineering to manufacture draglines. The first draglines were mounted on rail trucks and moved along rail tracks. Around 1920 Page Engineering introduced a dragline with the capability of moving with a walking motion. Some smaller machines were fitted with crawler tracks for movement. Chief competitors of Page in dragline manufacture were Bucyrus and Marion Steam Shovel Company. Bucyrus marketed its first dragline in 1910 and in 1912 introduced electricity as a power source for draglines. Marion Power Shovel Company which supplied many of the steam shovels used in construction of the Panama Canal and the ditches in the lower portion of the Little River Drainage District also marketed draglines in competition with Bucyrus. Bucyrus acquired the Marion company in 1997.

In a 1917 article, chief engineer B.F. Burns discussed the construction procedure for the diversion channel and levee and the equipment used:

> A strip is cleared approximately 400 feet wide. From this all brush, logs, and debris are removed. The stumps on the berms are cut to twenty-four inches above the ground, but elsewhere they are cut to such heights as will enable them to be removed with stump pullers [steam powered machines used to remove tree stumps] stump pullers and skidders being a necessary part of the contractors equipment. As the work goes forward the floodway strip, 900 feet in width, is cleared and, before the final completion of the system, all logs, brush and debris are removed so as to permit the free movement of the flood water over it. Following the clearing of the channel and levee base area the stumps are broken with dynamite and removed and the roots grubbed out so that the material will be practically free from fibrous matter when excavated from the channel and placed in the levee.[17]

Burns further elaborates on the specific type of draglines used: "On the main work Bucyrus drag line excavators are being used exclusively and on the Ramsey Creek Diversion Channel a Monighan drag line and an small Lindgerwood machine are being used." Burns then explains the use of electric draglines and how electricity was supplied: "All of the main Bucyrus machines, with one exception, are operated by electricity. A high tension line carrying 13,200 volts is strung along the channel. This current is generated at Cape Girardeau and is stepped down to 440 volts by transformers at the machines. On the work east of Allenville the transformers are located on barges floating in the channel. This facilitates their movement as the work progresses."[18]

Three of the four Bucyrus machines had 100-foot booms and one had a 125-foot boom. Buckets were either four and a half or three and a half cubic yards in capacity. The excavators worked continuously, 24 hours per day, six days a week. Sundays were used for repairing equipment. Each machine had an operator and an oiler. The operator controlling the equipment and the oiler taking care of maintenance and operated the machine while the main operator ate lunch so the work never stopped. The men worked

Top: Steam-powered stump puller removing stumps from route of the diversion channel. Once the stumps were removed they were piled and burned. *Bottom:* One of the draglines used in construction of the Little River Drainage District ditches. This unit moved on tracks laid along side the channel being constructed (both photographs Little River Drainage District Collection, Missouri State Archives).

10. Little River: Planning and Construction

A steam-powered floating dipper dredge chews its way through the mud and debris while working on one of the ditches in the lower district. This type of machinery was used in constructing all of the ditches in the lower district (Little River Drainage District Collection, Missouri State Archives).

in eight hour shifts. The machines also had an electric fan positioned near the operator's seat to keep mosquitoes and flies away.[19]

As mentioned earlier, work on the ditches in the lower section of the district was carried out by floating dipper dredges. Contractors used dredges manufactured by several companies including American Steel Dredge Company, Marion Power Shovel, and Fairbanks. Theses machines were shipped by rail as close as possible where digging was to begin and assembled there. Typically the dredges were equipped with a 45 boom and a one-and-a-half yard dipper and were powered with a steam engine which also powered a generator to provide lighting so that operation could be 24 hours. The hulls of these dredges were 16 to 18 feet wide and about 80 feet long. They were operated by a day crew of three or four men, two actually operating the dredge and one tending the fire for the boiler.

Before digging actually began, the right of way was cleared of brush and trees. Trees were cut into firewood and stacked along the right of way for use by the dredges although some did utilize coal for fuel. Stumps which would present problems for removal by the dredge were removed with dynamite. The district engineers marked the route of the ditch with stakes so that the dredge operators always had view of a line of stakes. As digging progressed, the dredge operator would pull up the spuds and allow the dredge to float forward, reset the spuds, and begin digging again. Accompanying each dredge was what was referred to as a cabin boat or houseboat which served as the contractor's office and as the mess and sleeping quarters for the dredge crew. A two-story cabin was erected on a hull built of heavy planks coated to make them waterproof. The lower story was divided into two rooms, one for the contractor's office and a break room for crew members when not working. The other room as the kitchen and mess room where meals were eaten. The cook was usually the wife of one of the crew members. The second story consisted of one sleeping room for the crew and another room with quarters for the cook and her husband. The houseboat would be launched after the dredge had dug enough of the ditch for it to float.[20]

Two world events in the 1910s impacted the Little River Drainage District and slowed construction progress. The first was the onset of World War I. President Woodrow Wilson asked Congress for a declaration of war against Germany April 2, 1917. At the end of January, the German government announced that all ships traveling to French or British ports were subject to attack by it submarines. In March, Germany sank three American merchant ships. The United States was now a part of World War I. A line of entrenchments extending from the English Channel to Switzerland constituted what came to be known as the Western Front. Combat along this line was at a virtual stalemate between the opposing forces. At the time of its entry into the war, the United States Army had a total strength of just over 200,000 men compared to European armies of more than one million. To increase the strength of the army, on May 18, 1917, Congress established a draft which initially included men from 21 to 30 but was later expanded to include those from 18 to 45. By the end of the war the size of the army had grown to 3.7 million men.[21] This large number of men going into military service hampered efforts by contractors to maintain sufficient workers for the Little River project.

Additionally, much of American industry was converted to manufacturing materiel for the war effort. The National Defense Act of 1916 established what eventually became known as the War Industries Board, overseeing economic and industrial mobilization for the war.[22] The focus of industry on the war effort resulted in a shortage of some supplies for

Houseboat following floating dredge. The houseboat provided eating and sleeping quarters for the crew as well as the contractor's office. Dredges generally operated 24 hours per day (Little River Drainage District Collection, Missouri State Archives).

the civilian market. In its 1918 report, the board of supervisors reported slow progress because of "the difficulty in securing repair parts, cable, fuel and supplies."

The second international event impacting the construction was the influenza epidemic of 1918. Influenza or the grippe as it was sometimes called has been with humankind for thousands of years but not often reaching the pandemic of 1918-1919. This version was often referred to as the Spanish flu although it did not have its origins in that country. Because Spain did not censor reporting of its problems in dealing with the influenza as did other European countries, the name became attached. In the early twentieth century its cause was still unknown. Although the germ theory, the idea that infectious microorganisms caused certain diseases, had been discussed since the early nineteenth century.[23] As the science of microbiology grew the concept of a contagion smaller than a bacteria was espoused by some scientists. Richard Shope of the Rockefeller Institute first identified the swine influenza virus in 1931. Further research lead to the isolation of the human influenza virus in 1939.[24] However, in 1918, many believed influenza had other causes such as miasma or toxic air produced by decaying organic material.[25]

Physicians had little to offer in way of treatment other than bed rest, sedatives, and "a nutritious diet of easy digestion" as suggested by the editors of the Journal of the American Medical Association in 1891.[26] Purveyors of patent medicines took advantage of the opportunity the influenza pandemic offered. Concoctions such as Paine's Celery Compound and Hunnicutt's Throat and Lung Cure were touted as remedies for the flu. An advertisement which ran in numerous newspapers described the Spanish influenza as "an exaggerated form of grip" and taking "larger doses than is prescribed for ordinary grip" of Laxative Bromo Quinine Tablets could actually prevent the disease.[27]

Americans were not unfamiliar with influenza as an epidemic surfaced in 1890-1891 but nothing comparable to what came in 1918. Influenza appeared in the spring of 1918 in the United States but was no worse than its usual annual appearance and it subsided by summer. Influenza began impacting combat troops in Europe in the spring of 1918 also and reappeared in Boston in August among sailors but by October influenza had traversed the entire country and proved to be a particularly virulent form of the disease.[28] It caused so much injury to the lungs that it became easy for pneumonia bacteria to attack. Deaths most often actually occurred because of the accompanying pneumonia. Although reporting was not complete, the first reported case in Missouri was October 11, 1918.[29]

Local officials across the country tried to slow the spread by closing public places such as schools, theaters, and even churches. In some cases they restricted the hours businesses could be open and asked people to wear gauze masks when in public. In southeast Missouri, beginning October 11, 1918, the Cape Girardeau city council closed all theaters, churches, conventions, and schools. Pool rooms were to close at 8 p.m. each day and all businesses were ordered to keep people from remaining on their premises after purchases had been made. The December 13, 1918, edition of *The Weekly Tribune* published in Cape Girardeau noted that police had been busy enforcing restrictions "around the various business houses by keeping the civilians from congregating in the stores and on the street corners. A few stores have had extra people on the busiest days to keep the crowds limited to about twelve people as much as possible." Fortunately, by the summer of 1919 the Spanish flu subsided and then disappeared.

The 1918 influenza pandemic was devastating. Although records of the time were not good, it is estimated that 20 to 50 million people were killed worldwide. In the United States, 25 percent of the population contracted the disease and 675,000 died.[30] The flu also made a strong impact on the economy through business closures and lost work. At times, entire families succumbed to the disease. Work on the Little River Drainage District suffered as well. The board of supervisors reported that "influenza has severely interfered in the progress of the work, and in some instances causing complete suspension of work."[31]

Work on the diversion channel portion of the original Plan for Drainage was nearing completion by 1918, although flooding in May of that year tested the diversion channel levee. The flood cut through the levee near Allenville and several other breaks occurred east of Dutchtown. The district's consulting engineers examined these breaks and found how they could be repaired and made more secure. Their conclusion was that, overall, the levee proved to be secure.[32] However, continued erosion along the diversion channel necessitated the installation of rip-rap and willow mats to prevent damage to the levee. This was done in 1920, which proved to be a landmark year for the district since it marked the completion of all the work under the original Plan for Drainage.[33]

A second bond sale of $600,000 was made October 15 to finance the diversion of Sal's Creek and additional work on Castor River. This year also marked the beginning of maintenance work on ditches in the lower district, as chief engineer L.L. Hidinger reported, "The maintenance work on the lower ditches could not be longer deferred, because their capacity was in some cases greatly diminished."[34]

Concern about the soundness of the levee south of the diversion channel led the district's board of supervisors and landowners to provide an extra measure of vigilance over the levee as recorded in the minutes of the 1924 landowners meeting by organizing "a flood patrol throughout the diversion system securing comptent [sic] men who will, in the event of a severe storm patrol the levees for the purpose of protecting them and reporting immediately any fault that may be found which might result seriously if neglected."[35]

A new phase of construction began with the letting of contracts in 1921 for ditches in the west extension of the district in Stoddard and Bollinger counties. This work was financed by the issuance of $750,000 in bonds. After completion of the original plan for drainage, it became apparent to the district and landowners that some areas were not being drained as well as others. A resolution from the landowners in their 1923 meeting requested the district to make necessary changes to the Plan for Drainage.[36] Theses modifications required enlarging some existing ditches and digging additional ones. Also a part of the revised plan was the purchase of land and construction of three retention basins south of the diversion channel in Scott and Stoddard counties to hold runoff from the hill areas in times of heavy rainfall. Two of these are in the Caney Creek Valley and the third is the Jenkins Basin south of Painton. A fifth and final bond issue in the amount of $4,000,000 was made in October 1924 to finance this revised plan.[37]

The drainage system built by the Little River Drainage District received its severest test in the flood of 1927. The first half of 1927 brought southeast Missouri about the same amount of precipitation it normally receives for an entire year. Levees along the St. Francis River broke in several places, sending a flow across the Kennett-Malden Ridge into the Little River Valley. The diversion channel levee sustained some slides and some serious damage but successfully held the flood. The lower district underwent additional severe flooding when the Mississippi River levee at Dorena failed, causing a flow to cross the Sikeston Ridge. In total, flood damage cost the district approximately $42,000 in repairs.[38] With the completion of modification to the original plan for drainage, which equalized the drainage benefits in all parts of the district and the west extension of the district into Stoddard and Bollinger counties, the district's work shifted from construction to maintenance of the ditches and levees constructed beginning in the late 1920s onward.

By 1925, the Little River Drainage District had spent almost $7,000,000 in just the construction of ditches, levees, and clearing right-of-way. This did not include engineering and surveying expenses, purchase of right-of-way, or administration. Total expenditures by the district since its inception approached $15,000,000, a major increase over the $400,000 estimated cost at the time of incorporation.[39] This represented approximately $30 owed on every acre within the district, a major factor in the financial peril the district would have to navigate in the next decade.

The future looked bright in the mid–1920s for the Little River Drainage District and southeast Missouri agriculture now that a means to successfully drain the entire area was in place and new land could be cleared and put into production. The conversion of the region from swampland to farmland was well underway.

CHAPTER II

Little River Drainage District: Floods, the Great Depression, Financial Failure and Recovery

The late teens proved to be a time of agricultural prosperity and expansion in the United States. World War I created a surge in the demand for food to be shipped to Europe even before the United States entered the war. The troop build up and deployment to Europe of American troops required additional large stockpiles of food. Farmers responded to this opportunity by increasing the production of livestock and crops.

The end of World War I brought change again as food shipments to Europe decreased. By 1920, surpluses began to collapse crop and livestock prices. With the progression of the 1920s, problems for farmers worsened, and the nation headed toward the economic depression of the 1930s. The depression for farmers actually began almost a decade earlier than it did for other sectors of the economy. Those farmers who had borrowed heavily during the war years to expand felt the effect of declining farm prices especially hard.[1] Historian David Danbom points out another reason farmers felt a depression economy in the 1920s: "One factor that contributed to rural hardship during the twenties was the reality that the prices farmers paid for the goods they purchased did not decline to the same degree as the prices they received. Hence, their real incomes were not as robust as they had been before the war."[2]

Although many businesses and industries flourished in the 1920s, agricultural commodity prices and land values declined steadily throughout the decade.[3] The decline in farm prices coupled with several successive years of weather-related crop losses proved disastrous for the Little River Drainage District. The district depended on landowners' payment of assessments to make interest and principal payments to bondholders, and farmers' income in turn depended on crop yields and prices that provided a profit from their investment in land and crop production costs. As the nation edged toward depression, this balance tilted away from the farmer, consequently tax collection by Little River Drainage district began suffering.

Until 1919, the tax collection rate had always been good, with less than 1 percent delinquent. In 1920, the delinquency rate jumped to almost 3 percent and the following year it climbed to 8½ percent. It was the policy of the board of supervisors to aggressively pursue lawsuits against landowners with delinquent taxes "within six months after the taxes became delinquent," according the their 1927 *Bulletin*.[4] The penalty on delinquent taxes was set at 2 percent per month. In 1921, the board changed its policy and stopped filing lawsuits within six months of taxes becoming delinquent. It recognized the difficult situation in which economic conditions had placed landowners.

As both land prices and agricultural commodity prices continued to fall, the tax delinquency problem worsened. The June 1927 semi-annual bulletin reported the following delinquency rates for land in the original district: "the percentage of the 1925 levy delinquent on October 1, 1926 was 15.7 percent while the percentage of the 1924 tax levy delinquent on October 1, 1925, was 13.4 percent." The situation in the Stoddard and Bollinger County Extension was even worse: "The percentage of the 1924 tax delinquent October 1, 1925, was 20.8 percent while the percentage of the 1925 tax levy delinquent October 1, 1926, was 32.2 percent."[5] Clearly, the situation was worsening year by year. In 1929, delinquency ran as high as 58 percent.

The district's board of supervisors again took a hard line attitude toward tax delinquencies and resumed preparing suits against all land on which delinquent taxes were owed. Some landowners requested the board to reduce or waive the 2 percent per month penalty on back taxes. however, the board refused to do this, claiming that it had no legal authority to do so.[6] The board even went so far as to hire a tax attorney, Richard B Russell, to help prepare cases involving delinquent taxes.

The year 1927 brought to the Mississippi Valley the most devastating flood in its history. The Diversion Channel levee sustained some serious damage but the district reported that "at no time was the water closer than 7 feet to the top of the levee."[7] Breaks in both Mississippi and St. Francis River levees caused severe flooding, with the St. Francis River levee breaking three places between Campbell and the Arkansas state line: one north of

St. Francis, Arkansas, another west of Gibson, Missouri, and a third north and west of Kennett. A report from the district described the flooding from the St. Francis this way: "The flood water ... flowed east across the Kennett-Malden Ridge and into the Little River District.... These overflows occurred repeatedly and almost continuously from February until the latter part of May."[8] At 4:15 a.m. on April 16, a crevasse formed in the Mississippi River levee at Dorena, flooding 200,000 acres of land. The report gives this description of the Mississippi River levee breaks: "In April, the Mississippi river levee broke at Dorena some 15 miles east of New Madrid. This water passed into the St. Johns Levee District and breached the backwater levee, extending from New Madrid to Farrenburg. The flood water crossed the New Madrid-Sikeston Ridge at a depth from 4 to 8 feet and several miles in width."[9]

According to a U.S. Weather Bureau report, water entered New Madrid and stood "1.5 feet higher inside the city levee than in the river in front of the town." Fortunately the Coast Guard steamer *Kankakee* was in the area and was able "to remove people from the flooded area."[10]

Precipitation during the 1926-1927 winter and the spring of 1927 swelled the river to record levels. The effects of the 1927 Mississippi River flood extended far beyond the southeast Missouri lowlands. The levee breach at Dorena was only the first of 42 major and 120 total levee crevasses, flooding 16,570,627 acres in seven states which resulted in $102,562,395 in crop losses. In some cases levees were opened with dynamite to reduce the river flow such as in St. Bernard Parish, Louisiana, which reduced flood pressure on New Orleans.

The magnitude of the flood quickly overwhelmed local resources and required a coordinated national effort to help those who were forced to leave their homes by the rising waters. To accomplish this, President Calvin Coolidge established a special commission to coordinate relief efforts and appointed Commerce Secretary Herbert Hoover to head this commission, giving him immense power. Coolidge directed that the commission work in concert with the American Red Cross whose chairman, James L. Fieser was also a member of the commission. The remainder of the committee was composed of the secretaries of the Treasury, War, Justice, and Navy along with members of the Red Cross Central Committee.[11]

To care for people forced out of their homes who had no other place to stay, the Red Cross established camps on high ground, usually along levees with the Army providing tents. In total, the Red Cross set up 154 camps, 13 of which were in southeast Missouri. A total of 325,554 people were housed in camps along the lower Mississippi River. More than two-thirds

The United States Coast Guard steamer *Kankakee* rescued victims of the 1927 Mississippi River flood in the vicinity of New Madrid (Collections of the St. Louis Mercantile Library at the University of Missouri–St. Louis).

of that number were black. Those staying in the camps were provided with food, clothing, and immunizations. Doctors and nurses were also available in most camps. While conditions were less than ideal, camp residents generally tolerated the situation well.[12]

In some camps, particularly in Arkansas, Mississippi, and Louisiana however, racial tension was present and complaints of mistreatment of blacks in the distribution of food, clothing, and other items were made. In addition, in some cases armed guards were present and blacks were not allowed to leave the camp and were forced to work at gunpoint without pay. Some planters feared that if blacks left the area they would not return and their farms would be faced with a labor shortage.

Racial animosity at the Greenville, Mississippi, camp seemed to be some of the worse. Author John M. Barry in his book about the flood, *Rising Tide*, notes that black men were paid "nothing for Red Cross work, which included the handling of all supplies, and the work was performed by men

11. Little River: Floods, Depression, Financial Failure and Recovery 139

Refugees from the 1927 Mississippi River flood crowded into Red Cross tents set up on levees (Collections of the St. Louis Mercantile Library at the University of Missouri–St. Louis).

working under guns."[13] In response to complaints, Hoover appointed the Colored Advisory Committee headed by Robert Morton of the Tuskegee Institute. The commission made two inspections of camps in Arkansas, Mississippi, and Louisiana and made numerous suggestions as to things that needed to be changed in its first report but little action was taken. Its second report made after a second tour in November dealt more with resettlement efforts following the flood and found blatant abuses of Red Cross policy. The commission found "that landlords were routinely stealing supplies designated for tenants, that black landowners were refused supplies, that thousands of colored victims had yet to receive clothing needed for the winter."[14] Such issues were left largely unaddressed. Although Hoover proved to be a master at managing the logistics of the flood relief effort, winning many accolades for his work and ultimately the presidency of the United States, the racial tensions that developed caused blacks to begin shifting their allegiance from the Republican to the Democratic party.

The 1927 flood changed the lives of individuals, communities, and the river itself. But, as author John Barry states perhaps the greatest and longest lasting effect of the 1927 flood was "the way Americans viewed government.

Prior to this event, Americans generally did not believe government had a responsibility for individual citizens."[15] This change in perception of the role of government has had and is still having a wide array of consequences as the federal government touches individual lives in such diverse ways ranging from marriage regulations to healthcare.

The magnitude of this flood made it clear that large floods along the Mississippi could not be contained without an overall, multi-state plan and without more money than could be raised locally. Thus all eyes turned toward the government for solutions. The result was the Flood Control Act of 1928. Although not all that its promoters wanted, it marked a step in the direction of federal responsibility for flood control along the Mississippi. The Little River Drainage District benefited from the act as well. A provision in the bill extended the limits of the planned work to Cape Girardeau. This meant that the Corps of Engineers could take over maintenance of the Headwater Diversion Channel Levee. The Corps assumed this responsibility in 1930 with the letting of their first contract October 14, 1930, for strengthening the levee.[16] The involvement of the government in levee maintenance marked the first time any government money had been put into the Little River Drainage District project. Heretofore all work had been carried out by the use of taxes paid by landowners of the district. This levee was and is still considered a first line levee protecting the St. Francis Basin.

The Corps of Engineers and the Mississippi River Commission made

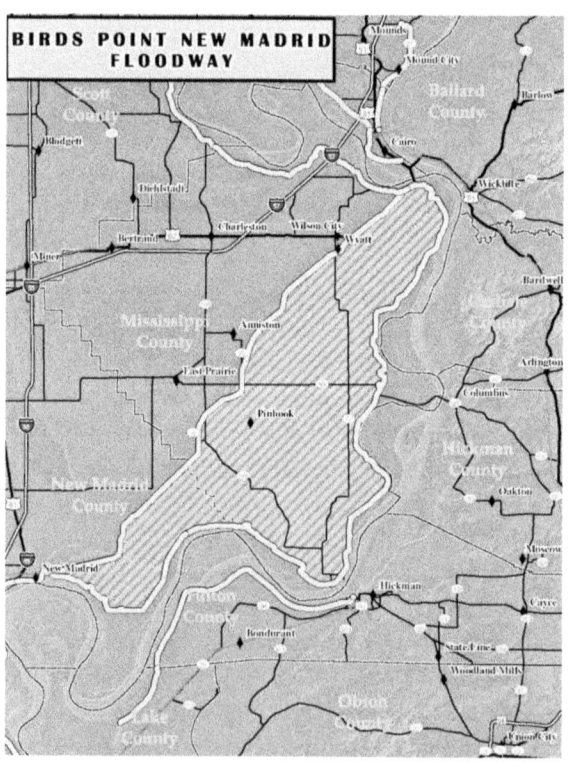

Map showing the location of the Birds Point–New Madrid Floodway established after the 1927 flood. The floodway has been activated only twice, 1937 and 2011 (U.S. Army Corps of Engineers).

other changes in southeast Missouri in regards to flood control as a result the Flood Control Act of 1928. A part of the Mississippi River and Tributaries Project was to take multiple approaches to flood control whereas previously levees had been the primary defense. This project established floodways and river straightening as other tools in controlling flood levels instead of only building higher levees. The Corps located one of these floodways in the southeast Missouri lowlands, the Birds Point–New Madrid Floodway. Its purpose was and remains to reduce flood elevations at and above Cairo, Illinois. The floodway is three to ten miles wide and is bounded on the east by the Mississippi River frontline levee extending 56 miles from Birds Point to New Madrid. On the west it is bounded by the 36-mile long setback levee. There is a 1,500-foot gap in the frontline levee near New Madrid which allows the flood water to drain back into the Mississippi River. Flow into the floodway is controlled by two sections of the frontline levee referred to as "fuseplugs." These sections of the levee are constructed to a lower elevation than the adjacent levee. One is an 11-mile section at the upper end of the frontline levee and the other is a five-mile section at the lower end. The floodway is activated when the river overtops these fuseplug sections or, at the discretion of the Corps of Engineers and the Mississippi River Commission, these or other sections of the levee are opened by explosives. The floodway encompasses just over 130,000 acres of fertile farmland. The Birds Point–New Madrid Floodway was added to Mississippi River Commission plans in 1927 by Major General Edgar Jadwin, Chief of Engineers. Jadwin rejected the Mississippi river Commission's plan to increase the elevation of the levees at Cairo largely based on costs and substituted his own plan which included the floodway.[17]

Opposition quickly developed to the floodway even though the federal government was required to compensate landowners for losses. At a January 17, 1928, meeting called by the board of supervisors of the St. Johns Levee District attended by representatives of banks, bond houses, and insurance companies a resolution was adopted opposing the Jadwin Plan. One of the most vocal opponents of the Jadwin plan was Missouri Senator Harry Hawes who referred to the plan as "the most murderous engineering document I have ever seen."[18] Otto Kochtitzky expressed his opposition to the Jadwin plan in a March 31, 1930, article in the *Southeast Missourian*: "This will not contribute to any flood control except, ... to limit the height of very great floods in the vicinity of Cairo. It will afford no benefit whatever to that portion of Mississippi County, Missouri, remaining outside the floodway, but will cause great property loss, inconvenience and injury to its citizens."[19]

Despite repeated protests by both area residents and legislators, on

December 11, 1928, President Coolidge authorized the purchase of flowage rights. Flowage rights paid a one-time indemnity to landowners to allow flooding of their land when the floodway was in operation. Construction of the setback levee began October 21, 1929, after disposal of lawsuits against establishment of the floodway and was completed in October of 1932. However, at that time only 44 percent of the needed flowage rights had been obtained. The federal government did not actually obtain full flowage rights until 1942 although the floodway was put into operation for the first time in 1937.[20] With tax delinquencies at record levels, having the federal government assume some costs of levee maintenance came at a crucial time for Little River Drainage District. However, even this support could not stave off the financial crisis facing the district within the next year as the nation's and southeast Missouri's economic conditions deteriorated.

The tax burden for 1927 proved even weightier with little or no crop production on most farms. By December of 1927, because of such extreme flooding, the district's board assumed a somewhat softer attitude toward the collection of delinquent taxes. In a resolution, the board provided that taxes could be paid during December with the penalty reduced from 2 to ½ percent per month.[21] Unfortunately, even this one month of penalty reduction did little to ameliorate the landowners' tax situation and the impending financial crisis looming in the Little River Drainage District's future.

The fact that not all land in the district was cleared and in a condition to cultivate and produce a crop magnified the real tax burden. Even in 1932, as reported in their *Bulletin* for that year, only 24 percent of the land was cleared of timber and stumps and cultivated. About 32 percent was partly cleared of timber and stumps and partly in cultivation, while 44 percent was in woods with most of the marketable timber removed but not in cultivation. This meant that approximately 40 percent of the land in the district was producing revenue for the landowners. That 40 percent had to pay the taxes levied against it and the remaining 60 percent of the district acreage. The taxes included general state and county assessments as well as drainage taxes. Having land situated in more than one drainage district added to the landowners' tax woes. Historian Leon Ogilvie notes that in 1920, 488,455 acres in southeast Missouri were in two or more drainage districts. By 1930 this number had risen to 888,758 acres.[22] Using some typical per acre assessments, it is easy to see how the relatively small amount of cultivated land magnified the tax burden. If a farmer was assessed $2 per acre from Little River Drainage District, $0.55 per acre general tax, and $0.25 per acre from other drainage districts his tax bill would be $2.80

per acre. But with only 40 percent of his land in production the real tax burden would be $7 per producing acre.

Especially detrimental to the income of drainage districts was default on tax payments by lumber companies holding thousands of acres of land. One example of this was the Wisconsin Lumber Company's decision in 1930 to stop paying taxes on 57,000 acres of its property in Pemiscot and Dunklin counties from which all usable timber had been removed. The company owned most of the land in the Elk Chute Drainage District and much of it was also in the Little River Drainage District. Wisconsin Lumber Company paid about $175,000 annually in property taxes. This amounted to a substantial loss of income for both the drainage districts and general operations of the counties. A Sikeston newspaper noted that Wisconsin Lumber Company's failure to pay tax its taxes caused Pemiscot and Dunklin counties to "face a severe financial crisis."[23] Another drainage district suffering the loss of tax revenue was the Inter-River Drainage District in Butler County which drained land lying between the Black and St. Francis rivers when American Sugar Refining Company stopped paying taxes on 60,000 acres it owned in the district in 1929. Again, the valuable timber had been removed so the company had no further use for the land and refused to continue paying taxes.

With its income dropping, the Little River Drainage District tried to remain solvent by scaling back expenditures for ditch maintenance through delaying needed projects and canceling some of its contracts. The district reported in 1930, "This year's [1929] maintenance program has been curtailed on account of shortage of funds." It further noted that "the contract with C.H. Moore for keeping the ditches and levees in the lower part of the District cleared and in condition was cancelled on account of lack of funds."[24] All efforts failed, and on October 1, 1929, the district defaulted in payments of principal and interest on bonds due on that date. The Board of Supervisor's report made at the October 28, 1929, landowners' meeting explained the situation this way: "Owing to the condition prevailing in the District during the past several years, resulting in large increases in the delinquent taxes, the payment of interest and principal on our bonds of October 1, 1928, wiped out entirely the surplus of approximately $265,000.00, which the district had at that time. The tax collections for the year 1928 were insufficient to pay both principal and interest due October 1, 1929."[25]

For Little River and other drainage and levee districts in default on bond payments, only two possible solutions existed. One was to reach some kind of agreement with the bondholders for reduced and deferred payments or, second, seek some help from the federal government, which at this time it was not eager to provide. The board of supervisors of the Little River Drainage District pursued both avenues of aid. Up until this point there was not the immediate reaction by individuals and groups to turn to the federal government for help on problems that is so prevalent today. But two disasters of unprecedented proportions, the 1927 Mississippi river flood and the Great Depression which began in the agricultural sector of the economy almost a decade before the stock market crash of 1929, coming close together, changed the nation's and local drainage and levee districts' response to such events and caused both individuals and special interest groups to look to the federal government for solutions.

Following the stock market crash, many consumers reduced spending for such things as automobiles and radios causing manufacturers to cut production thus resulting in large numbers of workers in urban areas losing their jobs. Without jobs, consumer loans could not be repaid and the downturn in retail sales meant that many businesses as well could not repay loans, placing severe pressure on the banking industry. Historians Larry Schweikart and Michael Allen argue that U.S. tax policy and failure to increase the money supply were major contributors to the depression spiral. They note that The U.S. money supply fell by one third. "Had no other factors been at work … this alone would have pushed the economy over the edge."[26] Unemployment reached 25 percent nationally and much higher in some localities. As banks struggled to meet their obligations, they sometimes foreclosed even on loans that were being repaid regularly resulting in hundreds of thousands of farmers losing their farms between 1929 and 1932. In some instances, farmers remained on the land, farming land they once owned as tenants. Agricultural surpluses continued to build causing prices to plummet even further.[27]

At the October 1929 Little River Drainage District's landowner meeting, a resolution was passed expressing confidence and support for the board of supervisors and their efforts to find a solution to the district's dilemma: "We commend the Board of Supervisors for starting negotiations and the efforts they have made to work out a plan of refinancing the bonded indebtedness of the district." The closing statement of the resolution reiterated their complete support of the board: "We express confidence in the Board of Supervisors and leave it to them to make the best terms possible."[28] All but one member of the board of supervisors at this time began his service in 1907 with the incorporation of the district. The president of the board of supervisors was John H. Himmelberger who was the most influential individual to ever serve on the board had been president of the board since its inception.

11. Little River: Floods, Depression, Financial Failure and Recovery   145

It was against the backdrop of and in the midst of the Great Depression that the board pursued efforts on two fronts to find a way out of its financial crisis. One was to work with the bondholders' protective committee formed to represent bondholders' interests to arrive at a payment plan. At the same time, the district actively sought to secure passage of legislation that would provide some measure of assistance from the federal government.

Prior to its default on bond payments, some members of the board of supervisors met with various St. Louis and Chicago investment houses that distributed the district's bonds. In St. Louis on October 22, 1929, holders of mortgages on land in the Little River Drainage District formed a committee consisting of representatives of mortgage holders and landowners to work with the board of supervisors and the bondholders' protective committee. Member of that committee and their affiliation were a s follows: L.L. Beavers, St. Louis (St. Louis Joint Stock Land Bank); Wood Netherlands, St. Louis (Federal Land Bank of St. Louis); W.A. Hemphill, Kennett (landowner); Julien Friant, Cape Girardeau (landowner); and W.D. Gibbs, St. Louis (Central Land Trust).[29] In order to protect and represent the interests of those who had invested in Little River bonds, two bondholders' protective committees were formed. One, headed by John W. Dennison, vice-president of the Continental Illinois Company, Chicago, represented bonds issued for the original district. Other members of the committee included Richard Pidgeon, Estabrook and Company, Boston; George Packard, Harris Trust and Savings Bank, Chicago; and J.D. McGee, Boatmen's National Company, Chicago. What became known as the Bliss Committee, chaired by W.K. Bliss, First National Company, St. Louis, represented holders of bonds for the Stoddard-Bollinger Counties Extension. Also serving on the Bliss Committee were James F. Quigg, Mississippi Valley Trust Company, St. Louis and P.C. Jones. The goal of the protective committees was to secure the outstanding bonds from the owners so that they could act with authority from the owners in planning for the refinancing the district. Eventually the two committees jointly formed the Little River Corporation to act in refinancing discussions. However, in order to carry out this function, those who had invested in district bonds had to be willing to surrender them to the corporation. While in some cases, owners refused to surrender their bonds, by 1933 the Little River Corporation held 90 percent of the district's outstanding bonds.

The district maintained membership in the National Drainage Association, an organization composed of drainage and irrigation districts across the nation. Their goal was to foster the passage of legislation to aid districts that found themselves in difficult financial situations, and such bills were being introduced in the legislature in 1929. The measure supported by the National Drainage Association and known as the Smith-Glenn Bill, passed the Senate in late 1929 but was not acted on by the House. Because the Little River Drainage District wanted to exert as much influence as possible to secure passage of this or a similar measure, they engaged the services of Julien Friant of Cape Girardeau as a lobbyist for the District from 1931 to 1933. Friant was an officer of the Himmelberger-Harrison Land and Investment Company form 1915 to 1925 and secretary-treasurer of the National Drainage Association from 1931 to 1922. In 1933, he became a special assistant to the Secretary of Agriculture, a position he held until his death in 1935.

Within the district meanwhile, to further generate funds for payment of the bonds, the board of supervisors in 1929 obtained judgments against land with past due taxes and tried to sell this land. Illustrating the depressed nature of region's economy was the fact that at each sale held, no one bid on the land. Missouri writer, social reformer, and farmer Thad Snow describes tax sales of farmland in Mississippi County this way: "The sheriff auctioned them off to the highest bidder. The law required the sales to be advertised, and they were public sales, but usually only the despoiled debtor and the legal agent of the outside creditor attended them."[30]

In 1929, cotton was selling for about 16 cents per pound only to drop to five cents in 1931. Wheat that sold for $1 per bushel in 1929, fell to 38 cents per bushel about a year later. Such prices simply made it impossible to buy land and realize enough from crops to pay for the land and pay the taxes.[31] The board of supervisors felt they had made significant progress toward refinancing efforts with the bondholders' protective committees when, in 1930, an agreement known as the Dennison Agreement was struck to reduce the payments required each year on the bonds. The original payment required was $900,000 each year, which the committee reduced to $400,000 for 1930, $450,000 for 1931, $500,000 for 1932, $550,000 for 1933, and $600,000 for 1934. Unfortunately, with farm prices at their lowest point in the twentieth century, there was little hope of these goals being met. For 1930, instead of $400,000, tax collections brought in only about $160,000.[32]

The board of supervisors felt this was a reasonable agreement and, as expected, was quite disappointed with the 1930 collections. In their report to the landowners, they chided those who for whatever reason had not paid their taxes: "It is not fair to those taxpayers who have paid their 1930 taxes and those who are desirous of paying the taxes for the next five years on the reduced basis offered by the bondholders to be prevented from doing so by landowners who either refuse or cannot pay the 1930 taxes."[33]

The less than a sympathetic attitude of the board of supervisors may be reflective in part of the make up of the board. The board was composed of owners of large holdings of land which most had owned for a long period of time and on which they owed little. The majority had connections with the timber industry and held accumulated assets which allowed them to continue to prosper even in the depression. In contrast, small farmers who had more recently purchased a few hundred or fewer acres of newly drained and cleared land on which to farm and support a family simply could not realize enough profit at the depressed commodity prices to make loan payments, provide a living for their family, and pay property taxes.

To the board of supervisors, the agreement with the bondholder protective committee represented a window of opportunity to bring the district's finances back to solvency, and it did not want that window closed. They decided to take strong, aggressive action in the form of lawsuits and foreclosures against those who had not paid their taxes, stating in Bulletin 45 that "it [the board of supervisors] must use every means within the law to secure the minimum amount required by the bondholders."[34] The bondholders' protective committee allowed the district to reduce the payment amount required to settle delinquent taxes. Taxes for 1927 and prior years could be paid at 30 percent without penalty, 1928 taxes at 40 percent without penalty, and 1929 at 50 percent without penalty, if 1930 taxes were also paid. To take advantage of these rates, landowners had to pay 1928 and prior years' taxes before December 1, 1930, and 1929 taxes had to be paid before January 1, 1931.[35] Despite these seemingly generous terms, depressed prices and drought of the early 1930s mad it impossible for large numbers of landowners to comply.

As if to add insult to injury, farmers faced several years of severe drought in the early 1930s on top of depressed farm commodity prices, earning the time period the moniker "the Dirty Thirties," referring to the dust storms originating in the Great Plains. While the worst drought conditions occurred in the Great Plains, all of the central United States and Mid-South suffered below normal rainfall, sharply reducing crop production. Thad Snow described the conditions "Swampeast Missouri" farmers faced when he wrote, "The first three years of the thirties were a nightmare. Everybody who had not already gone broke attended to the matter in one of those years."[36] Landowner C.E. Willis wrote a two-page letter addressed to the district's board of supervisors and the bondholders' protective committee on September 7, 1932. In this letter, Willis who owned 280 acres, outlined clearly the difficulty landowners faced in trying to pay taxes. Willis, writing from Edwardsville, Illinois, was apparently an absentee landowner, as were numerous other land owners in the Little River Drainage District. Willis had to continually put more money into his farm and explained his situation this way: "Have owned this land twelve (12) years. Have very good tenants, raise fair crops. Have paid over $7000 in taxes in all of the twelve years. I have not in any one year received enough rent to pay the taxes on the land. Last year 1931 I raised over 7,000 bushels of corn but my ⅓ of the crop did not pay the taxes, to say nothing of the up keep, repairs, depreciation or any interest on my money invested." Willis further explained the dilemma farmers and landowners were in: "If, I with my land paid for, no mortgages and good tenants cannot make it go, how can the man who owes for a good part of his make a living."[37]

Not only could landowners not pay the taxes on their land, they could not pay their mortgages either. Thus, ownership of land continued to be transferred to mortgage holders as they foreclosed on mortgages. Julien Friant, testifying before a House of Representatives committee, estimated that through 1929, mortgage holders had taken title to as much as 300,000 acres in southeast Missouri.[38] The number of acres in foreclosure increased substantially in the thirties. Some of the largest lenders were insurance companies, thus they gained title to large land holdings in southeast Missouri. Thad Snow wrote, "In the Delta the insurance companies who were the biggest lenders took ownership of most of the land, and they set up agencies in every town of importance to operate their vast holdings."[39]

In the midst of its financial crisis, the district lost significant leadership with the death in 1930 of John H. Himmelberger. Himmelberger was by far the most influential member of the board. He served as member of the board of supervisors and as president of the board from 1907 until his death in 1930. W.P. Anderson replaced Himmelberger as president.

Tax collections for 1931 fared no better than those for 1930. On July 14, 1932, John Dennison, on behalf of the bondholders' protective committee, sent the board of supervisors a letter informing them that "the recommendations [in the Dennison Agreement] are now withdrawn and the subject matter of the memorandum is considered void and without effect."[40] This basically brought to a halt efforts to negotiate a refinancing agreement with the bondholders' protective committee and federal legislation to help drainage districts in default had not yet been enacted, making the situation facing the district grim indeed.

Julien Friant worked nearly full time trying to secure federal legislation for the refinancing of drainage districts. He went to Washington first in

1929, to testify before Senate and House committees. In a letter to Russell L. Dearmont, he outlined his efforts for the district. "I contacted hundreds of people from the man who is now President of the United States, his advisors, cabinet officers, most of the Senators and Congressmen, the officers of most of the leading life insurance companies in the United States, including the Presidents of several of them, down to officers of drainage, levee, and irrigation districts all over the country."[41]

Because of his tireless efforts on behalf of the district, Friant expressed to Dearmont that he felt the $7,500 the district paid him for his work was not enough compared to what had been paid to Burett Oliver for his work as district attorney, and he considered asking the board for an additional $10,000. In addition to his work directly for the district, he helped raise funds for the National Drainage Association, which also worked for the passage of legislation which would have been favorable for Little River.

It was not until June 1933, that federal help was available for drainage districts. Section 36 of the Emergency Farm Mortgage Act of 1933 allowed the Reconstruction Finance Corporation to make loans to drainage districts in financial trouble. The Reconstruction Finance Corporation was established under the Hoover administration but was not extensively used. It was authorized to make loans to financial institutions, state and local governments, and railroads. The RFC was greatly expanded under Roosevelt to include aid to agriculture. The board of supervisors did not waste any time in making an application to the RFC, completing their application by August 1933. After receiving the application, the RFC made their own study of the ability of landowners in southeast Missouri to pay. Following this assessment, in December the RFC offered to loan the district $2,191,414. The loan carried an annual interest rate of 4 percent. The RFC eventually increased the amount of the loan to $2,405,000. At the time of its default, the principal amount on the district's outstanding bonds amounted to $8,018,000. Unpaid interest amounted to $1,041,826.25 resulting in a total outstanding debt of $9,059,826.25.

Obviously the amount of this loan was far less than the indebtedness of the district, which meant that bondholders were going ultimately to receive only a portion of the face value of their bonds, which amounted to 27.3 cents per dollar if they accepted the RFC terms. However, they had little chance of collecting that amount if they instead resorted to litigation forcing the district into bankruptcy.

The district now faced the challenge of long negotiations with the bondholders' protective committee to gain their acceptance of the loan. Part of this process was to convince owners of bonds to deposit them with the committee and accept terms of the RFC loan. Negotiations were long and arduous between the Little River Corporation and the Bondholders' Protective Committee represented by Roy Kercheval, Wyllis Blyth, and John Dennison, and the Little River Drainage District represented by Robert Burett Oliver of the Oliver Law Firm. Julien Friant also continued to work extensively on the RFC loan for the district after becoming an assistant secretary of agriculture. Friant was instrumental in carrying out all of the negotiations with the bondholders' committee.

The Bondholders' committee first asked the RFC to increase the amount of the loan to $6,000,000,000, which the RFC refused to do. Eventually negotiations resulted in an increase in the amount that would be paid for the bonds, based on the percentage of the bonds turned over to the committee. The amount ranged from 27.7 to 30 cents. This final arrangement was not agreed to until October 1937. By the time all parties reached a final agreement, the amount owed by the district in principal and accrued interest amounted to $12 million. The rate of payment to bond holders was determined to be 29.8 cents per dollar. This represented a substantial loss for those who had invested in the original bonds of the district. However, given the economic conditions of the country and southeast Missouri at the time few other alternatives remained.

The RFC required the district to issue new or refunding bonds in two series: Series A bonds for the amount of the loan were held by the RFC and Series B bonds as collateral for the first series held by Boatmen's National Bank of St. Louis acting as trustee under the RFC agreement. Once the refunding bonds were issued, the original old bonds of the district were returned to the district. The RFC loaned the district a total of $2,405,500 to be repaid over a period of 20 years with a 4 percent interest rate. Tax assessment had to be sufficient to make the annual payment plus the 4 percent interest in addition to an assessment for maintenance.

It had taken almost ten years for the Little River Drainage District to finally come to terms with its outstanding debt, but with the refinancing arrangement worked out through the RFC, taxes could be reduced to an amount more in line with the land's ability to produce and the prices being received for the crops harvested. For example, the 1929 assessment was $2.12 per acre while the 1937 average assessment was $1.18. This meant it was much more likely that landowners would be able to pay their assessments. With the refinancing plan in place, the Little River Drainage District was once again on its way toward financial solvency. The board held a ceremony at Morehouse in 1938 to burn the original bonds returned to the district as part of the refinancing. As the economy slowly improved, so did the percentage of land on which taxes were paid. Tax collections again produced sufficient revenue to make principal and interest payments and once again carry out regular maintenance. By 1940, tax collections rebounded significantly. The *Bulletin* of December 1940 reported that levies for 1934 through 1938 were more than 90 percent paid and the 1939 levy was 88.8 percent paid. Following some discounting, the district was able to pay off the RFC bonds in April 1952. Since that time the district has remained financially stable.

Reconstruction Finance Corporation refinancing also enabled other, smaller Bootheel drainage districts to regain their financial foothold. A total of 21 drainage and levee districts in the Bootheel received RFC refinancing following default on their bond payments. Only the three districts of Elk Chute, Inter-River, and St. John Levee District were able to refinance through negotiations with bondholders without RFC assistance.[42]

Assistance from the federal government also came to Little River and other districts in the form of labor from the Civilian Conservation Corps. The CCC was one of the numerous programs started by President Franklin Roosevelt during the first 100 days of his first term. The program focused primarily on outdoor projects such as replanting trees, building parks and hiking trails, constructing forest access roads, fighting forest fires, and drainage projects. It employed unmarried men ages 18 to 26. Camps were organized in a quasi-military fashion. Workers were paid $30 per month with $25 of that amount being sent back to their families. Literacy and other classes were offered in the camps enabling the men to learn trades and skills marketable in other jobs. It has been considered by many historians to be the most successful New Deal program. Camps were established in every state. Many of the buildings they constructed in state and national parks still stand. The program was disbanded in 1942.

In 1935, the CCC established camps at Delta, Hayti, and New Madrid. The CCC made available three draglines for work on ditch maintenance. The district paid for fuel, supplies, and material, but labor was from CCC members, allowing the work to be done at considerable savings to the district. The CCC also provided extensive manual labor for clearing brush and building bridges and fences.

The district also benefited from another New Deal program, the Works Progress Administration. The WPA, created by executive order from President Roosevelt in 1935, built roads and many public buildings across the country. The district won approval for new projects resulting in the completion of important maintenance work before the WPA program ended in 1943.

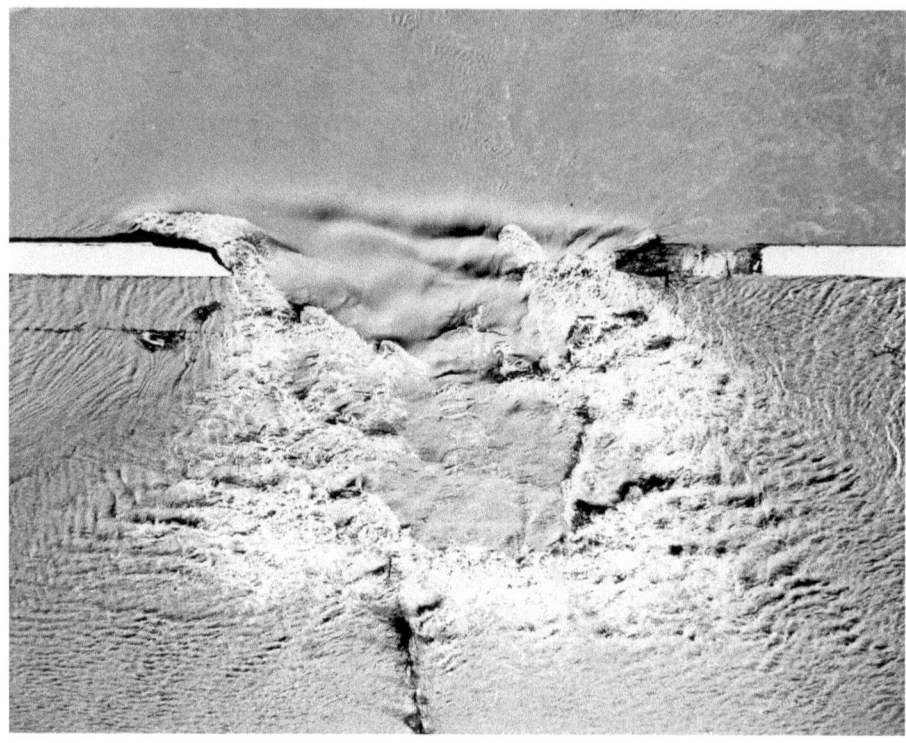

Water flowing through the dynamited levee into the Birds Point–New Madrid Floodway during the 1937 flood. This was the first time the Birds Point–New Madrid Floodway was activated. The floodway was activated in the same manner again in 2011 (Library of Congress, Prints and Photographs Division, FSA/OWI Collection [reproduction number, LC-USF-344-003835-ZB]).

Within a decade of the historic 1927 flood in the Mississippi Valley, nature challenged the southeast Missouri lowlands again with another flood. This one coming in 1937. The new year began with heavy rainfall throughout the Ohio Valley. Tributaries carrying runoff to the Ohio River from Pittsburg to Cairo caused the Ohio to reach flood stage by the middle of January, affecting towns all along its course such as Cincinnati, Louisville, Paducah, and Cairo and ultimately reaching the Mississippi River and the southeast Missouri lowlands. The disaster began January 24 when as much as 14 inches of rainfall fell on parts of Kentucky and Tennessee. It became apparent to the Corps of Engineers that this was going to be more than just a seasonal flood as they kept their eye on the river gauge at Cairo. According to plans, the Birds Point–New Madrid Floodway was to be placed into operation when the reading at Cairo reached 60 feet.

To make conditions even more miserable for those facing evacuation of their homes to escape flood waters, the weather turned colder, changing the rain to sleet which accumulated as much as six inches.[43] Tributary streams overflowed first forcing large numbers of people in southeast Missouri to leave their home. By January 19, six breaks occurred in the St. Francis River levee in Dunklin County near Kennett which flooded 50,000 acres of farmland.[44] Ice and sleet downed utility lines disrupting electricity and telephone service to the area. In response, the Red Cross established relief centers in Hornersville, Senath, Cardwell, Arbyrd, and Rives. Railroads also supplied boxcars to be used as shelter for some of the 500 or more refugees. In Kennett, the courthouse, city hall, churches, and empty buildings were being used to shelter flood victims.[45] The first warning of a major flood possible on the Mississippi went out from District Engineer Lt. Col. Eugene Reybold January 15. On January 24 Reybold issued a memorandum stating that a flood of 62 feet on the Cairo gauge was possible with 60 feet being the trigger to open the Birds Point–New Madrid Floodway. The memorandum also ordered turning over operations along the St. Francis to local officials with all Corps personnel returning to Memphis to prepare for operations along the Mississippi. The following day Reybold convened a conference in Memphis attended by government officials of various levels along with representatives of railroads, highway departments, and levee boards. The purpose was to inform them of the potential of a catastrophic flood. Prior to this conference, on January 21, the Corps advised residents of the floodway to begin evacuation. Broadcasts were made on Memphis radio stations and printed handbills were distributed notifying residents of the need to evacuate the floodway. Major R.D. Burdick was placed in charge of opening the levee. Rumors spread of armed local farmers resisting efforts by the Corps to breach the frontline fuseplug levee. The story even appeared in various newspapers across the country. The crew charged with placing explosives became frightened when they saw a shotgun wielding man running around the levee and retreated back to Cairo without completing their task. Reybold ordered two companies of regular army troops to protect the dynamite crew.

However, the actual events surrounding the "battle of the fuseplug" turned out to be a humorous story and somewhat of an embarrassment for the Corps. It has now become a part of southeast Missouri folklore. Mississippi County farmer Thad Snow learned what actually happened and wrote a letter to the editor of the *St. Louis Post Dispatch* a few days later. It turned out that the "armed farmers" consisted only of one local, well-known, hunter and trapper named Budge Cobb. Budge wasn't interested in interfering with the Corps. He knew rabbits would be headed toward the levee ahead of rising water so he was positioning himself to shoot them. When the workers saw a man with a shotgun and heard frequent firing, they misunderstood his intent and left the area. Thus the story circulated that armed farmers drove the Corps off the levee much to the embarrassment and tarnished prestige of the Army.[46]

One beneficial thing did come out of the delay in blowing the levee: it allowed time for more people to evacuate. The cold, icy conditions were making it difficult for residents to leave the floodway area. Snow describes the floodway as being "thickly populated, mostly with black and white work people."[47] Actual population of the floodway at that time was around 3,000.[48] Snow, whose farm was located outside of the floodway but along a main highway leading out of the area, described the scene on this highway: "All day long an unbroken line of traffic passes by. Sometimes a solid mile-long line of trucks goes by in low gear, waiting to break through herds of tired, dispirited cattle which no man can urge on out of their weary gait or out of the ice-broken roadway straight ahead. Some poor people carried out a little bedding on their backs; more often the utmost they could do was to carry out the children."[49]

Author David Welky adds this description of residents leaving the floodway derived from Red Cross reports: "Lines of sharecroppers trudged along, their hands folded into their coat sleeves and rags wrapped around their head to fend off the cold wind."[50] On January 25, the Corps was finally able to breach the frontline levee. The following day more openings were made for a total of 14 crevasses in the levee allowing water to rush into the floodway. The floodway functioned but only lowered the river level at Cairo by about half what had been projected earlier. Airplanes from the 110th Army National Guard Observation Squadron monitored conditions as the floodway filled, often spotting stranded residents, many who had simply refused to leave earlier, and directing rescuers to their location. Tragedy struck when a barge carrying levee workers struck a snag causing at least two dozen to drown in the frigid water.[51] The Corps of Engineers, Missouri Highway Department, Red Cross, local law enforcement, and individuals all participated in rescuing residents from the floodway.

The number of flood refugees in 1937 was staggering. Author David Welky notes that "people from Pittsburgh's Golden Triangle to Cairo's alluvial triangle, from Bird's Point in Missouri to Friars Point in Mississippi ran for their lives." The make up of the refugees cut across racial lines and social status. Welky continues, "They left home in luxury cars, trains, jalopies, rafts, and wagons, on horses and on their own two feet. They came from

Farmland near New Madrid flooded by the 1937 flood. The flooding displaced hundreds of residents, particularly in the Birds Point–New Madrid Floodway (Library of Congress, Prints and Photographs Division, FSA/OWI Collection [reproduction number, LC-USF341-010204-B]).

every race and social class, although poor whites and African Americans tended to live closer to the river and suffered disproportionately."[52] Local communities were often overwhelmed by the number people to be cared for. Some 3000 took refuge in Charleston and 2,500 in Kennett.[53] During the first week of the flood, 60,000 sheltered in Memphis at a camp set up at the fairgrounds.[54] In Arkansas, 1,000 went to Jonesboro, 3,500 to Marianna, and 12,000 to Forest City, a town of only 5,500.[55] In total, more than 85,000 families were rescued and transported to shelters across 20 states.[56]

As in the 1927 flood, the Red Cross took the lead in relief efforts although other groups such as the American Legion and the Salvation Army also provided help. The highly effective public relations effort of the Red Cross downplayed the contributions of other groups to bolster their own image.[57] Conditions in camps varied. For some sharecroppers, conditions there were better than what they had before the flood. However, most camps were overcrowded and undersupplied and in some cases widespread influenza, pneumonia, and other diseases were present. Many camps tried to improve

Flood refugees housed in Baptist Church at Sikeston. Those displaced by the flooding were forced to find shelter wherever they could. The fact the flood occurred during winter added to their misery (Library of Congress, Prints and Photographs Division [reproduction number, LC-USF34-010466-D]).

the long-term conditions of refugees by providing classes on personal hygiene, basic nutrition, and household sanitation. Camp directors also offered entertainment and recreation programs to boost morale.[58] Racial tension also surfaced in camps during the 1937 flood just as it had in refugee camps during the 1927 flood. Camps were segregated and charges of discrimination in the distribution of supplies and conscripted work surfaced. While the national office of the Red Cross had a strict policy against discrimination, author David Welky notes that "because the Red Cross needed local chapters to run operations on the ground, it was impossible to enforce the national office's colorblind guide."[59] The Red Cross did take accusations of discrimination seriously and invited members of the National Urban League, the Southern Tenant Farmers Union, the black press, and other organizations to visit some of its camps. Most charges of discrimination were found to be false. However, the Red Cross tolerated pay differences. For example, white doctors in Paducah, Kentucky, were paid $300 a month plus hotel and food while black doctors received $60 a month and nothing for housing or food.[60] Planters were concerned that sharecroppers might not return to their farms after the flood which brought into question the survival of the cotton economy thus some planters who in many cases also headed local Red Cross chapters pressured sharecroppers to commit to returning to work in exchange for receiving certain supplies.[61]

The Southern Tenant Farmers Union, a new organization which came into existence a few years prior to the flood tried to use the treatment of sharecroppers to increase its influence and membership. The STFU formed in July 1934 in Tyronza, Poinsett County, Arkansas, with the goal to bring about changes in the sharecropping system prevalent in the Delta regions of southeast Missouri and northeast Arkansas. Socialists H.L. Mitchell and H. Clay East were instrumental in forming the organization. Unique to the STFU and new for the time was that it included both black and white members and embraced women as well. The STFU leaders and lawyers pressured the Red Cross about conditions in some camps but investigators were not welcomed by most local community leaders who were generally opposed to unions. STFU members from the Bird's Point area also exerted pressure on the federal government to help improve the conditions of sharecroppers since it was the federal government that caused them to be homeless in the first place. But, the dispersal of sharecroppers during the flood made communication difficult for the STFU which immerged from the flood without funds and out of contact with its members.[62]

By February the flood began to subside. Overall the Jadwin plan which included floodways, channel straightening, and higher levees had succeeded. There were no levee breaks on the Mississippi other than those where floodways were employed.[63] Gradually those exiled by the flood began to return home. Red Cross officials assisted local landowners in getting sharecroppers back to their farms as soon as possible. Sometimes even sooner than it was safe to do so.[64] In some cases, sharecroppers lived in tents until houses destroyed by the flood could be rebuilt. Sharecroppers returned to the Birds Point–New Madrid Floodway and other farms throughout southeast Missouri but more conflict was soon to come as government farm policy brought about a clash between landowners and sharecroppers.

While the Birds Point–New Madrid Floodway may have saved Cairo, it, unlike other Ohio River towns such as Paducah and Louisville, never really recovered. Whereas Paducah and other towns experienced a revival after the flood, Cairo continued its slow decline. Use of the floodway, while considered successful by engineers, left deep-seeded animosity between local farmers and the Corps of Engineers which has persisted. The floodway was not used again until 2011 when its use was no less controversial. As the flood in the spring of 2011 began to threaten Cairo the Corps began making plans to once again activate the Birds Point–New Madrid Floodway. Farmers in the affected area filed lawsuits against the Corps and Missouri state officials intervened in an effort to block use of the floodway. Ultimately the Corps prevailed in court and detonated explosives just after 10 p.m. May 2 to allow a portion of the Mississippi River to flow into the floodway, destroying homes, farm buildings, farm equipment, and causing severe damage to some of the 130,000 acres of farm land in the floodway. While the Corps contended that the operation of the floodway was successful, the decision really came down to choosing whose property would be destroyed. Major General Edward Markham, the Chief of Engineers during the 1937 flood felt the impact of the use of the floodway. His testimony before a congressional committee on flood control not only expressed how he felt about the decision to open the floodway in 1937 but also echoes how residents felt about the 2011 use of the floodway when he stated, "I am now of the opinion that no plan is satisfactory which is based upon deliberately turning floodwaters upon the homes and property of people, even though the right to do so may have been paid for in advance."[65]

CHAPTER 12

Land Promotion, Post-Drainage Agriculture and Social Change

Organizations, railroads, and real estate investors began to actively promote the southeast Missouri lowlands toward the end of the nineteenth century. The Missouri Immigration Society published the *Hand-Book of Missouri* in 1880, describing conditions of climate, soil, agriculture, mining, and manufacturing in all areas of the state in order to stimulate interest in individuals and companies to locate within the state. In the section devoted to the lowlands of southeast Missouri, Louis Houck painted a very positive although exaggerated picture of the lowlands when he stated, "After every rain, the water rapidly drains away."[1] This was true for areas like the Sikeston Ridge and Kennett-Malden Prairie, but for the Little River Valley, adequate drainage was lacking.

Promotional efforts for southeast Missouri started to change in the 1890s as railroads began crisscrossing the area making timber harvesting attractive to large lumber companies. By 1920, all parts of the Bootheel lay within six and a half miles of a railroad.[2] Between 1890 and 1910, the population of all Bootheel counties either doubled or tripled.

Railroads were among the first to extensively promote the region. They published pamphlets and advertised in magazines and even offered tours at reduced rates. In 1889, Missouri Pacific issued a 94-page booklet, *Statistics and Information Concerning the State of Missouri*, detailing Missouri farm land along its route, such as this description of Dunklin County: "The beautiful prairies of Dunklin County, which are now a succession of the handsomest farms in Missouri were classed as swamp and overflow. When the timber is removed, it will be found that there are not 40,000 acres of actual swamp in southeast Missouri and that all of this can be drained at small expense."[3] The Frisco Railroad published a pamphlet in the early 1900s titled *Supersoil Along the Frisco Lines, Southeast Missouri and Northeast Arkansas* which touted the productivity of soils in this area. In 1912, the company released a new thirty-page pamphlet called *The Mississippi Valley Northeastern Arkansas and Southeastern Missouri* featuring a color cover. In an effort to sell its land and increase traffic, Frisco formed a development department that aided individuals wanting to locate in the area. They made available to newcomers assistance from specialists in various aspects of agriculture. Likewise, the Iron Mountain Railroad and the Cotton Belt Railroad also published pamphlets during this time, extolling the virtues of southeast Missouri. As with other railroads, they hoped to attract buyers of land they owned and increase traffic from timber and farm products.

During the late 1880s, immigration societies formed in several counties. In 1889, a region-wide effort was made at promotion in the formation of the Southeast Missouri Society, to which counties sent representatives to a convention in Cape Girardeau. Otto Kochtitzky was among those in attendance. However, the group met with little success since the various counties provided limited financial support. Residents of eight counties organized the Southeast Missouri Agricultural Bureau in 1919, with its headquarters at Dexter. The Bureau succeeded in getting articles about southeast Missouri published in a variety of farm publications such as this ad which appeared in *The Prairie Farmer*: "Southeast Missouri Alluvial Empire: the finest of corn and alfalfa lands at rock bottom prices and easy terms."[4] The organization also issued a small pamphlet of its own which emphasized drainage improvements, the variety of crops grown, road improvements, and the advantage of the region's location between north and south.

The Southeast Missouri Agricultural Bureau reorganized in the mid–1920s hiring A.I. Foard, a former editor of the *Journal of Agriculture* as secretary. Thad Snow of Charleston served as president. Other board members included Xenophon Caverno of Canalou, C.A. Vandivort of Cape Girardeau, W.H. Sikes of Sikeston, S.P. Reynolds of Caruthersville, Dwight H. Brown of Poplar Bluff, Norman D. Blue of Puxico, and R. Irl Jones of Kennett. At the same time, the organization moved its headquarters to Union Station in St. Louis, where it established a permanent exhibit. The group continued advertising and publishing articles in farm magazines, primarily those with a midwestern readership. Their pamphlets again emphasized that southeast Missouri was "where north joins south." The group also called attention to the variety of crops grown: corn, wheat, cotton, alfalfa, vegetables, fruits, melons, cowpeas, soybeans, and pecans. The Bureau even produced a three-reel film in 1924, describing opportunities in the area.[5] The film, called "One Hundred Years in Ten," was shown in towns all over southeast Missouri, in nearby states, and at Farmers' Week in Columbia hosted by the University of Missouri College of Agriculture.[6]

A.I. Foard resigned as secretary in 1924, and the focus of the bureau began to change. The group abandoned its exhibit at Union Station in St. Louis and moved its offices to the Chamber of Commerce building in St. Louis. It also decided to concentrate its efforts on advertising "in farm and livestock papers and direct attention will be given to the papers in the South."[7] This change in focus for the organization coincides with the major increase in the amount of cotton planted in southeast Missouri that year. The organization changed its name to The Southeast Missouri Agricultural and Industrial Association in 1926. Despite all of its efforts, the organization never succeeded in attracting the numbers of farmers it hoped it would. Although A.I. Foard claimed that in the fall of 1922 "new settlers arrived ... at the rate of 1,500 a day due to the publicity given Southeast Missouri by the Southeast Missouri Agricultural Bureau."[8]

Real estate firms also took an active role in promoting southeast Missouri land to farmers. Realtors circulated booklets extolling the advantages of buying farm land in the region. They pointed to improved drainage, railroads, schools, churches, roads, and climate as well as its location between north and south. Booklets from three firms, Southeast Realty Company, Little River Valley Land Company, and C. F Bruton Real Estate and Investment Company, illustrate the promotion by real estate agents.

In the early 1920s, Southeast Realty Company in Cape Girardeau, managed by Arthur C. Bowman, published a twelve-page illustrated booklet featuring land throughout southeast Missouri. The land offered for sale included timberland, cut-over land, and partially cleared land. Prices quoted ranged from $10 per acre to $50 per acre.

About 1913, the Little River Valley Land Company of Cape Girardeau published a 60-page booklet titled *Southeast Missouri: The Garden Spot of the Mississippi Valley*. The firm was headed by A.L. Harty, a member of the Littler River Drainage District board of directors. This publication begins with a description of the location and climate. Some of the claims were at best exaggerations, for example, "cyclones and tornadoes are never experienced."[9] The drainage and amount of rainfall might also have been misrepresented. "It [rainfall] has never been known by the oldest settlers to fail ... it is never sufficiently heavy to damage growing crops."[10]

The booklet goes on to describe each county and its towns, crops, and transportation.

In 1919, C.F. Bruton Real Estate and Investment Company located in Sikeston, published a 32-page booklet called *The Modern Promised Land*. The booklet mentions several prominent southeast Missouri farmers, has a testimonial written by one of Bruton's clients, and features numerous photographs of crops, farms, and houses. Bruton discusses the Littler River Drainage District and how it is improving drainage. Also included are discussions of various crops and livestock produced, weather data, soils, water availability, transportation, and businesses.

Bruton's booklet mirrors a common racial bias of the region. Bruton writes, "No Negro farmers where we sell land. Very few towns have any Negroes in them."[11] Bruton's publication was made only a couple of years before the arrival of large numbers of black sharecroppers from the old cotton south which changed the racial makeup and agriculture of the lowlands. Land sellers of the time didn't anticipate the shift to a sharecropper based cotton economy for the southeast Missouri lowlands. Although all promotional literature mentioned cotton as an important crop, promotional efforts at this point targeted primarily midwestern farmers who were focused on growing wheat, corn, and other grains along with hay and livestock production.

Disposal and development of newly cleared and cut-over land became a major issue for lumber companies not only in the southeast Missouri lowlands but throughout the delta land along the Mississippi River through Arkansas, Mississippi, and Louisiana where bottomland hardwood forests had been logged as well as areas in the upper Midwest and Great Lakes regions where extensive logging had taken place. The Himmelberger-Harrison Lumber Company tried to sell some of its cut-over land by issuing pamphlets and placing advertisements in numerous farm publications like this one in *Wallace's Farmer*: "Southeast Missouri rich alluvial made soil; cut-over, no cash down, no interest four years, then 33 years time, 6 percent."[12] They even set up a separate division to handle land sales. First called the Himmelberger-Harrison Land Selling Company it was headed by John and Julien Friant. Later the name was changed to Himmelberger-Harrison Land and Investment Company.[13] This push to sell and develop this vast area of cut-over land gave rise to magazines devoted to the subject. One such publication, *Cut-Over Lands* published in St. Louis by James E. Gatewood carried articles on a wide range of topics such as how to convert cut-over land to livestock pasture, drainage issues, growing crops, soils, equipment for logging and land clearing, and reports from various states. The magazine also carried extensive advertising from timber companies, many in southeast Missouri, trying to sell their cut-over land. For example, the May 1919 issue featured three ads from southeast Missouri firms. W. Caleb Smith of Sikeston offered "farms and cut-over land in large and small tracts." Little River Farms in Kennett had 15,000 acres touted as being great for "wheat, corn, cotton, and alfalfa" while Gideon-Anderson Lumber and Mercantile Company in Gideon featured "fine lands for wheat and corn."[14] Another publication originating in St. Louis, *Mississippi Valley Magazine*, published by the Mississippi Valley Association described itself as "Devoted to the exploitation of America's greatest basin." It published a wide variety of articles relating to the development of industry and agriculture in the Mississippi Valley including the development of cut-over land. It also featured ads for the sale of southeast Missouri land.

Once the Wisconsin Lumber Company, a division of International Harvester with southeast Missouri headquarters at Deering, had removed most of the timber from its 60,000 acres in Pemiscot and Dunklin counties it, like other timber companies, needed to dispose of its cut-over land. The company really took two approaches to dealing with this land. One was to actually clear some of the land and engage in farming and the other was to sell land to farmers.

After the lumber mill at Deering closed in 1928 the company cleared some of the land and established a farming operation using sharecroppers. Grover Wicker was the first farm manager of what became known as Deering Plantation.[15] Beginning a few years earlier, Wisconsin Lumber Company published pamphlets and began trying to sell cut-over land, devising a financing plan which allowed farmers to purchase land without making any payments other than taxes the for the first two years. The land usually sold for $60 per acre. The farmers were allowed to space the remaining payment over 15 years. The first payment would be $1 per acre with the payment each successive year increasing by $1 per acre so that at the end of 17 years payments were complete. However, the company continued losing as much as $70,000 to $140,000 a year.[16] In 1935, Charles B. Baker, Dunklin County land manager for Missouri State Life Insurance Company, purchased Deering and 2,600 acres of cleared farm land from Wisconsin Lumber Company for $110,000. Baker established other businesses there and operated the plantation until 1956 when he sold it to A.T. Earls for $1,000,000.[17] Deering Plantation issued, as did other plantations and some lumber mills at the time, their own medium of exchange. Workers needing credit to purchase farm or other supplies would be issued metal coins referred to as "brozine" or paper coupons redeemable in merchandise only at the plantation store. Some companies even paid workers for labor with this type of coinage.

An influx of three distinct groups of new settlers arrived from 1880 until the mid–1930s into the southeast Missouri lowlands. The first wave of settlers moved into southeast Missouri beginning in the late 1880s as the timber industry was beginning to flourish. These settlers were poor white people primarily from the hills of western Tennessee and Kentucky, although many also came from the Ozarks of Missouri and Arkansas. They were trying to improve their standard of living by taking jobs in the timber industry. Logging operations and mills both offered numerous job opportunities for many as did work on drainage projects. Others worked at clearing cut-over land. Thad Snow explains how those working to clear land were paid. "The clearing families did not work for day wages but at so much per acre, usually $8 to $12, depending on the nature and density of the growth to be cleared, and somewhat on the landowner's ability or willingness to pay. In general, speculative landowners paid conservative rates for the clearing. That is, for a clearing job that would have cost $30 or $40 per acre at prevailing wages, which were very low at the time, landowners would pay $8 or $10 by the acre."[18] Snow goes on to describe the people doing the work of clearing cut-over land: "They were poor people, of course, and they came from poor hill country where the going was hard, and they showed it. But you can't generalize even about woods people; they were good, bad and indifferent like everybody else. Some were hard customers and had tales to tell about how they had cut this or that man's guts out, back in the hills. Most were just ordinary work people who had never had much chance in the hills."[19]

In his book about the pioneering Matthews family of Sikeston, Edward C. Matthews III describes the life of those working as timber cutters: "Many of the timber cutters in those days were hoboes recruited from passing trains. The logging camps where the lumberjacks lived were canvas cities, with a huge circus tent serving as a mess hall surrounded by much smaller lodging tents. As the timber was harvested … the logging camps were periodically moved to a new location. The usual wages were from 20 to 24 cents an hour, plus food and lodging. The workdays were said to be ten hours, but in reality went from dawn to dusk."[20]

Eventually some of these families were able to buy farms. However as the timber resources diminished, most were left with few options but to work as day-labor on farms or become sharecroppers. Since much of the land was owned in large blocks by timber interests and insurance companies, land tenancy was especially high in the Bootheel.

A wave of what native residents termed "Yankee" farmers came to southeast Missouri between 1900 to 1915. These were the Midwestern farmers that promoters hoped to attract. Coming mostly from Indiana, Illinois, and Ohio, these farmers were looking for a fresh start in a new land, some perhaps looking for a "frontier" experience. As available land was taken up in their native states, these farmers came to Missouri hoping to obtain more land than they had owned previously, while others hoped to own their own farm for the first time. Thad Snow, who came to Mississippi County in 1910 from Indiana, typifies this type of farmer. Snow wrote, "I was going somewhere to a different sort of country. If I could find it I wanted it to be a 'new' country that I could spread out in, and one where a lot remained still to be done."[21] Snow found the kind of country he was looking for and although he suffered through droughts, floods, and bankruptcies he ultimately became a successful farmer and landowner in Mississippi County.

Another Indiana farmer, Hugh Studabaker, who came to southeast Missouri from Bluffton, Indiana, about the same time that Snow came didn't find conditions of land, and climate as it had been portrayed by the real estate companies. He also found the methods the real estate companies used in collecting commissions to be questionable and encountered harsh terms when he needed credit. So frustrated was Studabaker with what he found in southeast Missouri that when he returned to Indiana in 1913 he penned a booklet, *What They "Showed Me" in Southeast Missouri*, to warn others about the difficulties they would face in moving to this region.

Studabaker purchased a 215-acre farm near Sikeston on the west side of the Sikeston Ridge from C.D. Matthews through C.M. Smith Brothers Land Company paying $75 per acre for this land. Studabaker paid an initial $2,000 and gave Matthews a deed of trust on the property. The balance was to be paid in ten annual payments of $1,412.80. Studabaker signed 11 notes to finance the deal. One for $500 which paid the balance of the land company commission not deducted from the $2,000 down payment. Matthews would not allow the land company to have their full commission of $1,075 in cash up front. A second note for $912.80 was the balance of the first payment and nine other notes for $1,412.80 covered the remainder of the payments on the farm. Each note also carried 6 percent annual interest. When he was not able to make his payment due in 1911 in full, Matthews then required an additional 2 percent interest to keep from foreclosing on his note. Studabaker also purchased from the previous tenant the current year's corn crop.[22] When Studabaker needed credit to cover living expenses and farm supplies purchased at Matthew's Farmer's Supply Company he learned that he had to give a mortgage on his wheat crop and his corn crop not yet planted to secure credit. Studabaker was controlled by Matthews since he purchased the farm from Matthews, and Matthews also owned the store where he purchased supplies and owned controlling interest in Scott County Milling Company where Studabaker sold his grain.[23] He discovered that much of his farm was so wet that he could get a crop in only in a drier than normal year. His family experienced malaria and its accompanying chills along with typhoid fever, pneumonia, and boils in addition to contending with snakes, flies, fleas, and mosquitoes.

Studabaker was eventually able to sell his farm at the end of 1912 and came out about $2,000 in debt. He suggested to others interested in coming to southeast Missouri that they "either try a rental proposition for a year or work for somebody else a season" before purchasing land.[24] These northern farmers wanted to grow crops such as corn, wheat, alfalfa, and oats as they had in their native states. Cotton was a crop unfamiliar to them and one in which they had little interest. This pattern of agriculture became particularly well established in Scott and Mississippi counties. It was not until 1910 that Mississippi County grew more than 100 acres of cotton and not until after 1919 that Scott County grew more than 100 acres of cotton.

The southern lowland counties of Dunklin, New Madrid, and Pemiscot had grown cotton from the time of their earliest settlement. Most of these first settlers were from Tennessee or Kentucky with a few from Arkansas, Mississippi, and Alabama. From the 1880s into the early twentieth century, farmers especially from Tennessee moved into these counties looking for more and better land than was available in their native state. They obviously favored southern crops with which they were familiar. While cotton was of minor importance in the northern Bootheel counties, it was a major crop in the southern counties, particularly Dunklin County, which had been a producing county throughout its history. In 1890, cotton grew on 16 percent of the land in farms in Dunklin and Pemiscot counties. The figure for New Madrid was 8 percent. By 1910, Dunklin County planted 25 percent of its farmland in cotton. Pemiscot County planted 20 percent, while New Madrid lagged with only 6 percent of its farmland in cotton.[25] Before 1900, Dunklin County had eight cotton gins: four in Kennett and two each in Malden and Cardwell. In addition, a cottonseed oil mill operated in Kennett.[26]

Three events in the early 1920s coincided to bring the third wave of settlers to southeast Missouri. As a result of enhanced drainage brought about by the Little River and other drainage districts, timber was removed and the cut-over land cleared for agriculture. This opening of large areas of land in the Bootheel happened at the same time that the boll weevil was moving northward over the mid-south cotton areas. The drop in grain prices and rise in cotton prices at this time resulting in widespread increase in cotton acreage in the Bootheel as a third factor in attracting settlers.

The boll weevil (*Anthonomus grandis*) is a small insect, about one-fourth inch long, that damages squares (flower buds) and small bolls by puncturing them for feeding and egg laying. This insect, not native to the United States, originated in Mexico and Central America and first appeared in the United States near Brownsville, Texas, in 1892. Spreading at the rate of 60 miles per year, the pest reached the Mississippi River by about 1907. It arrived in the Carolinas in 1922. While the boll weevil was first detected in Missouri in 1913, southeast Missouri's usually cold winters kept their numbers low.[27] Because the boll weevil reproduces several generations each year losses can be huge, in some cases total crop failure. Before frost, adults enter a hibernation or diapause phase to survive the winter. They bury themselves under leaf litter and other plant debris to protect themselves from the cold. Adults emerge in the spring and begin feeding on the terminals of seedling cotton plant and start egg laying when squares first appear. Mild winters in the South allowed the boll weevil population to expand in the early 1900s. Farmers, entomologists, and plant specialists struggled to find a solution to the problem of the boll weevil. They looked for earlier maturing varieties and effective insecticides in addition to experimenting with cultural practices such as early stalk destruction.

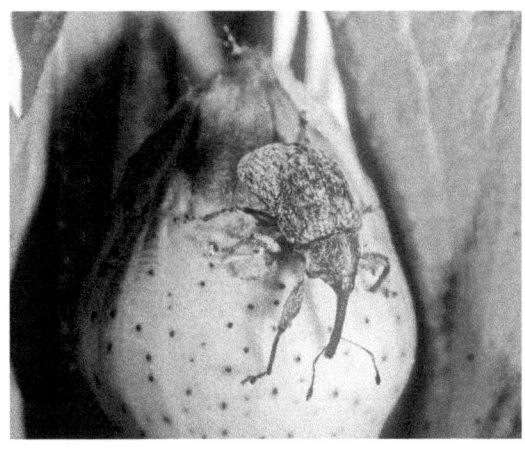

The boll weevil devastated much of the old cotton South in the late nineteenth and early twentieth centuries, resulting in large numbers of sharecroppers, both black and white, moving to southeast Missouri where the insect had not yet become established (courtesy United States Department of Agriculture, Agricultural Research Service).

The boll weevil was only brought under control in the late twentieth and early twenty-first century with the boll weevil eradication programs. In these programs, growers are assessed a fee for each acre of cotton grown which is used to pay for placing pheromone traps to monitor the population coupled with widespread spraying. In an eradication program, every acre of cotton is sprayed with an insecticide several times during the growing season. The eradication program started in Virginia and North Carolina in the late 1970s and expanded across the cotton belt. In southeast Missouri, the boll weevil population took longer to develop than in areas farther south. But by the late 1980s and early 1990s, boll weevil numbers reached damaging levels. An eradication program was started in the Bootheel in August of 2001. By 2008 the pest was considered eradicated in Missouri's cotton growing area and, in 2009, 98 percent of the cotton acreage in the United States was considered free of boll weevils.[28]

Enterprise, Alabama, erected this monument to the boll weevil because its damage to cotton forced farmers in the region to diversify and grow other crops. This change in agriculture brought new prosperity (photograph by the author).

But in the 1920s nothing stemmed the boll weevil's conquest which devastated the southern cotton growing areas, forcing farmers to switch to other crops. One town, Enterprise, Alabama, even erected a monument to the boll weevil because its damage to the area's cotton crop spurred farmers to switch to peanuts and other crops, bringing new prosperity to the city and region. This move away from cotton across the south displaced many thousands of cotton sharecroppers. Some moved to northern urban centers to look for work, leaving agriculture altogether, while others migrated into southeast Missouri and northeast Arkansas where the boll weevil had not reached damaging levels in the 1920s. There they looked for opportunities to obtain a sharecrop. The majority of these sharecroppers were African Americans from Mississippi, Alabama, and southern Arkansas. Along with them came some white sharecroppers and small farmers looking for opportunities to grow cotton without the plague of the boll weevil.

The combined high cost of land clearing and drainage taxes and the decline in grain prices following World War I made landowners eager to find an alternative crop from which to make a profit. With the region's consistently high yields and an increase in cotton prices between 1920 and 1924, growers saw cotton as a possible answer. Cotton sold for 21.5 cents per pound in 1922 then rose to 32.5 cents in 1923.[29]

The convergence of these three factors, the opening of new agricultural land, spread of the boll weevil across the old cotton south, and high cotton prices, brought about a large increase in cotton acreage in the region. In 1924, there seemed to be a turning point. Every Bootheel county vastly increased its cotton acreage that year; even the northern counties of Mississippi and Scott joined the cotton bandwagon. Each of these counties grew more than 50,000 acres of cotton. Dunklin County, traditionally the largest cotton-producing county in the state more than doubled the acres grown from 1919, planting 93,448 acres in cotton. Pemiscot County grew cotton on more than 50 percent of its farmland with 129,637 acres. New Madrid County grew 90,114 acres of cotton.[30] There was not only a shift in the crops grown but a change in the sociological make up of the region as thousands of African American sharecroppers spilled into the region.

African American Population (based on U.S. Census data)

County	1900	1910	1920	1930
Dunklin	205	96	147	461
Mississippi	2,265	2,006	1,311	3,997
New Madrid	2,027	2,097	1,950	5,617
Pemiscot	862	1,533	3,865	10,040
Scott	505	545	365	1,531
Stoddard	47	24	17	1,692

Along with the sharecroppers also came farmers looking to rent land and investors looking to build gins and stores to take advantage of this new cotton country. Thad Snow described this migration into "Swampeast Missouri" during the winter and spring of 1924: "So in the winter and early spring of 1924 cotton growers, big and little, black and white, from mere croppers up to 'rarin' back' planters, moved up into Missouri and spread out all over the land. Along with them came ginners, traders, moneylenders and adventurers on-the-make who had an aptitude for making money out of the confusion that unavoidably attends so sudden a movement of people

Many new cotton gins opened throughout the Bootheel in the 1920s as cotton acreage increased. This one was located in Kennett (courtesy Tony Byrd, Kennett, Missouri).

into unfamiliar surroundings. It was said that ten thousand Negro croppers crossed the state line during January and February of 1924."[31]

While Snow probably exaggerates the suddenness of this change to cotton, the 1920s was a period of major social change for the southeast Missouri lowlands. Landowners welcomed the influx of black Southern sharecroppers. They quickly built makeshift box construction houses on farms for them or provided lumber and nails for them to build their own houses. As can be seen from the table above, the majority of these new sharecroppers moved into the counties of Mississippi, Scott, New Madrid, and Pemiscot. In these counties, most of the large blocks of timberland owned by lumber companies, insurance companies, or individuals were being converted to farmland. Conditions differed in Dunklin County. Few African Americans had ever lived in Dunklin County and little desire existed on the part of residents to use their labor. Most of the land where cotton was grown in Dunklin County had been in cultivation for many years compared to the vast areas of newly converted farmland in the other counties. Farms also tended to be smaller although many farmers did have white sharecroppers to assist with the labor.

Hastily built sharecropper houses dotted the southeast Missouri landscape. Such structures were built to accommodate the large influx of sharecroppers moving into the region in the 1920s (Library of Congress, Prints and Photographs Division, FSA/OWI Collection [reproduction number, LC-USF33-011525-M3]).

This large influx of African American sharecroppers increased racial tension in the Bootheel although such tension existed in the southeast lowland counties prior to this influx of sharecroppers. In the 1910s landowners sometimes brought in black laborers to clear land when the local labor force was insufficient. There were also black migrants who came to the Bootheel in the fall to pick cotton. White laborers living in the Bootheel generally opposed the use of black labor. Historian Irvin G. Wyllie argues that the basis for this racial conflict was primarily economic. Wyllie writes, "Planters and landlords hailed the Negro as an agent of progress and welcomed him to the Bootheel. But the poorer class of whites, fearing higher rents and lower wages, tried to drive him out. The Bootheel's sordid record of violence cannot be understood apart from this simple conflict of economic interests." The conflict was really between these white workers and large landowners and businessmen. In October 1911, a group of a group of poor whites tried to run off black migrant workers in Caruthersville by burning the boarding house where they were staying.[32]

H.R. Post of Parma ran into conflict with local white workers when he brought in blacks to help clear land even though he had a petition with 60 signatures of local landowners and businessmen approving his action prior to bringing in the black workers. One of his workers was attacked and Post was threatened. Post's father appealed to Missouri governor, Herbert S. Hadley, who did send the state adjutant general to investigate however the governor took no action other than to refer the matter to the New Madrid County sheriff who had no intention of taking action for fear of being unable to retain his office in the next election.[33] In September 1911, four black cotton pickers were shot in night raids in southern New Madrid County while a few weeks later a mob ran black cotton pickers off a plantation in northern Pemiscot County.[34] The fall of 1911 was particularly lawless in Pemiscot County. A black man was jailed for knifing two white men in a street fight. Sentiment in the local paper suggested that people should take care of the matter and not depend on the law. Caruthersville law officials removed the man to Kennett. Some 40 individuals commandeered a locomotive and coach and headed to Kennett to retrieve the offender. Officials at Kennett apparently got word of their intentions and removed the man to another location before the mob arrived. Kennett officials refused to divulge his location and the group returned to Caruthersville unfulfilled.[35] On October 10, two black men were removed from the jail at Caruthersville and one was killed by the mob. A grand jury was convened but no charges were brought. As a result, large numbers of black cotton pickers left the Caruthersville area which seems to have been the intent of the perpetrators.[36]

In May 1919, John Riley of Sikeston encountered conflict when he hired African American workers to clear stumps on his Stoddard County farm. According the *Sikeston Standard* he had employed white workers but they all quit, preferring to spend the spring fishing rather than working. He even offered them more money but to no avail. In a effort to get part of his farm in cultivation that season, he hired African American workers. A group of white workers confronted Riley and informed him they would not tolerate the black workers. Consequently Riley dismissed them and went as far as St. Louis trying to find white workers.[37] Lynching, instances of shooting into houses, and other forms of intimidation throughout the region continued into the first three decades of the twentieth century. Schools were segregated, as were residential areas of most towns. The main ditch or ditch number one of the Little River Drainage District served as an unofficial "deadline" west of which African Americans were generally unwelcome.[38]

Violence against African Americans, landowners, and businesses led to the organization of several groups of "Night Riders" in southeast Missouri between 1910 and 1915. These groups, usually wearing masks and riding horses, would attack the homes of landowners or their businesses with gunfire or dynamite at night and would also physically whip some individuals. They usually first sent threatening letters to the target of their attacks. The *Hayti Herald* reported April 13, 1911, that night riders in Stoddard County posted signs on several farms near Advance "demanding that the renters of the various farms, shall not give up one-half their crop as was intended, but to give only one-third." The *Cape County Herald* reported that W.H. Taylor of Sikeston had left the area after receiving threatening letters. Taylor was a key witness in the case of seven night riders indicted by a Federal Grand Jury for sending threatening letters in the mail. Letters were also received by Scott County Milling Company officials and lumberman W.H. Baker, Sr.[39]

While the issues differed, the night riding tactic existed in neighboring states a few years before it began in southeast Missouri. In Obion County, Tennessee, in 1908, there were several months of night riding incidences by local residents protesting the West Tennessee Land Company's claim to ownership of Reelfoot Lake. Subsistence farmers used the lake for fishing and hunting to supplement their income. West Tennessee Land Company purchased all claims, controlled access, and planned to drain part of the lake for cotton ground. The night riders committed numerous crimes between April and October 1908. In October, the night riders murdered Quentin Rankin, an attorney and investor in West Tennessee Land Company. Several night riders were convicted but the verdict was eventually over turned by the Tennessee Supreme Court. The issue was finally resolved when the state of Tennessee took possession of the lake giving open access.[40]

In western Kentucky in what is known as the black patch tobacco area, at the beginning of the twentieth century, tobacco marketing was controlled by the American Tobacco Company and two other groups from overseas. These three groups made an agreement not to compete thus controlling the price paid to farmers for their tobacco, bringing prices down to a level below the cost of production. In 1904, growers formed the Planters' Protective Association to pool their production and market it cooperatively thus giving leverage in obtaining a better price. However the success of this effort required all growers to participate. Some growers refused prompting PPA growers to organize night rider groups that used violence to coerce other growers to join the cooperative effort. They burned buildings and carried out beatings. The state intervened with militia and eventually obtained several court convictions. Within a couple of years, the pooling of crops and the U.S. Supreme Court ruling that the American Tobacco

Company had violated anti-trust laws eventually brought higher prices and an end to the violence.[41]

In its October 30, 1915, issue, the Scott County *Kicker* reported that 50 to 80 night riders attacked the town of Tallapoosa. There were frequent reports of night rider activity in Scott, Stoddard, New Madrid, Pemiscot, and Dunklin counties. According the March 4, 1915, *Hayti Herald* the following notice had been posted in several locations around Hayti: "Warning! Negros [sic] Read and run if you can't read run anyway. All negros of Pemiscot County Missouri, are hereby warned to leave the said county or take the consequences. This means ten days from date. 2-27-15. To white people: Do not hire negros at your peril. Do not disregard this notice. Signed Night Riders."

Violence by the night riders reached a pinnacle the night of November 1, 1915, when 27 white men wearing masks arrived at M.B. Adkisson's home three miles south of Gideon near the Dunklin County line. Adkisson was a landowner and farmer. This is how the *Dunklin Democrat* newspaper described the events: "Particulars reached Kennett yesterday of renewed activity of the band of night riders in New Madrid County, who last Monday called on Pete [apparently a nickname] ... who resides three miles south of Gideon, near the Dunklin County line, and took him from his home and whipped him and after they turned him loose and bade him return home in a hurry, they fired a fusillade of shots, ... a stray bullet struck him in the heel."

Members of the night riders wrote threatening letters to local landowners and Gideon-Anderson Lumber Company. The Himmelberger-Harrison Land and Lumber Company also received threats.[42] Their demands included increasing the rate for land clearing from $6 to $10 per acre, reducing rents paid by tenants, and firing all black laborers, hiring only whites. They made threats to burn Gideon and Clarkton if their demands were not met. Landowners in the area hired six men to work as detectives to find the responsible parties. These six men had been staying in a shack on the Heisserer-Smith farm a mile and a half southeast of Clarkton when they were attacked by night riders about two weeks after the Adkisson event. Around midnight the night riders approached the cabin and began shooting.

One of the detectives stated, "I guess we shot back and forth an hour before they finally began to pull off. Then they began to bunch up in front of the house, and we concentrated our fire on them there. That must have dispersed them for they began to get away." Two of the detectives were wounded along with several of the night riders. A posse of citizens from

Clarkton and Campbell used bloodhounds to track down and arrest seven of the night riders.[43]

Eventually authorities arrested a total of 67 men in connection with the attacks on Adkisson and the attack on the detectives. Their trial was held in New Madrid in January 1916. All of the defendants were either tenant farmers or timber workers. Most were married and had families. These families traveled to New Madrid and stayed in their wagons during the trial. By contrast, a group of landowners with extensive holdings formed the New Madrid Citizen's Committee which contributed money to the prosecution and rented the Fairfield Hotel in New Madrid for journalists, law enforcement officials, and witnesses testifying for the prosecution.[44] All charged in the night riders case were convicted but only eight received prison sentences: John Osborn, John Elder, Riley and Tude Miskel, A.J. Wallace, Dick Gamble, Walter Willoby, and John Stinnett. Some were released because of their testimony and the remainder were sentenced and paroled.

John Case, an editor for *Missouri Ruralist* visited southeast Missouri in 1915 and offered his opinion on the conflict between tenants and landowners. Case believed that part of the problem was with the leases. The custom throughout the region was to give only one-year contracts to tenants. This provided little security for the tenant and provided little incentive for him to make improvements in the farm. Case also believed it "doubtful if the class of tenants who now till the land ever will do much better and the landowners aren't going to spend an unnecessary dollar." He saw the landowners as being "standpatters" who didn't want to make any changes to improve conditions for their tenants and workers.[45] Ultimately, both racial and class conflict became a part of the social climate of the Bootheel as new land opened to agriculture.

CHAPTER 13

New Political and Religious Movements and the Sharecropper Demonstration

From 1907 until 1916, racial tensions and the frustration of white sharecroppers and wage workers as evidenced by the night riding incidences gave rise to two social movements: one political, the socialist party and the other religious, Pentecostalism. Many who had come to the Bootheel to work cutting timber found themselves with little opportunity after the timber was removed other than clearing land or becoming tenants or sharecroppers on the newly cleared farm land. Dissatisfaction with both rental charges for land whether crop rent or cash rent and rates for wage work led many to look for some outlet to express their disdain for their economic situation. This discontent became fertile ground for the rise of the Bootheel Socialist Party and a new religious experience in the form of Pentecostalism. To some extent the two groups overlapped, both appealing to the white working class. Testimony given in the night rider trial at New Madrid linked two of the leaders, John Elder and Dick Gamble to both movements.

Socialist newspapers played a key role in promoting socialist ideology in the Bootheel. The movement took root first in Scott County with Phil Hafner's establishment of his newspaper, the *Kicker* in 1901. Hafner, in his paper, did not support the night riders actions but understood them, stating, "These outbreaks are the result of unjust conditions." Hafner maintained that change had to come through voting: "The robbed and starving farmers strike at individuals instead of the system. They are getting exactly what they vote for."[1] He believed that if the tenants and workers would vote for socialist candidates change would take place. Hafner elaborated further: "After they have struggled blindly and gone thru much suffering they will eventually learn that it is not the landlord, but the LAND SYSTEM that is getting their goat. When they reach that stage of intelligence, they will quit night-riding and vote out the system that enslaves them."[2]

Hafner, while advocating public ownership of agricultural land and railroads, seemed to favor a gradual approach to change and was as much concerned with breaking up the control of local politics by the Democratic Party and its inherent corruption as in establishing socialism. However, Hafner clearly wanted to change the status quo and saw socialism as the means to that end when he wrote, "The landlord in town or in city or in foreign land, who does no useful work and who now sits in his comfortable home and, by reason of his paper titles to the land, forces the producers to bring him 'all above a living,' might have to hunt up a pick and shovel and apply for a job on the section. It is the aim of Socialism to eliminate rent, interest, and profit."[3]

In the 1910 election, the Scott County socialists garnered 900 votes, a sizable share of the vote in an area dominated by the Democratic Party. Hafner commented on the reason the vote was not larger: "we had very little organization and less money." He further believed that "organization will carry Scott County at the next election."[4] In addition to the press, socialists used public meetings to familiarize people with their position. These meetings often took the form of a picnic or barbecue. Hafner reports on one such meeting held in Blodgett: "It was a great time the people had at Blodgett last Saturday at the picnic given by the Socialists. By noon a tremendous crowd had gathered, variously estimated at from 1500 to 2000 people. And the barbecued meat was fine." Hafner noted that Clarence Darrow was one of the speakers. Although not invited by the socialists according to Hafner, in his speech Darrow spoke about prohibition from the "Socialist view point."[5] At the time, Darrow was well-known as a labor lawyer having represented labor activist Eugene Debs a few years earlier. However, in 1911 he was dropped as a lawyer by labor organizations after he was accused of trying to bribe a juror. In 1925, Darrow achieved nationwide attention when he defended John T. Scopes, a Dayton, Tennessee, biology teacher, against charges he violated a Tennessee law prohibiting teaching human evolution. Darrow was pitted against William Jennings Bryan who was hired by the prosecution in a trial that received national attention.

Other noted socialist speakers at various times in the Bootheel meetings included Eugene Debbs, a union organizer and five-time Socialist candidate for president; Kate Richards O'Hare; and Rose Pastor Stokes. O'Hare grew up in Kansas City and joined the socialist party in 1901, becoming a popular speaker and writer on socialism. In 1910, she ran for the U.S. House of Representatives. She then moved to St. Louis and was the Socialist Party candidate for the U.S. Senate in 1916. O'Hare was convicted of violating the Espionage Act after making a speech opposing World War I. Sentenced to five years in prison, she served 14 months of her sentence in the Missouri State Penitentiary before having her sentence commuted by President Woodrow Wilson in 1920. After her release, O'Hare focused much of her efforts on reform of the American prison system.[6] Stokes, born in Poland in 1879, moved with her mother and step-father to the United States in 1890. While writing for the Jewish newspaper, *Yidishes Tageblat*, she met a wealthy social reformer, Graham Phelps Stokes, whom she later married. In 1906, they both joined the Socialist Party of America. Rose became one of the most popular speakers, describing herself as a voice of the worker. On March 23, 1918, she was arrested by the FBI in Willow Springs, Missouri, for violation of the Espionage Act as a result of a speech she made in Kansas City and a letter she sent to the *Kansas City Star*. A jury convicted Rose but after two appeals her conviction was overturned. In 1919, she became a founding member of the Communist Party of America.[7]

The August 31, 1912, edition of the Kicker carried a large ad for a "Socialist Picnic" to be held at Morley. The event would feature "Music, Dancing, Refreshments." While Hafner's attacks on large landowners and timber companies did generate support, the socialist vote dropped to 649 in 1912 and to only 150 in 1914. Historian Jarod Roll suggests that improved economic conditions along with dropping tenancy rates in Scott County account for the decreasing socialist support.[8]

The center of socialist activity and influence shifted to Dunklin County in 1912 where Socialist candidate for the state senate, John G. Scott garnered 984 votes although his democrat rival overshadowed him by receiving more than 2,700 votes. Eugene Debs, the socialist presidential candidate, out polled both Republican William H. Taft and Progressive Theodore Roosevelt in the county. The following year Scott began publication of a socialist newspaper in Kennett, the *Justice*. Scott's ideas included retuning land rented out and held for speculation to the state. At least initially, he urged a gradual socialism and making changes at the ballot box. In fact, each issue of the *Justice* carried the following slogan: "Workers of the world unite at the ballot Box. You have nothing to lose but hard work and poor pay. You have the whole world to win through socialism."

Scott also tapped into the racial conflict caused by the use of black workers in the Bootheel since this was one of the points of contention between white tenants and wage-workers and landlords. Socialists compared what they called the "wage slavery" of white tenants and workers to chattel slavery. The *Justice* complained, "Several slaves hunting masters around here, but they are not so fortunate as the niggers were who always had a master and grub furnished them."[9] Scott further contended that there were fields where "only negroes ... were employed."[10] It is not difficult to see why some residents associated the socialists with the night riders since both were challenging the same societal issues.

Scott and other socialists also employed Biblical and other religious references in driving home their point that tenants should not have to pay for their use of the land. In April 1914 Scott wrote: "The landlord says 'pay me a fourth or a third or a half of what God and you produce.' We don't have to pay any earthly rain-lord or air-lord or sunshine-lord so why pay a landlord.... Landlordism is ungodly and opposed to true Christianity; it places the Rule of Gold above the Golden Rule.... Lets unite and possess the lands of Dunklin County for ourselves, for God made, not for the Sheltons, Elys, Byrds, Hunters, Douglass and other big landlords but for the common people to use and enjoy."[11]

Some socialist tenants believed landlords should be expelled with force just as Christ expelled the moneychangers from the Temple.[12] Scott promoted the socialist party in Dunklin County in ways similar to those used by Hafner in Scott County by holding picnics and public events with invited socialist speakers. For example, in January 1914 Scott announced in the *Justice* that a socialist rally would be held at the Cardwell school featuring speeches and bidding for box suppers with the proceeds going to support publication of the *Justice* newspaper.

Scott's writing in the *Justice* became more violent. In April 1914 Scott advised "every laboring man in Dunklin County to lay by a part of his earnings and invest it in a good repeating rifle to keep in his home." He further opined that "if every working man and tenant farmer in Dunklin County had a good repeating Winchester rifle at home together with about 200 rounds of ammunition, do you believe that anarchy and mob violence would prevail in Kennett?"[13] In May 1914 he wrote that "fighting must be done" and added, "Now we socialists are peaceful people, trying to get our rights peacefully at the ballot box. But if we are persecuted ... we will do exactly what every other downtrodden class has done—revolt and fight."

Scott published the socialist platform for Kennett and Dunklin County in the *Justice* in July 1914. Some of the changes the socialists were pushing included: an eight-hour work day; minimum wage; an old age pension for every worker over 50 years of age; restoration of 62,000 acres of land; and continued reclamation of swampland by the state and such land to be held in the public domain. Earlier, Scott published a list of things he wanted to see accomplished for the city of Kennett. It is interesting to note that several of the improvements Scott was promoting did eventually happen, such as a city owned light plant, library, public parks and playgrounds, paved streets, and drinking fountains on the square.[14] In April 1914, Scott was attacked and beaten as he was exiting the Kennett post office. He was threatened and told to leave Kennett.[15] Shortly after this episode, Scott moved his publication to Gibson where it was published only a few months until he left the area effectively ending the Socialist Party's influence in the region.

However, into this climate of labor unrest and racial tension the Pentecostal revivals emerged, with preachers often holding services under large tents. White Pentecostal evangelists moved from the Ozarks into the lowlands bringing a new kind of religious experience that emphasized emotional outpourings, spiritual gifts, particularly speaking in tongues and healing, and hope for a brighter future with Christ's return. They also criticized materialism, wealth, and worldly influence—some of the same issues addressed by the socialists. These evangelists were not always well received by the mainline churches—Methodist, Baptist, and Presbyterian—who usually counted among their membership large landowners and those with interests in the region's timber. This new religious group was sometimes referred to by locals and in the press by the derogatory term "Holy Rollers."

Pentecostalism's roots can be traced first to Charles F. Parham who believed and taught that speaking in tongues was evidence of baptism of the holy spirit which was the defining characteristic of the movement. On January 1, 1901, at his Bethel Bible School in Topeka, Kansas, students spoke in tongues giving rise to his ministry that followed known as the Apostolic Faith Movement. From Topeka Parham went to Kansas City; Galena, Kansas; Joplin and several other locations in Missouri. He then moved to Orchard, Texas, and finally to Houston where he met and taught William Seymour.[16] Seymour, who had been influenced by holiness preachers in Cincinnati, Ohio, traveled with help from Parham to Los Angeles where he became the leader of the Apostolic Faith Mission at 312 Azusa Street. Stories of the meetings that became known as the Azusa Street Revival spread across the country. Many people traveled to witness the events taking place there at the largely black though interracial meetings. The services included highly emotional displays of dancing, shouting, singing, falling on the floor, and speaking in tongues as evidence of baptism of the holy spirit, somewhat reminiscent of events at the 1801 revival at Cane Ridge Meeting House in Bourbon County, Kentucky, during the Second Great Awakening. Parham visited Azusa in 1906 and strongly criticized Seymour's services at Azusa, particularly their interracial nature.[17] Before World War I, the influence of preachers who experienced the Azusa Street Revival led to the formation of numerous Pentecostal denominations such as the Assemblies of God, the Church of God in Christ (Memphis), the Church of God (Cleveland, Tennessee), and the Pentecostal Holiness Church.[18]

Pentecostalism arrived in the Bootheel in 1910 when evangelist John Davis from Thayer, Missouri, and others first held meetings in Senath followed by revivals in Kennett and Cardwell. From Dunklin County, Pentecostal churches spread throughout southeast Missouri with the efforts of evangelists such as Walter Higgins. Higgins writes that "they did various things to hinder services." Things done to hinder services included throwing cayenne pepper. He notes that "one night ... there was so much pepper in the air that you felt you could hardly breathe."[19] Higgins received threats of physical violence when he was holding meetings in Canalou in New Madrid County. Services were disrupted and his storefront church was broken into and the contents vandalized. He received no support from local police who made it clear that the intent was for Higgins to leave town. Eventually he was physically attacked but he did not leave and in fact the attacks only seemed to bring more people to their revival meetings.[20] Historian Jarrod Roll notes that "the teaching spread fastest among poor people because it gave them the power, both individually and collectively to confront evil. Pentecostals converted thousands of followers in the Bootheel in the early 1910s, most of them from timber camps, gangs of land clearers, and tenant families."[21] This was the same group from which the socialists drew most of their support as well.

Joseph Snyder, an evangelist in Kennett, reported in the *Christian Evangel* of the successful meetings there: "House is crowded. Some are getting right with God and the saints are getting straightened up with their neighbors and each other. We need preachers here who will preach Christ in the place of doctrine."[22] Another evangelist, R.W. Skelton, reported on his work in Holcomb: "I came to Dunklin County about a week ago and began to give the word to the people who soon saw their need of salvation. The sinners are under great conviction, having dreams of Christ's soon coming."[23] Other evangelists from across southeast Missouri reported in Pentecostal publications about the large number of people attending services. In August of 1913 the Senath and Cardwell area continued to be a strong area for the Pentecostals. J.N. Golf reported that the southeast Missouri camp meeting would be held at Cardwell. The meeting was scheduled to last nine days with meals and cots being provided free of charge for those attending.[24] The new Pentecostal religion and socialist ideas meshed since both were appealing to the same socio-economic group. John Scott in his *Justice* newspaper publicized Pentecostal churches and their activities while denigrating mainline churches. This alliance benefited both groups. It was predominately the white timber workers and tenants attending the Pentecostal churches in southeast Missouri. At the same time, Scott railed against landowners bringing in black workers to pick cotton and clear land. A division existed among Pentecostals on the issue of interracial services stemming from Charles Parham's rejection of such services by William Seymour at Azusa. The Assemblies of God denomination, established at Hot Springs, Arkansas, in 1914 as a white Pentecostal denomination, flourished in the Bootheel.

Socialist influence in the southeast Missouri lowlands was short lived. Without the voice of Hafner and Scott, socialist voting declined. In the 1916 presidential election the socialist candidate received only 375 votes in Dunklin County. In the 1918 election for senator, the socialist vote dropped to only 64 in Dunklin County and 23 in Scott County.[25] The Democratic Party continued its strong control of elections throughout the lowland counties. The socialist movement's decline in southeast Missouri was also spurred in part by its connections to the night rider incidents and better conditions for farmers at the onset of World War I. Historian Leon Ogilvie observed that "it is doubtful that Socialism could have continued to grow even under other more favorable circumstances. Increasingly coming into the area were people who considered the region a land of economic opportunity rather than one of economic exploitation."[26] By contrast, Pentecostalism, particularly the Assemblies of God, continued to flourish. Jarod Roll suggests that "with one less alternative, Bootheel workers turned even more to the Assemblies of God, many no doubt disillusioned by socialism."[27] As churches in this new denomination acquired property and built buildings in communities across the lowlands they as Roll notes, had "an increasing stake in these rural communities and suggests how far Pentecostalism had come in making peace with the dominant social and economic powers in the area."[28] In short, they began to appear more mainstream and less radical than when they first appeared on the scene with rowdy tent revivals and camp meetings.

Although night riding incidences waned after 1916 the farm tenancy system in the Bootheel created a climate for potential conflict. Farm tenancy differed in this region from the rest of the state. In most of the state, land was farmed by the owner. By contrast, in the Bootheel a different pattern emerged because of the large tracts acquired by lumber companies who sought to turn it into farmland after timber removal. The Bootheel had a much higher tenancy rate than the remainder of the state, and the rate increased as more land was cleared after removal of timber. The following table illustrates this.

Tenancy Rates (based on U.S. Census data)

Year	State	Dunklin	Miss.	N. Mad	Pem.	Scott	Stod.
1900	30.5%	63.5%	62.1%	70.0%	60.0%	55.0%	39.8%
1910	29.9%	67.4%	71.7%	81.0%	76.5%	60.5%	51.2%
1920	28.8%	64.3%	72.0%	79.1%	71.9%	55.9%	46.4%
1925	32.6%	72.4%	92.2%	91.0%	85.1%	80.1%	53.6%
1930	34.8%	76.2%	87.5%	90.9%	87.4%	70.8%	51.5%

Tenancy took several forms. Some land was operated by salaried managers with day labor. But much more common was either the cash lease or a crop-share arrangement. In a cash lease, the landowner is paid a set amount per acre and the tenant then farms the land providing all inputs and receiving all income. Most frequently seen was a crop-share lease, particularly after drainage assured a much better chance of making a crop each year. In this arrangement, the landowner furnishes a percentage, usually ⅓ on grain and ¼ on cotton, of the crop production costs such as fertilizer and seed, and receives the same proportion from the proceeds. The tenant provides the remainder of fertilizer and seed costs, provides all equipment and labor, and receives the larger share of crop sales. In a second type of share arrangement, the landowner furnished half of the crop production costs and all of the equipment but none of the labor, and received half of the crop. This kind of tenant, usually referred to as a sharecropper or simply cropper, furnished half of the crop expenses and all of the labor and received half of the crop. In addition, in most cases, the sharecropper was provided a place to live and space for a garden. The landowner also often furnished living expenses for the cropper and his family until crops were harvested.

Tenants who had equipment often rented several times more land than they could farm. To handle this extra land, they would have several sharecroppers working the land. Before the advent of tractors and other mechanized equipment, one family with one team of horses or mules could handle 40 acres. In these farming arrangements, the landowner and the tenant would each receive one-fourth of the crop and the sharecropper half.

The landowner and tenant each paid one-fourth of the expenses; the sharecropper paid the other half.

The sharecropper system developed throughout the South following the Civil War. Landowners during Reconstruction who were strapped for cash to pay wages for farm labor began offering a share of the crop in return for labor to produce the crop. The practice become common and widespread in the Bootheel during the 1920s, 30s, and 40s on farms growing cotton. Cotton was a much more labor intensive crop than grain, thus landowners employed the system mostly on cotton farms. Sharecropping began to wane in the 1950s and was virtually gone in the 1960s. The advent of power equipment, chemicals to control weeds which eliminated chopping, and mechanical pickers made unnecessary the large amount of hand labor required to grow cotton. Landowners customarily gave only one-year contracts to both tenants and sharecroppers, even though the same families often farmed the same land for years.

The sharecropping and tenant-farming systems have been portrayed in strongly negative terms by many sociologists and historians, equating sharecropping with a form of slavery. Unquestionably, it was subject to abuse in southeast Missouri as elsewhere in the South and many sharecroppers lived in deplorable conditions. On some large plantations sharecroppers were overseen by managers sometimes referred to as "riding bosses" who also often held the position of deputy sheriff. Landowners provided all necessary items for the sharecropper to put in a crop and advanced cash for the family's food and other living expenses until a crop was harvested. These items were referred to as the sharecropper's "furnish." Frequently, the large landowners who had many tenants or sharecroppers operated on a plantation system in which all supplies were obtained from stores or commissaries owned by the landowner and often exorbitant interest was charged for items purchased on credit. H. L Mitchell, co-founder of the Southern Tenant Farmers Union, noted in his autobiography that the prices were always higher at company stores and that "an interest rate of 40 percent annually was considered normal."[29] To insure that sharecroppers only purchased supplies from plantation stores, they issued advances in the form of coupons or coins that were only valid at the plantation store. In addition, many plantations also operated their own cotton gin. Thus the sharecropper had only one place to sell what he produced. He had to pay what the landowner said he owed and received only what the landowner wanted to pay for his share of the crop. Unscrupulous landowners took advantage of this situation. Sometimes the sharecropper was left with little or nothing to show for his year's work. In a year of poor crops, the sharecropper might actually owe the plantation more than the crop brought, thus he was obligated to continue in his circumstances another year hoping a good crop would enable him to "pay out."

Despite such abuses, the tenant and sharecropping system was not inherently bad. Like any business arrangement, its success depended on the integrity of all partners. As long as the sharecropper was paid fairly for his portion of the crop and not saddled with excessive interest on loans, each party in the arrangement received equity based on their contribution to production of the crop. Many sharecroppers were happy to work for the same tenant or landowner over a period of years and made a comfortable living. Even education was tailored to the sharecropper system. Most schools in the Bootheel and the South in general adjusted their schedules to accommodate the need for children to be a part of the labor force during the cotton harvest. School would start in late July and continue about six weeks when it would dismiss for six weeks during the cotton harvest. This practice disappeared in the late 1950s and early 60s as mechanical cotton pickers became the norm.

In a 1996 interview with Ray Brassieur, Maxwell Williams, who managed farmland from 1934 to 1938 for General American Life Insurance Company in the Bragg City area and later for Gideon-Anderson in the Gideon area and was a long-time member of the Little River Drainage District Board of Supervisors, shared his perspective on land tenancy on the farms he managed.

> Yes, they were tenants, and that was all right, there was nothing wrong with it. You hear or read about these people speaking of sharecropping as if it were slavery or something. As a matter of fact, the farmer would rent land, and he would—money was scarce for wages—he would sharecrop his cotton land to sharecroppers. His rent was 25 percent of the cotton. He would sharecrop it to a family and so they get half—the tenant got a fourth, and landlord got a fourth, the sharecropper got half and picked it. But it was all an equitable thing and the sharecropper was well paid for his labor; he was better off than if he was working for wages. It gave him a definite equity and also it gave him a motive, it gave him an interest in the crop, it was part his.[30]

The Great Depression of the 1930s exacerbated the difficulties in making a profit from agriculture for landowners, tenants, and sharecropper alike as was discussed in Chapter 11 in relation to the financing the Little River Drainage District. Efforts by the Department of Agriculture under the New Deal programs to help bolster prices of farm commodities inadvertently made conditions worse for sharecroppers in some areas of the Bootheel. The Agricultural Adjustment Administration (AAA) program required acreage reduction for crops such as corn, wheat, and cotton and made payments to farmers for this reduction. The AAA required that payments be made to landowners, tenants, and sharecroppers according to their respective interest in the crop. In other words, if a cropper was to receive half of the crop then he was to receive half of the government payment. To avoid dividing the payment, some landowners simply evicted their tenants and sharecroppers and replaced them with day labor. This left the sharecroppers not only without income but also without any place to live since most were furnished housing by landowners. Additionally, the houses furnished were poorly constructed and in many cases sharecroppers were not allowed space to have a garden or keep a cow or other livestock for their own use.

While the large landowners which included banks and insurance companies took advantage of the program by dismissing the sharecroppers, some justification can be seen in the case of small landowners who also were farmers. These farmers usually had a mortgage in addition to the property and drainage taxes. When a portion of a farm was idled by the AAA program, the farmer was placed in a bind to be able to make the required payments. If he further divided the government payment on the acreage not in production with a sharecropper then he might face the prospect of losing his farm by being unable to make mortgage and tax payments. The payments under the AAA programs while helpful did not provide as much money in most cases as a good cotton crop.[31]

The sharecropper's difficulties led to the formation of the Southern Tenant Farmers' Union in July 1934 in Poinsett County, Arkansas, under the leadership of H.L. Mitchell and Clay East. Socialism and an interest in organizing protests against the plight of sharecroppers gained a greater stronghold in the eastern Arkansas Delta than in the Missouri Bootheel to the north. H.L. Mitchell had been a sharecropper for his in-laws in the Halls, Tennessee, area. His father who lived and operated a barbershop in Tyronza, Arkansas, encouraged his son to move there. After declining an offer to sharecrop on a plantation, Mitchell finally moved to Tyronza in 1927 to open a dry cleaning business. Even before moving to Arkansas, Mitchell was strongly influenced in his youth by his reading of socialist writers such as Upton Sinclair. Later he discovered the Little Blue Book series sold by socialist publisher Emmanuel Haldeman-Julius of Girard, Kansas. This series included works by well known writers of the day such as Calerance Darrow, Oscar Wilde, Upton Sinclair, Edgar Allan Poe, Jack London, Ralph Waldo Emerson, and many others. Some of the works were reprints while others were written for Haldeman-Julius. and covered a variety of topics. According to Mitchell it was through this series that he became acquainted with Karl Marx's *Das Capital* and Frederick Engel's *Communist Manifesto*.[32]

The Southern Tenant Farmers Union Museum operated by Arkansas State University in Tyronza, Arkansas, preserves the history of the union's organization and activities in northeast Arkansas and southeast Missouri as well as the history of cotton growing in the region (photograph by the author).

In Tyronza, Mitchell influenced a friend, Clay East, to embrace socialism. East operated a gas station in Tyronza next to Mitchell's cleaning business. Mitchell and East organized a Socialist Party local in Tyronza in 1932 then both became involved in Socialist politics on the state and national levels, making a trip to Washington, D.C. to attend a national Socialist convention.[33] In July 1934, a group of 11 white and seven black sharecroppers met in a school near Tyronza with Mitchell and East to form the Southern Tenant Farmers Union. It was decided at the initial meeting that both blacks and whites would be included in the organization. The union grew rapidly, moved its offices to Memphis, and by the end of 1934 had over 1,000 members and planned to start organizing in other states.[34]

Some of the union's first contacts in Missouri came through the efforts of John L. Handcox. Handcox, born in Brinkley, Arkansas, in 1904, struggled to make a living as a sharecropper in the 1920s. In 1935, he went to Mitchell's office in Memphis and asked him to publish in the STFU's publication, the *Sharecropper's Voice*, a four-line poem he had penned.[35] Mitchell encouraged Handcox to write more songs, resulting in Handcox becoming

H.L. Mitchell's cleaning business in Tyronza restored as it looked in the 1930s. The cleaners was located adjacent to Mitchell's father's barbershop. Mitchell was one of the founders of the STFU.

known as the "Sharecropper Troubadour." Handcox so impressed Mitchell that he titled his autobiography after the name of one of Handcox's songs, "Mean Things Happening in This Land." His songs became important parts of STFU organizational meetings when the union was trying to recruit new members. These meetings sometimes took on the atmosphere of Pentecostal revival meetings common in the area at that time including singing hymns, prayers, and powerful oratory.[36] While on a fundraising tour for the Socialist Party in 1937, Handcox recorded several of his songs at the Library of Congress for the Archive of Folksong. Since he did not much like speaking to groups, he used his songs to get the message of the union across at meetings.[37]

Handcox and the STFU first reached the Bootheel in 1936 when the union sent him to Mississippi County to start chapters of the organization there. One of his first stops was the farm of prominent Mississippi County planter Thad Snow. Snow's reception of Handcox so impressed him that he wrote a poem about this first encounter, "Out on Mr. Snow's Farm." Snow invited Handcox to talk to his sharecroppers and Handcox even stayed with a family on Snow's farm for several months and organized an STFU

13. New Movements and the Sharecropper Demonstration

Clay East's service station next door to Mitchell's cleaners in Tyronza. The building has been restored by the Southern Tenant Farmers Museum to its appearance in the 1930s when operated by East. East helped H.L. Mitchell organize the STFU.

local in the area. He found sharecroppers in Mississippi County receptive to the message of the STFU: joining the union was the only way to bring about positive change to their lives. Locals also formed in numerous parts of New Madrid and Pemiscot counties.

While in southeast Missouri, Handcox met Owen Whitfield, a black minister and sharecropper. Whitfield hand been a sharecropper in eastern Arkansas and moved to Mississippi County in 1922 as the explosion in cotton acreage was beginning in the region. In 1924, he began preaching at several area black churches, aligning himself with the Missionary or Primitive Baptist traditions.[38] He soon became a leader in the Mississippi County sharecropper community. Flooding in 1927 forced Whitfield and his family to leave southeast Missouri for a time and move to Cache, Illinois. However they returned in 1929 to rent 120 acres and actually have two sharecropper families working for them.[39] The 1933 Bankhead Cotton Control Act mandated acreage reduction under the AAA programs but government payments meant to pay for the lost income from reduced acreage were paid directly to landowners who were to distribute it proportionately to tenants and sharecroppers. Whitfield's landlord withheld some of what Whitfield was entitled to receive. In 1935, Whitfield moved with his wife, Zella, and his large family to a farm near Pinhook in Mississippi County and once again began serving as minister to several area churches.[40]

While the STFU had been actively organizing in southeast Missouri, Whitfield remained aloof from the organization. But in November 1936, one of the members of Whitfield's church at Crosno in Mississippi County asked to use the church for an STFU meeting. Whitfield was reluctant especially since one of the speakers was a white radical preacher, Claude Williams, who was director of the New Era School of Social Action and Prophetic Religion in Little Rock, Arkansas. Whitfield attended and was so impressed with Williams's message of condemnation of the sharecropper system and his enthusiasm for the power of joining the union that Whitfield joined the STFU. Following this meeting, Whitfield began working with John Handcox in organizing for the union. It is at this point that Whitfield becomes the STFU's most ardent supporter in southeast Missouri and a leader seeking to better the quality of life for the sharecroppers. In 1937, the STFU revoked the small stipend it had been paying Handcox as an organizer in southeast Missouri. However, Whitfield was added to the STFU National Executive Committee and he began receiving payment as a field staff member.[41] Whitfield becomes immersed in union activities and attends national conventions, eventually being elected vice-president of the STFU.[42]

The STFU affiliated with the Congress of Industrial Organizations (CIO) in 1937 by becoming a part of the United Cannery Agricultural Packing and Allied Workers of America (UCAPAWA). A conflict developed between H.L. Mitchell and UCAPAWA leadership over the collection of dues and control of the STFU. Whitfield's support of the STFU dwindled when he was elected vice president of UCAPAWA although at the same time he was also vice president of the STFU. He saw a connection to the larger more powerful CIO through UCAPAWA as beneficial to the sharecropper's struggles.[43]

Whitfield was an energetic minister and organizer when he met Mississippi County planter, Thad Snow in 1936. In Snow, he found an ally and friend. Historian Louis Cantor notes that "Whitfield openly discussed the problems of the Bootheel sharecropper with Thad Snow."[44] The owner of a large plantation operated by several sharecropping families, Snow possessed a paternalistic attitude toward his black sharecroppers.[45] He was an enigma: sympathetic to the difficulties of the sharecroppers yet he profited from sharecropper labor on his farm and the government farm program payments to which he was not opposed. He nonetheless, saw the system as flawed and was a frequent writer of letters to the *St. Louis Post Dispatch*, discussing conditions in what he referred to as "Swampeast Missouri." He also had enough political connections to be conversant with congressmen, the governor of Missouri, and the secretary of agriculture.[46]

In anticipation of January evictions, Whitfield developed his own plan, independently of the union, for drawing attention to the situation with sharecroppers in southeast Missouri. Landowners in the region had a common, long standing practice of issuing eviction notices to sharecroppers in December for them to vacate in January. This facilitated the movement of sharecroppers to another farm if they were dissatisfied with their current location. In most years, not all receiving eviction notices were actually evicted since landowners offered contracts to farm the following year. However, as has been noted, because of the AAA acreage reduction programs many sharecroppers were switched to becoming day-laborers thus they often had to vacate the house in which they were living. Louis Cantor writes that reports of large-scale eviction prior to 1938 "had been grossly exaggerated." Based on FSA investigations, only "twenty-one families were evicted from Sikeston and twenty-five from Wyatt, Missouri."[47]

The FSA began an experimental program in an effort to help displaced farm workers by establishing cooperative farming communities known as Southeast Missouri Farms. The FSA purchased 6,700 acres near La Forge and built enough four- or five-room homes to accommodate 100 sharecropper families. The government also loaned each family $1,300 to purchase livestock, feed, and farm equipment. The FSA allotted a portion the farmland to each family and also provided a cotton gin, store and other facilities. Hans Baasch, director of the La Forge Project strongly supported the cooperative farming concept and became close friends with Whitfield.[48] Whitfield's friendship with Baasch and Snow enabled him obtain one of the newly built La Forge homes for his family.

Whitfield's plan was for a peaceful demonstration along two major highways in southeast Missouri, 60 and 61, to draw attention to the sharecroppers and the problems they faced. This was not a strike since the participants had been evicted and it took place during the part of the year when no farm work was being done. The sharecroppers would peacefully move on to the sides of the highways. Whitfield had actually opposed STFU organized strikes in Arkansas the year before.[49] While he shared his plans with Thad Snow, Snow had nothing to do with organizing the demonstration although because he supported it and the sharecroppers grievances, suspicions began to build that he was behind it. He did little to dispel this

One of the houses provided to former sharecroppers at the cooperative farming community called Southeast Missouri Farms near La Forge (Library of Congress, Prints and Photographs Division, FSA/OWI Collection [reproduction number LC-USF34-031287-D]).

image and in fact seemed to enjoy the accusation. Eventually he published a tongue-in-cheek "confession" about how he planned the whole affair. Snow did direct Whitfield to Sam Armstrong, a reporter for the St Louis Post Dispatch.[50] Whitfield invited Armstrong to a meeting at the First Negro Baptist Church in Sikeston January 8.[51] Armstrong persuaded Snow to go to the meeting at the church with him where Whitfield and his assistants would make final plans for the demonstration. Following the meeting, Whitfield gave Armstrong permission to print an account of plans for the demonstration in his paper. The story appeared in the January 8 edition but few people believed it would happen and largely discounted the prospect.

Whitfield didn't notify the STFU office in Memphis of his plans either. In December 1938, he did mention to H.L. Mitchell that evicted croppers had plans to move their household goods to the side of the highway. He said no more to Mitchell. Historian Louis Cantor observes that "when the Bootheel sharecroppers moved to the highways in January of 1939, it came as complete surprise to Mitchell and the union, for it was secretly organized, planned, and directed entirely by Mr. Whitfield."[52] Whitfield had concerns

Sharecroppers gathered along Highway 60 in New Madrid County. During the night of January 9, 1939, both black and white sharecroppers moved their few possessions along the highway (Library of Congress, Prints and Photographs Division, FSA/OWI Collection [reproduction number LC-USF33-002927-M1]).

about protection of the croppers from cold weather and contacted Congressman Orville Zimmerman of Kennett about getting tents from the state. Zimmerman told him to tell Thad Snow and that he and Snow were going through Jefferson City in a few days and they would talk to the governor and head of the Missouri National Guard. Details of their trip are sketchy and conflicting but both Governor Stark and Adjutant-general Lewis Means were alerted to the possibility of the demonstration.[53]

During the night of January 9, 1939, both black and white sharecroppers began moving their meager belongings to the side of Highway 60 east and west of Sikeston and along Highway 61 north and south of Sikeston. More came on the morning of January 10. The FBI and Missouri Highway Patrol reported that around 1,161 individuals camped along the highways and included both black and white sharecroppers.[54] Those moving to the roadside had little other than a few blankets and strips of canvass to protect them from the January cold. Owen Whitfield was not among the campers. With his wife and family housed at their La Forge Project home, he went to St. Louis, fearing for his safety. Later, his wife, Zella, and his children

Sharecroppers trying to keep warm during the highway demonstration. The demonstrators had only makeshift tents and stoves to protect them from the January cold (Library of Congress, Prints and Photographs Division, FSA/OWI Collection [reproduction number LC-USF-33-002947-M4]).

joined him in St. Louis. The demonstration did bring the attention he hoped for as reporters from major newspapers descended on the area. There was local concern about protection from the weather for the demonstrators. C.L. Blanton, editor of the *Sikeston Standard*, sent a telegram to Lewis Means head of the National Guard in Jefferson City inquiring about tents. Ultimately neither the National Guard nor Red Cross provided any assistance. All relief came from private charities, individuals, the STFU, and CIO.

The local press sought to emphasize that much of the stimulus for the demonstration came from outside the area and that some of those camped on the roadside were not even sharecroppers as one case reported in the *Sikeston Standard*: "The bouquet in this city goes to Frank Davis, negro employee of Mrs. Jennie Sikes, who has not worked a crop in four years. He left his job here and joined the camp beside the city."55 A letter written to southeast Missouri businessman and special assistant to the secretary of agriculture, Julian Friant from a Portageville resident Albert Beis illustrates the feeling that the demonstration was influenced by individuals outside of the area: "It is all the work of agitators, labor heads."56 The *Standard* also reprinted an article from the *St. Louis Globe-Democrat* reporting the results

13. New Movements and the Sharecropper Demonstration

This marker along Highway 60 east of Charleston in Mississippi County commemorates the 1939 Sharecroppers Demonstration (photograph by the author).

of its investigation of the demonstration. The *Globe's* report seems to be at odds with articles appearing in the *Post-Dispatch* which were largely sympathetic to the demonstrators. The *Globe's* report revealed that 15 percent of the croppers in the demonstration had already been offered contracts for the coming year and that some camped along the highways were neither tenants or sharecroppers.[57] Some landowners believed that a major factor contributing to unemployment among day laborers and sharecroppers who participated in the demonstration was the acreage restrictions placed on certain crops. R.B. Oliver, Little River Drainage District attorney, made such an argument in a letter written to Julian Friant: "The reason for the moving of these poor people is because of the fact that the landowners are unable to farm enough of their land to give them employment." Oliver went on to explain the unique situation in southeast Missouri: "The few counties in Southeast Missouri and one or two counties in Kentucky and Tennessee are the only counties, so I have been informed where *three* major crop restrictions are in force, namely wheat, corn, and cotton, possibly tobacco may be also included in the Kentucky and Tennessee counties Oliver urged changes in the law so that landowners would have to comply with acreage reduction on only one crop."[58]

The demonstration drew national attention and became an embarrassment for state officials. Dr. Harry Parker, state health commissioner toured the area on Friday, January 13, and declared the site of the camps to be a public health hazard. The following day the campers were told they would have to leave. Perhaps as many as half of them returned to the farms from which they had moved while the while others chose to find work in other places.[59] Historian Louis Cantor notes that "A large number, however, objected to leaving, and in several instances camps had to be broken up by police." The highway patrol and the Mississippi and New Madrid County sheriff's department loaded about 100 families into highway department trucks and moved them to a 40-acre area in the Birds Point–New Madrid Spillway owned by New Madrid County not far from La Forge. Smaller groups were moved to the levee near Dorena and to the Sweet Home Baptist Church near Wyatt.[60] Conditions for those placed in these camps was little improved from what they experienced on the roadside.

Twenty-five landowners from several southeast Missouri counties met and signed a petition denying that their actions had anything to do with the demonstration and requested an investigation.[61] Following the demonstration, the FBI made an investigation. Its report appeared in the March 14 issue of the *Sikeston Standard*. The FBI report stated that landowners failed to understand that the demonstration was about the "economic system prevailing in the area." According to the report, the demonstrators interviewed "were not protesting against any specific landlord or group of landlords but against the condition in which they found themselves, which they described as 'economic slavery.'" The report described their economic condition as one of "poor houses, lack of property, inadequate diet, and income too low to provide a decent standard of living." It also noted that the customary food the sharecroppers ate consisted of "salt pork, corn pone, dried beans, and occasionally a few vegetables." The report also suggested that the reason landowners did not know the demonstration was going to occur was their apathy toward the sharecroppers' conditions. The report also found that the majority of the sharecroppers had received notices to vacate their premises by first of the year.[62]

Lincoln University students became involved in bringing aid to some of the sharecroppers in camps after their removal from the highways. Lincoln history professor Lorenzo J. Greene visited the Sweet Home Baptist Church camp after speaking to students and teachers at Charleston High School. Greene made pictures and interviewed individuals, taking the information he obtained back to Jefferson City to share with faculty and students. Students responded enthusiastically and Greene states that "there

Missouri officials ordered the demonstrators removed from the roadsides. Here demonstrators' possessions are being loaded onto Missouri Highway Department trucks under the supervision of the Missouri Highway Patrol (Library of Congress, Prints and Photographs Division, FSA/OWI Collection [reproduction number LC-USF-33-002930-M2]).

followed now, a whirlwind campaign to help the sharecroppers."[63] The students collected food, medicine, and clothing and several of the students accompanied Greene to southeast Missouri to deliver the supplies. Greene contacted black newspapers which resulted in aid coming to the sharecroppers from across the country.[64] Greene and the Lincoln University students continued helping the sharecroppers after about 100 families who were without a place to live moved to a 95-acre tract in Butler County near Harviell, southwest of Poplar Bluff, that became known as Cropperville.

In St. Louis, Whitfield worked to help organize the St. Louis Committee for Rehabilitation of the Sharecroppers. Josephine Johnson and Fannie Cook, St. Louis writers, headed the committee which also involved representatives from UCAPAWA, the St. Louis CIO, and St. Louis Urban League, church leaders, and officials of the St. Louis Industrial Council. This group raised money for the purchase of the land near Harviell. Eighty black and 15 white families moved there on June 17, 1939. They encountered local hostility to their presence and had to rely on relief agencies for food. Before the next planting season additional land had been cleared and the

One of the locations behind the Mississippi River levee to which sharecroppers were moved by Missouri officials to get them off the highways. Conditions were no better there than on the roadsides (Library of Congress, Prints and Photographs Division, FSA/OWI Collection [reproduction number LC-USF33-002956-M4]).

FSA made grants to the group. Some young men joined the CCC and others worked with the WPA. Eventually residents began to drift away during World War II to find better opportunities and within several years most had left.[65]

While Whitfield's demonstration didn't bring immediate wholesale change for the sharecroppers, change did come. The demonstration also foreshadowed the widespread peaceful protests for racial equality and voting rights lead by Martin Luther King, Jr., and others that were to come in the 1960s. It also showed that peaceful demonstrations could bring about change. One change that took place quickly was that the landowners began to take seriously the sharecroppers condition. The *Sikeston Standard* reported the results of a meeting of 65 Mississippi County landowners in December 1939 who unanimously passed a resolution which stated that "we believe cotton labor under the reduced acreage program is entitled to share in the Government payments in accordance with the law, and must be permitted to do so if we desire to attain social peace and stability." The resolution went

Cabins built by displaced sharecropper who relocated to land in Butler County purchased partially through the efforts of Owen Whitfield. The community became know as Cropperville (Library of Congress, Prints and Photographs Division, FSA/OWI Collection [reproduction number LC-USF34-029179-D]).

on to urge Congress and the Department of Agriculture to enact measures "that will make it impossible for a landowner or tenant to receive that portion of Government payments set up for the sharecropper, unless the owner or tenant in addition to performing his functions as such, had done also the bodily work of making the cotton crop."[66]

Missouri officials much wanted to avoid another demonstration so Governor Stark convened a conference in St. Louis January 6, 1940, inviting landowners, sharecroppers, and officials of both state and federal agencies. The Governor invited Owen Whitfield to represent the sharecroppers.[67] As a result of the conference, Governor Stark appointed a six-member committee which included Whitfield to work closely with the Farm Security Administration to implement their programs.[68] Among the programs the FSA hoped to implement were loans, subsistence income during times when little farm work was available, and the construction of homes for farm laborers.[69]

Probably the most visible and longest lasting action by the FSA involved the building of homes for farm laborers. This project, known as Delmo Labor Homes, constructed ten communities across the Bootheel. Mildred Smith who worked as an FSA Home Management Supervisor with the Delmo Homes describes them this way: "these homes were to be permanent homes, occupied by farm workers who were seasonally employed but who remained in the area most of the year."[70] Construction began on these homes in 1940. Each house consisted of three bedrooms, kitchen, living-dining area, closet, and pantry, and a concrete lined cellar under the house accessed from the living-dining area. Electrical wiring was provided in each house for lighting only with no outlets provided. A concrete lined sanitary privy was constructed for each house along with a well equipped with a pitcher pump. Each location had a central public building equipped with hot and cold running water, flush toilets, and shower and laundry facilities. There was also space at each house for a garden and some of the remaining land was farmed cooperatively.[71] The communities were racially segregated and each community varied between 50 and 80 units. The locations of the Delmo Homes and their racial makeup were as follows:

> East Prairie, Mississippi County (white)
> Gray Ridge, Stoddard County (white)
> Kennett, Dunklin County (white)
> North Lilbourn, New Madrid County (black)
> South Lilbourn, New Madrid County (white)
> Morehouse, New Madrid County (white)
> North Wardell, Pemiscot County (black)
> South Wardell, Pemiscot County (white)
> North Wyatt, Mississippi County (black)
> South Wyatt, Mississippi County (white)[72]

Residents living in the Delmo homes were expected to pay a modest rent of $3 per month and each family was to give four hours of work per week to tasks assigned by the camp manager. Residents working at non-farm employment could pay as much as $12 per month. Camp managers experienced difficulty in collecting rent, at times delinquency rates ran high.[73] Other problems faced by the project included low acceptance of the program by local residents, occupants of the homes working in non-farm jobs, and opposition to FSA programs in Congress.

When the government placed the Delmo Homes up for sale in 1945, the same individuals and groups in St. Louis that organized to aid those involved in the 1939 roadside demonstration formed the Delmo Housing Corporation to purchase the Delmo Homes and then sell them to the residents. H.L. Mitchell and the STFU also provided assistance in this effort. After considerable negotiation, the Delmo Housing Corporation was able to purchase nine of the ten projects for a price of $285,000.[74] By 1954, all of the homes in the Delmo communities had been sold. The Delmo Housing Corporation which still exists has become a nonprofit social service agency. While the program experienced problems, it did provide for many families their first decent home and enabled many to become home owners for the first time.[75] Most of the houses have changed ownership several times, some have been torn down or burned, and others remodeled. The pattern in which the communities were built and houses arranged is still recognizable in aerial photographs however the Kennett location is no longer distinguishable.[76]

Chapter 14

Politics and Farm Labor Changes

The large influx of sharecroppers from the South influenced the politics of the Bootheel counties for several decades. Most residents of the Bootheel had sympathized with the Confederacy during the Civil War and the region was politically strongly Democratic. However, the black sharecroppers migrating to the Bootheel in the 1920s identified with the Republican party.[1] In elections between 1924 and 1928, Republicans made strong showings, especially in Pemiscot and New Madrid counties. Republican candidates generally out polled their Democratic rivals in those precincts that had larger numbers of black voters.[2] Historian Will Sarvis notes, "The disfranchisement of blacks and poor whites that followed Reconstruction in the Deep South never occurred in Southeast Missouri." To the contrary, politicians actually courted the black vote and encouraged multiple voting among black sharecroppers which became commonplace and widespread in the Bootheel.[3] Instead of disfranchisement, Bootheel political leaders sought to manipulate the black vote. Party loyalty of black voters changed in the 1930s. With the introduction of Roosevelt's New Deal programs, black voters felt they were better served by the Democratic Party thus began voting primarily for those candidates, nationally as well as in southeast Missouri. Consequently, the Bootheel remained solidly Democratic. Few Republican candidates could be elected, especially to county offices. Who would hold an office was generally decided in the primary election.

Vote manipulation took several forms. Missouri had no state-wide voter registration requirement until 1973 making voter fraud relatively easy and widespread. Much Bootheel voter fraud occurred in the form of multiple voting or "repeating" the vote. Sarvis observes that multiple voting "has become one of the great legends of Bootheel political history, probably somewhat exaggerated, but with much basis in fact."[4] Multiple voting involved transportation of voters from one precinct to another allowing them to vote multiple times. This technique was usually referred to as "hauling" voters. Politicians would pay an individual with a car to transport voters who supposedly would vote for the candidate providing their transportation. Sometimes voter transportation was even more blatant. Vic Downing who served in the Missouri House of Representatives for 20 years stated in an interview with historian Will Sarvis for the State Historical Society of Missouri Oral History Program that "they would pick up truckloads of people, farm laborers and all and they'd take them—maybe vote them four or five times over the county. They'd just haul them from one place to the other and vote them."[5] Farm laborers could even be brought in from Arkansas to vote in precincts that lay close to the state line. Tom Cash describes this involving voting in the south end of Pemiscot County near the Arkansas state line: "They had trailer truck loads of voters. They went to Hemondale. This fellow, Pappy Brown ('Harry' Brown was his name) owned a [cotton] gin at Hermondale. Hermondale was right astriddle to the county line down there. They could go into Aransas or Missouri, either one. They'd just go by precinct and vote them, they'd go to the next one and vote them again."[6]

Voter manipulation also took place in the form of out right bribes. Vic Downing describes how large landowners might influence the vote. "A lot of the time, they would pay them so much to vote. They'd get a truckload of them and maybe give them five dollars a piece or something, and just haul them around and vote them around. Or they'd buy them a fifth of whiskey."[7] At times, landowners and businessmen used economic pressure to influence voting. Large landowners would "suggest" to their tenants and sharecroppers who they should vote for, leaving the impression that the landowner could determine who a particular tenant voted for and if their vote was not for the correct candidate the tenant or sharecropper might lose his land. Similar influence was exerted at times by gin owners who also usually controlled a large amount of land. In the 1930s and 40s, gins frequently loaned farmers money to make a crop thus had economic influence over these customers. Gins and other businesses also influenced employees to vote for certain candidates. Jack Stapleton, long-time publisher of the *Dunklin Democrat* commented in an interview with historian Will Sarvis that "back in those days there was not any hesitation to direct your employees to vote one way or the other."[8] At times voting was not even done at the polling place. John M. Alford, Pemiscot County clerk explained: "Believe it or not, when I was a kid, I can remember seeing the polling places taken to the cotton fields. At that time they used a lot of hand labor, manual labor. When they [cotton pickers] turned around on the end [of a row], everybody votes; all the field workers vote. They don't go to the polling place."[9]

Control of the vote sometimes occurred at the polling place when paper ballots were used. In tallying the ballots, votes that should have gone to one candidate could be given to another. Additionally, election judges could help particular candidates by marking ballots for people who did not even show up to vote or as in some cases marking ballots for deceased voters. Most of these problems disappeared with state-wide voter registration and the use of machine counted ballots.

The political machine also existed in some Bootheel counties into the 1960s. Most noted was J.V. Conran's "organization" in New Madrid County. Conran served as prosecuting attorney for New Madrid County. This group decided which candidates to support and it was those candidates who usually won the election. Hal Hunter, Jr., who followed Conran as prosecuting attorney described the organization this way: "It was simply a group of mostly large landowners who, of course, had a lot of employees or a lot of tenants. They were interested in good county government. And J.V. was smart enough to realize that's what they wanted, and of course that's what he wanted. They tried to choose candidates that they thought would be helpful. Part of it was they wanted to pick candidates that could control a certain number of votes, too, and help the organization."[10]

A political machine also existed for a time in 30s and 40s in Stoddard County headed by Kip Briney and Yewell Lawrence. Although it never became as organized or as effective as the Conran organization.[11] One way political organizations strengthened their control over county politics was in the awarding of jobs. In the 30s and 40s political appointments to government jobs such as those with the WPA, postal service, and the Agricultural Stabilization and Conservation Service (ASCS) usually depended on the recommendation of politically influential individuals in the county.

Along with demonstrations and government programs, technology also brought change to the farm labor condition in southeast Missouri during the 1930s and 40s. At the beginning of the twentieth century, most farm work in Missouri was accomplished with horses or mules. By mid-century, the tractor had replaced the horse and mule as the primary source of farm power. In the transition period between 1920 and 1940, tractor use steadily increased. The economic difficulties of the 1930s slowed the progress somewhat slowed since tractors required a cash outlay for gasoline that many could not afford. Even as late as 1940, some farmers still employed horses and mules. The 1919 *Missouri Year Book of Agriculture* listed 3,332 tractors in the state on June first of 1919. By November first, the total had swelled to 7,200, prompting E.A. Logan and Jewell Mayes, authors of "Tractor Survey, Missouri 1919," to comment that "the tractor business is just beginning to get underway and both dealers and farmers of Missouri now realize that the tractor has come to stay."[12]

A major advance in tractor design and utilization came in 1924 when International Harvester introduced its Farmall series, designed for multiple uses on the farm. It featured a power takeoff shaft to operate mowers and other equipment. Competitive companies soon introduced similar models such as the John Deere GP (for General Purpose) in 1928 which had a hydraulic power lift making it possible to raise and lower implements without dismounting the tractor. In 1932, Allis-Chalmers replaced the iron lug wheels with pneumatic tires, increasing ride comfort and tractor speed. Henry Ford added the first "three-point hitch" to his tractors in 1939. This more refined power lift system kept implements at a constant preset depth and allowed the transfer of weight to the rear wheels when the load on the engine increased too much. Tractors increased productivity and reduced costs. When not in use they required no fuel in contrast to horses or mules which had to be fed and cared for even when not needed for farm work. Additionally, land set aside for the growing of feed for draft animals could now be utilized for growing cash crops. This all meant that less labor was required to make a crop.

Even with the advent of tractors, cotton remained a labor intensive crop when it came time to harvest. It had long been the dream of inventors and engineers to design a machine to take on the drudgery of the task of picking cotton. As early as 1850 Samuel S. Rembert and Jedediah Prescott of Memphis received the first patent for a cotton picking machine. Inventors tried about every conceivable mechanism for removing cotton from the boll in the ensuing years. Most experimenters focused on the following methods: pneumatic, using air to either vacuum or blow cotton from the boll; electrical, using static electricity to attract the cotton; thrasher which cut down the plant; stripper which combed the entire plant with teeth; and the spindle picker which used rotating fingers to remove cotton from open bolls, leaving foliage and unopened bolls on the plant.[13]

Angus Campbell began experimenting with pickers using barbed spindles in the late 1800s, receiving several patents and eventually partnering with Theodore H. Price to build the Price-Campbell Cotton Picker patented

Picking cotton by hand require a large labor force and was difficult work (Charles Trefts Photographs [P0034] 34-2295; The State Historical Society of Missouri Photograph Collection).

in 1912, however their machine never became efficient and dependable. Likewise, Hiram M. Berry in Greenville, Mississippi, also invented a picker with barbed spindles that never became commercially viable.[14] Peter Paul Haring first developed a cotton harvesting machine using spindles in 1891. By 1929 he patented a machine he believed could be commercially viable. Unfortunately, the Great Depression ruined his chances of securing investors to manufacture the machine.

John D. Rust and brother Mack, a mechanical engineer, began working on a cotton picker in the 1920s. The Rusts initially experimented with a barbed spindle but after John remembered how his finger stuck to cotton wet with dew when he picked cotton by hand switched to a smooth spindle which was also moistened. The Rusts successfully tested their machine at the Delta Experiment Station at Stoneville, Mississippi, in 1933, picking five bales a day.[15] This demonstration raised hopes that a commercial cotton picker loomed on the horizon, but their machine still needed development

Top: Brothers John and Mack Rust successfully demonstrated their mechanical cotton picker in 1933. *Bottom:* A view of the spindles in the Rust cotton picker. Rust used moistened straight, smooth spindles. Machines based on the Rust design were manufactured by Allis Chalmers and Ben Pearson (both courtesy Library of Congress, Prints and Photographs Division, FSA/OWI Collection [reproduction numbers LC-USF33-030549-M4 *top*; LC-USF33-030618-M4 *bottom*]).

Early International Harvester cotton picker mounted on a Farmall tractor (Library of Congress, Prints and Photographs Division, FSA/OWI Collection [reproduction number LC-USF33-030548-M1]).

and the Rusts were hampered by lack of financing. In 1944, they licensed patents to Allis-Chalmers for the production of cotton pickers. Allis-Chalmers produced cotton pickers using the Rust smooth spindle design while John Rust worked as a consulting engineer for Allis-Chalmers. Rust also granted a license to Ben Pearson, Inc. in 1949 to manufacture Rust cotton pickers.[16] Allis Chalmers manufactured its pickers in Gadsden, Alabama, while the Ben Pearson machines were made in Pine Bluff, Arkansas.

International Harvester purchased the Price-Campbell patents in the early 1920s and began work on a spindle picker using the barbed spindle concept. They also adopted Rust's idea of moistening the spindles. However, World War II material shortages meant commercial scale manufacturing could not begin until the post-war era. Harvester mounted the picker on one of its Farmall tractors and in 1948 built an assembly plant in Memphis to become the first large-scale manufacturer of cotton pickers, producing 1100 units the first year.

John Deere entered the market after purchasing Hiram Berry's patents. By the mid–1950s, all four manufacturers, International Harvester, John Deere, Allis Chalmers, and Ben Pearson, made both one-row tractor

A view of the spindles in the International Harvester cotton picker. International used a tapered, barbed spindle, a design which became the industry standard and used by both International and John Deere, the only two manufacturers of pickers after Ben Pearson and Allis Chalmers stopped making them (Library of Congress, Prints and Photographs Division, FSA.OWI Collection [reproduction number LC-USF33-030548-M2]).

mounted models and two-row self-propelled models.[17] An interesting side note is that ultimately the moistened, barbed spindle design prevailed after manufacturing of machines based on the Rust design ceased. Today John Deere dominates the cotton picker market.

While the use of the cotton picker steadily grew in southeast Missouri, it required nearly two decades before all cotton was machine harvested. During the 1955-1956 season 24 percent of the Missouri crop was machine harvested.[18] Even in the early 1960s some Bootheel landlords stipulated in rent contracts that cotton was to be harvested by hand because of their concerns with loss of crop during harvest and quality. During this time it was not uncommon for farmers to hire hands to pick the ends of cotton rows so that the machine would not waste cotton during turns. Cotton breeders worked to develop varieties more suited for machine picking while agricultural chemical companies compounded chemical defoliants to remove cotton leaves prior to harvest resulting in much cleaner picked cotton which improved the grade after ginning. Gins also added additional cleaning equipment to remove extra trash in machine picked cotton.

More social change came to the southeast lowlands as mechanization of farming expanded. Historians refer to the movement of large numbers of both white and black farm workers from southern states to industrial urban centers especially in the North from 1910 to 1970 as the Great Migration. While large numbers of the sharecroppers leaving the South in the 1920s because of the reduced cotton acreage resulting from the boll weevil infestation moved to northeast Arkansas and southeast Missouri looking for opportunities on farms there, many left agriculture altogether and moved to northern cities such as St. Louis, Chicago, or Detroit to find better paying jobs. Farm population nationwide showed a steady decrease from 1920 until 1931. The next three years brought a slight increase to the farm population but further decline began in 1934, reflecting the movement of people to improve their situation during the Great Depression. Decline continued during the war years as rural farm workers sought better paying jobs in war industry plants and many young men entered military service.[19] All seven of the southeast Missouri lowland counties experienced population increases

Cotton pickers now are capable of picking multiple rows of cotton at a single pass (courtesy United States Department of agriculture, Agricultural Research Service).

from 1900, peaking between 1940 and 1950. Population decline for most of these counties has continued, relieving the over supply of labor that resulted from the large influx of sharecroppers in the 1920s and 30s.[20]

Historians have debated whether the cotton picker caused the migration from cotton producing areas as machines replaced hand labor or if the decreased labor supply resulting from migration spurred more rapid adoption of the cotton picker and other technologies. In southeast Missouri, farm population decreased steadily after 1950, changing farm tenancy as well. The sharecropper system disappeared in the 1960s as did the myriad of small houses which dotted nearly every 40 acres of the countryside. Schools abandoned the fall break during harvest season since the labor of students was no longer needed in the cotton harvest. Those remaining to work on farms needed to acquire new skills to operate and maintain more complex tractors, combines, and cotton pickers. They also had to learn techniques of applying chemicals and fertilizers. As farms became larger some farmers began to pay their workers as full-time employees, providing year-round employment instead of seasonal work. Larger farms meant farmers needed to gain managerial skills and knowledge to manage larger capital expenditures. Instead of paying low-wage workers or using sharecroppers, farmers increased their investments by purchasing machinery. Farming gradually moved from being a labor intensive enterprise to a capital intensive one.

CHAPTER 15

End of an Era

With the arrival of the mid–twentieth century, the transformation from swampland to farmland in the southeast Missouri lowlands was complete. By 1935, the giant tracts of virgin timber were removed, and the large lumber mills lay silent.[1] Nearly all land suitable for agriculture was cleared and in cultivation by 1950.[2] Unlike some other forested regions of the nation, no effort was made to conserve and restore the Bootheel forests, making agriculture the economic focus of the region.[3]

This transformation was possible because of the drainage provided by small drainage districts throughout the region combined with the Little River Drainage District. H. Riley Bock, in his historical sketch of the Little River Drainage District, *Formation of a Drainage District*, points out that the change from timber to agriculture as the primary economic force in the region was reflected in the make-up of the board of supervisors following the fiftieth anniversary landowners' meeting in December 1957. With the election of two new supervisors at that meeting, all of the supervisors, with the exception of S.P. Reynolds, represented agricultural interests and had no ties to the early timber industry. Reynolds was the only original board member reaming. He came on the board in 1907, as a representative of Wisconsin Lumber Company.[4] Several significant issues arose at both its 1956 and 1957 landowners' meetings. these issues reflected not only the changing make-up and interests of the district's leadership but also the changing economic focus of the region as a whole. One proposal made was to move the district offices from Cape Girardeau to Morehouse. The offices had been in Cape Girardeau in the Himmelberger-Harrison Building on Broadway since its inception. Minutes of the 1956 meeting show that such a resolution was voted on and passed 92,179 to 85,461. Another resolution voted on at this landowners' meeting was to change attorneys for the district. This resolution was approved 91,802 to 85,800.[5] Apparently no action was taken toward moving the office before the 1957 landowners' meeting. A resolution on moving the office was once again brought to a vote. This time the resolution was overwhelmingly defeated 209,132 to 27,743.[6] The office remained in Cape Girardeau in the Himmelberger-Harrison Building until 2000 when the district purchased an office building on Kurre Lane in Cape Girardeau. The Oliver law firm remained attorneys for the district only until 1959 when they were replaced by Merrill Spitler. High fees charged by the Oliver firm is cited as the reason for the change.[7] The legal incorporation of the district expired in 1957, thus at the 1956 landowners meeting, a resolution was approved requesting the board of supervisors to petition the Butler County Circuit Court to extend the incorporation into perpetuity.[8] Because 1957 was one of the wettest years on record in southeast Missouri (from January 1 to November 30 Kennett received 93.34 inches) the 1957 landowners' meeting held a discussion of an interesting proposal from Everett B. Gee to construct a ditch to divert water from the floodway ditches in the lower district to the Mississippi River to provide a quicker outlet for flood waters. Eventually consultation with Corps of Engineers revealed such a project would be too expensive.

The original organizers of the Little river Drainage District could have hardly imagined the geographical and sociological changes that would take place in the southeast Missouri lowlands following its drainage. In summary, the changes resulting from drainage and clearing of the lowlands can be seen as the convergence of events over the first half of the twentieth century. Interest in the vast timber resources of the region did not peak until a network of railroads were built, mostly a result of the efforts of Louis Houck. Logging brought new settlers to the area as families and individuals came to find jobs in the bustling lumber industry. Timber removal left thousands of acres in need of drainage and clearing at a time when there was a favorable attitude nationally toward the drainage of wetlands so they could be used more productively. Planning and construction on the Little River project began as the Panama Canal was being completed, which meant engineers with drainage expertise were readily available and dredging contractors were looking for the next big project. Invention of the floating steam dipper dredge in the late 1800s made available for the first time equipment with the capability of eating its way through the tangled mass of vegetation to dig the ditches in the lower district.

The convergence of events also brought change to the region's social

Five parallel ditches of the Little River Drainage District east of Kennett in Dunklin County (Gerald Massie Photographs [P0016] 16–295, The State Historical Society of Missouri Photographic Collection).

structure. The opening of new agricultural land in the Little River Valley coincided with the spread of the boll weevil across the South, causing thousands of sharecroppers to move northward looking for areas where cotton could be grown without the threat of this insect. The new immigrants this time, instead of being people from the Ozarks and the hill country of Tennessee and Kentucky, mostly of Scotch-Irish descent, were in large part African Americans from the Arkansas, Mississippi, and Louisiana Delta country and other cotton growing regions of Mississippi and Alabama. They arrived at a time when farmers in southeast Missouri were shifting toward cotton and way from grain crops because of falling prices for grain, thus ushering in the widespread use of the sharecrop tenancy system. As all prices dropped during the Great Depression years of the 1930s, efforts by the federal government to bolster farm income actually helped create new problems for sharecroppers when many landowners changed to day labor to draw all of the government payments made for taking land out of production. Although federal agencies experimented with numerous programs, no really satisfactory solution for the sharecropper problem emerged. The Depression of the 1930s ravaged the economy of the region and carried Little River Drainage District and many farmers to the brink of bankruptcy. World War II ended most unemployment and brought an increase in farm prices, ending the Depression and returning tax collections for Little River Drainage District to higher levels.

With the complete transformation from swampland to farmland for the southeast Missouri lowlands by the fiftieth anniversary of the Little River Drainage District and with the era of a timber economy over, the region was poised for rapid expansion of mechanization and technology in the era of modern agriculture. While there has been some location of industry in southeast Missouri, the Bootheel's economy is based on agriculture. The region's swampland has become some of nation's most productive farmland. The major crops of the region include cotton, corn, rice, wheat, soybeans, grain sorghum. Horticultural crops including watermelon, peaches, sweet corn, and peas have become important as well.

Unfortunately, along side this productive farmland lie pockets of poverty, poor healthcare, high infant mortality rates, and high unemployment. While the geographic transformation from swampland to farmland was complete by mid–twentieth century, social change is still occurring as the region grapples with these vexing problems. Just as it takes a concerted effort to tackle social problems, drainage and levee districts remain vigilant and dedicated in their efforts to maintain drainage and provide protection from flooding in order for the region to remain farmland with its present high level of productivity. Otherwise, nature would encroach and return the farmland to swampland.

Chapter Notes

Introduction

1. Gary Lane McDowell, "Local Agencies and Land Development by Drainage: The Case of 'Swampeast' Missouri" (Ph.D. dissertation, Columbia University, 1965), 1.
2. *The Little River Drainage District of Southeast Missouri: 1907–Present*, 6.

Chapter 1

1. Roy B. Van Arsdale, et al., "The Origin of Crowley's Ridge, Northeastern Arkansas: Erosional Remnant or Tectonic Uplift?" *Bulletin of the Seismological Society of America* 85, no. 4 (August 1995), 963–85.
2. Arkansas Earthquake Center, University of Arkansas, "The Reelfoot Rift," http://quake.ualr.edu/public/reelfoot.htm (accessed 7/26/2016).
3. William James Braile, "Crustal Structure of the Northern Mississippi Embayment and Reelfoot Rift From Seismic Refraction/Reflection Profiling" (master's thesis, University of Texas El Paso, 1993), 15.
4. *Ibid*.
5. *Ibid*.
6. Robert T. Saucier, *Geomorphology and Quaternary Geologic History of the Lower Mississippi Valley* (Vicksburg: Mississippi River Commission, 1994), 67.
7. *Ibid.*, 68.
8. *Ibid*.
9. *Ibid.*, 97.
10. Tammy M. Rittenour, et al., "An Optical Age Chronology of Late Pleistocene Fluvial Deposits in the Northern Lower Mississippi Valley," *Quarterly Science Reviews* 22 (2003), 1109.
11. Rittenour, et al., "Fluvial Evolution of the Lower Mississippi River Valley During the Last 100 K.Y. Glacial Cycle: Response to Glaciation and Sea-level Change," *Geological Society of America Bulletin* 119, no. 5–6 (2007), 601–02.
12. Saucier, *Geomorphology*, 136.
13. Paul A. Delcourt and Hazel R. Delcourt, "Paleoclimates, Paleovegetation, and Paleofloras of North America North of Mexico During the Late Quaternary," in *Flora of North American North of Mexico*, ed. Flora of North American Committee, 1, ch. 4 (1993), http://floranorthamerica.org/Volume/V01/Chapter04 (accessed 7/26/16).
14. *Ibid*.
15. Paul A. Delcourt, et al., "Late Quaternary Dynamics in the Central Mississippi Valley," in *Arkansas Archaeology: Essays in Honor of Dan and Phyllis Morse*, ed. Robert C. Mainfort, et al. (Fayetteville: University of Arkansas Press, 1999), 15–28.
16. *Ibid*.
17. James E. King and William H. Allen, Jr., "A Holocene Vegetation Record from the Mississippi River Valley, Southeastern Missouri," *Quaternary Research* 8 (1977), 320.
18. Walter Schroeder, *Presettlement Prairie of Missouri*, Natural History Series No. 2

(Missouri Department of Conservation, 1983), 15.

Chapter 2

1. Ted Goebel, et al., "The Late Pleistocene Dispersal of Modern Humans in the Americas," *Science* 319 (2008), 1499.
2. Bruce Bradley and Dennis Stanford, "The North Atlantic Ice-Edge Corridor: A Possible Paleolithic Route to the New World," *World Archaeology* 36, no. 4 (2004), 460.
3. *Ibid.*, 466.
4. *Ibid.*, 472.
5. Goebel, 1500.
6. Julie Morrow, "The Paleoindian Period in Arkansas," *Arkansas Prehistory and History in Review* 331 (2006), 3.
7. Donald K. Grayson and David J. Meltzer, "Clovis Hunting and Large Mammal Extinction: A Critical Review of the Evidence," *Journal of World Prehistory* 16, no. 4, (2002), 313.
8. Michael J. O'Brien and W. Raymond Wood, *The Prehistory of Missouri*, 99.
9. Dan F. Morse and Phyllis A. Morse, *Archaeology of the Central Mississippi Valley*. (New York: Academic Press, 1983), 67–68.
10. O'Brien and Wood, 100.
11. Morse, 104.
12. O'Brien and Wood, 167.
13. *Ibid.*
14. Morse, 111–12.
15. *Ibid.*, 115–25.
16. O'Brien and Wood, 171.
17. Morse and Morse, 143.
18. *Ibid.*, 141.
19. O'Brien and Wood, 161.
20. *Ibid.*, 211 and Morse and Morse, 143.
21. Morse and Morse, 143.
22. Robert C. Mainfort, Jr., "Woodland Period," *Encyclopedia of Arkansas History & Culture*, http://www.encylopediaofarkansas.net/entry-detail.aspx?entryID=543 (accessed 7/26/16).
23. O'Brien and Wood, 218.
24. *Ibid.*, 232.
25. *Ibid.*, 281–82.
26. J.E. Kelley, "The Emergence of Mississippian Culture in the American Bottom Region." In *The Mississippian Emergence*, ed. B.D. Smith (Washington, D.C.: Smithsonian Institution Press, 1990), 117.
27. O'Brien and Wood, 251.
28. *Ibid.*, 251–52.
29. *Ibid.*, 295.
30. Carl H. Chapman and Eleanor R. Chapman, *Indians and Archaeology of Missouri*. (Columbia: University of Missouri Press, 1983), 84.
31. Robbie Ethridge, *From Chicaza to Chickasaw* (Chapel Hill: University of North Carolina Press, 2010), 12–14.
32. O'Brien and Wood, 289.
33. Chapman and Chapman, 75.
34. Charles R. Cobb. "An Appraisal of the Role of Mill Creek Chert Hoes in Mississippian Exchange Systems," *Southern Archaeology* 8, no. 2 (Winter 1989), 79.
35. O'Brien and Wood, 309.
36. Morse and Morse, 282.
37. O'Brien and Wood, 344.
38. *Ibid.*, 335.
39. *Ibid.*, 343.
40. Phillip L. Walker, et al., "The Causes of Porotic Hyperostosis and Cribra Orbitalia: A Reappraisal of the Iron-Deficiency-Anemia Hypothesis," *American Journal of Physical Anthropology* 139 (2009), 116.
41. *Ibid.*, 109–25.
42. *Ibid.*, 114.
43. Michael J. O'Brien, *Cat Monsters and Head Pots: The Archaeology of Missouri's Pemiscot Bayou* (Columbia: University of Missouri Press, 1994), 345.
44. William E. Foley, *The Genesis of Missouri* (Columbia: University of Missouri Press, 1989), 2.
45. Ethridge, 126.
46. O'Brien and Wood, 357.
47. Louis F. Burns, *A History of the Osage People* (Tuscaloosa: University of Alabama Press, 2004), 3–4.
48. Robert S. Douglass, *History of Southeast Missouri*, vol. 1 (Chicago: The Lewis Publishing Co., 1912), 41–42.
49. *Ibid.*, 45.

Chapter 3

1. Houck, *History of Missouri*, vol. 1, 105.
2. Douglass, *History of Southeast Missouri*, vol. 1, 81–82.
3. Frederic L. Billon, *Annals of St. Louis* (St. Louis: G.I. Jones and Company, 1886), 264.

4. *Report of the Commissioner of the General Land Office* (Washington, D.C.: Government Printing Office), 1866, 50.
5. Reuben Gold Thwaites, *Early Western Travels, 1748–1846* (Cleveland: The Arthur H. Clark Co., 1904), 282.
6. *Goodspeed's History of Southeast Missouri* (Chicago: Goodspeed Publishing Co., 1888), 106.
7. Thwaites, *Early Western Travels*, 283.
8. Max Savelle. "The Founding of New Madrid, Missouri," *Mississippi Valley Historical Review* 19, no. 1 (June 1932), 30–34.
9. *Ibid.*, 33.
10. Foley, *Genesis of Missouri*, 59.
11. Savelle, 35–42.
12. George Morgan letter to Don Diego De Gardoqui, 1789, quoted in Louis Houck, ed., *Spanish Regime in Missouri* (Chicago: R.R. Donnelley & Sons, 1908), 292–93.
13. Savelle, 40.
14. *Ibid.* 45–46.
15. Foley, 62–63.
16. Savelle, 52–53.
17. *Ibid.* 54–55.
18. Houck, *History of Missouri*, vol. II, 283.
19. *Ibid.*
20. Savelle, 55.
21. *Ibid.*
22. Floyd C. Shoemaker, "New Madrid, Mother of Southeast Missouri," *Missouri Historical Review* 49, no. 4 (July 1955), 320.
23. LaForge's letter to Delassus from Billon, *Annals of St. Louis*, 271.
24. *Ibid.*, 268.
25. *Ibid.*, 270.
26. *Ibid.*
27. Amos Stoddard, *Sketches, Historical and Descriptive of Louisiana* (Philadelphia: Mathew Carey, 1812), 211.
28. William Foley, *History of Missouri, Volume I, 1673–1820* (Columbia: University of Missouri Press, 1971), 136–38.
29. Fortescue Cuming in Thwaites, *Early Western Travels*, vol. 4, 281.
30. Foley, *Genesis of Missouri*, 99.
31. Edwin James in Thwaites, *Early Western Travels*, vol. 14, 103.
32. Cuming, 283.
33. Christian Schultz, *Travels on an Inland Voyage*, vol. 2. (New York: Isaac Riley, 1810) 103.
34. *Ibid.*

35. Douglass, 100.
36. *Ibid.*, 102.
37. *Ibid.*
38. Otto A. Rothert, *The Outlaws of Cave-in-Rock*. (Cleveland: The Arthur H. Clark Co., 1924), 157–272.
39. Douglass, 108–09.
40. Houck, 161.

Chapter 4

1. James L. Penick, Jr., *The New Madrid Earthquakes* (Columbia: University of Missouri Press, 1981), 8–9.
2. Myron L. Fuller, *The New Madrid Earthquake* (Washington, D.C.: Government Printing Office, 1912), 17.
3. Arch Johnston and Eugene S. Schweig, "The Enigma of the New Madrid Earthquakes of 1811–1812," *The Annual Review of Earth and Planetary Sciences* 24 (1996), 339.
4. Eliza Bryan, letter written n 1816 published in *The History of Cosmopolite or the Four Volumes of Lorenzo Dow's Journal* (Wheeling, WV: Joshua Martin, 1848), 344.
5. *Ibid.*
6. *Ibid.*, 345.
7. John Bradbury, *Travels in the Interior of America in the Years 1809, 1810, and 1811.* (Liverpool: Smith and Galway, 1817), 204.
8. John Shaw, "New Madrid Earthquake," account of Col. John Shaw, *Missouri Historical Review* 6 (1912), 92.
9. *Ibid.*
10. Zadok Cramer, *The Navigator*, 9th ed. (Pittsburgh: Cramer, Spear, and Eichbaum, 1817), 160–61. University of Missouri Digital Library. http://digital.library.umsystem.edu/cgi/t/text/pageviewer-idx?c=umlib;cc=umlib;sid=a4a8a215e54d6ba327bc2bea743f11b4;rgn=full%20text;idno=umlc000008;view=image;seq=161 (accessed 12/2/14).
11. Matthias Speed earthquake account published in the *Bardstown Repository* March 2, 1812. http://www.memphis.edu/ceri/compendium/eyewitness.php (accessed 7/27/16).
12. *Ibid.*
13. James Fletcher's letter to the *Pittsburg Gazette*, February 14, 1812. http://www.memphis.edu/ceri/compendium/eyewitness.php.
14. Daniel Bedinger's journal, published March 14, 1812, in the *National Intelligencer*,

Washington, D.C. http://www.memphis.edu/ceri/compendium/eyewitness.php (accessed 7/27/16).

15. Johnston and Schweig, 352.

16. David Stewart and Ray Knox, *The Earthquake That Never Went Away* (Marble Hill, MO: Guttenberg-Richter Publications, 1993), 144–49. David Stewart became cutoff from and lost much support of the mainstream seismological community after he gave credence to Iben Browning's forecast and his forecast methodology of an increased probability of a large earthquake along the New Madrid seismic zone December 2–3, 1990. No earthquakes occurred during that time. Nonetheless, Stewart's emphasis on the importance of earthquake preparedness for the area has now become a standard policy of state and federal emergency response agencies. His three books on the region provide a highly readable discussion of past earthquakes and numerous photographs of earthquake features still visible such as sand blows.

17. Bill Lueckenhoff, "The Story of a Leaky Lake," *Land and Water Magazine* 47, no. 1 (2003), 8–13. http://www.landandwater.com/features/vol47no1/vol47no1_1.html.

18. Ibid.

19. Fuller, 65.

20. A.N. Dillard quoted in J.W. Foster, *The Mississippi Valley: Its Physical Geography* (Chicago: S.C. Griggs & Co., 1869), 21.

21. Margaret J. Guccione, et al., "Origin and Age of the Manila High and Associated Big Lake 'Sunklands' in the New Madrid Seismic Zone, Northeastern Arkansas," *Geological Society of America Bulletin* 112, no. 4 (April 2000), 579.

22. David Stewart and Ray Knox, *The Earthquake America Forgot* (Marble Hill, MO: Guttenberg-Richter Publications, 2000), 214.

23. Fuller, Plate I, 8.

24. Johnston and Schweig, 377–79.

25. Ibid., 342.

26. Penick, 28.

27. Stewart and Knox, *The Earthquake America Forgot*, 209.

28. Ibid., 219.

29. Conevery Bolton Valencius, *Lost History of the New Madrid Earthquakes* (Chicago: University of Chicago Press, 2013), 85.

30. Goodspeed, *History of Southeast Missouri*, 221.

31. Douglass, 104.

32. Foley, 250–51.

33. Floyd C. Shoemaker, "New Madrid, Mother of Southeast Missouri," *Missouri Historical Review* 44, no. 4, 326.

34. American State Papers, 3: 427–28.

35. Shoemaker, 326.

36. Timothy Flint, *Recollections of the Last Ten Years in the Valley of the Mississippi* (Boston: Cummings, Hilliard, & Co., 1826). Reprint, George R. Brooks, ed., Carbondale: University of Southern Illinois Press, 1968, 165.

37. Alphonso Wetmore, *Gazetteer of the State of Missouri* (St. Louis: C. Keemle, 1837). Reprint, New York: Arno Press, 1975, 130–31.

38. Tom Kanon, "'Scared from Their Sins for a Season': The Religious Ramifications of the New Madrid Earthquakes, 1811–1812," *Ohio Valley History* 5 no. 2 (Summer 2005), 22.

39. Barton W. Stone, *The Biography of Barton Warren Stone* (Cincinnati: J.A. & U.P. James, 1847). Reprinted in *The Cane Ridge Reader*, ed. Hoke Smith Dickinson and Robert Wesley Steffer, Cane Ridge Preservation Project, 2006.

40. Kanon, 25.

41. Shaw, 91.

42. Kanon, 27.

43. Penick, 116.

44. Ibid., 34.

45. Kanon, 27.

46. Ibid., 31.

47. Johnston and Schweig, 372.

48. Yong Li, et al., "Evidence for Large Prehistoric Earthquakes in the Northern New Madrid Seismic Zone, Central United States," *Seismological Research Letters* 69, no. 3 (1998), 274–75.

49. Martitia P. Tuttle, et al., "The Earthquake Potential of the New Madrid Seismic Zone," *Bulletin of the Seismological Society of America* 92, no. 6 (2002), 2080.

50. Carl W. Stover and Jerry L. Coffman, *Seismicity of the United States, 1568–1989*, U.S. Geological Survey Professional Paper 1527 (Washington, D.C.: U.S. Government Printing Office, 1993).

51. J.H.B. Latrobe, *The First Steamboat Voyage on Western Waters* (Baltimore: Maryland Historical Society, 1871), 23.
52. *Ibid.*, 26.

Chapter 5

1. Houck, *History of Missouri*, vol. 1, 7. Max L. Kelley, "John Hardeman Walker—Cattle King," *Missouri Historical Review* 25, no. 2 (January 1951), 383–85.
2. Missouri Revised Statutes, Chapter 7, "State Boundaries," 7.001.1, http://www.moga.mo.gov/mostatutes/chapters/chapText007.html (accessed 7/27/16).
3. S. Lyle Johnson, "The Fight for the Pre-emption Law of 1841," *Arkansas Academy of Sciences Proceedings* 4 (1951), 165.
4. Russel L. Gerlach, *Settlement Patterns in Missouri* (Columbia: University of Missouri Press, 1986), 3.
5. H. Tyler Blethen and Curtis W. Wood, Jr., *Ulster and North America* (Tuscaloosa: University of Alabama Press, 1997), 1–3.
6. Wetmore, 219.
7. *Ibid.*, 128.
8. *Ibid.*, 222–23.
9. *Ibid.*, 223.
10. United States Census, Decennial Census Records: http://www2.census.gov/prod2/decennial/documents/1840a-04.pdf; http://www2.census.gov/prod2/decennial/documents/1850a-24.pdf; http://www2.census.gov/prod2/decennial/documents/1860b-06.pdf.
11. U.S. House of Representatives, "Swamp Lands in Missouri and Arkansas," Report No. 130, 30th Congress, 2nd Session, February 28, 1949, 11.
12. Thomas Beckwith, *Settlement and Settlers of Mississippi County* (East Prairie, MO: East Prairie Eagle, 1978), 29.
13. *Ibid.*, 5–10.
14. *Ibid.*, 24.
15. *Ibid.*, 26.
16. Douglass, 106.
17. 1860 Census of Agriculture, www2.census.gov/prod2/decennial/documents/1860b-08.pdf (accessed 1/16/14).
18. Floyd C. Shoemaker, "Kennett: Center of a Land Reborn in Missouri's Valley of the Nile," *Missouri Historical Review* 52, no. 2 (January 1958), 109.
19. Douglass, 342–43.
20. *Ibid.*, 339–40.

Chapter 6

1. North Todd Gentry, "Plank Roads in Missouri," *Missouri Historical Review* 31 no. 3 (April 1937), 237.
2. Laws of the State of Missouri, 15th General Assembly, 1849, 293–96; 16th General Assembly, 1851, 432–35; 18th General Assembly, 1855, 128–32 and 312–13.
3. Otto Kochtitzky, *The Story of a Busy Life* (Cape Girardeau: Ramfre Press, 1957), 74.
4. *Ibid.*
5. T.E. Page, "History of the Pole Road," *History of Dunklin County*, vol. 1 (Kennett, MO: Dunklin County Historical Society, 1951), 13.
6. Jeff Thompson, Letter to Solomon G. Kitchen, *Index to the Miscellaneous Document of House of Representatives for the Second Session of Forty-Seventh Congress, 1882-83* (Washington, D.C.: Government Printing Office, 1883), 742.
7. Kochtitzky, 74.
8. Laws of the State of Missouri.
9. Kochtitzky, 74.
10. Perry McCandless, *A History of Missouri*, vol. II (Columbia: University of Missouri Press, 2000), 147.
11. John Hall Dalton, Jr., "Dunklin County, Charles P. Chouteau, and the Courtship of the Iron Horse," *Missouri Historical Review* 82, no. 1 (October 1987), 73.
12. Douglass, 498–99.
13. Dalton, 83.
14. Douglass, 499–500.
15. Dalton, 92.
16. Kochtitzky, 76–77.
17. Jacob E. Anderson, "Eighty Years of Transportation Progress: A History of the St. Louis Southwestern Railway," *Cotton Belt News*, October 1957, http://www.ttarchive.com/Library/Articles/Cotton-Belt_80-Years-Progress.html#3 (accessed 7/27/16).
18. Kochtitzky, 116.
19. Joel P. Rhodes, *A Missouri Railroad Pioneer: The Life of Louis Houck* (Columbia: University of Missouri Press, 2008), 71.
20. William T. Doherty, Jr., *Louis Houck: Missouri Historian and Entrepreneur*. (Columbia: University of Missouri Press, 1960), 12.

21. William T. Doherty, Jr., "The Missouri Interests of Louis Houck" (Ph.D. diss., University of Missouri, 1951), 63–100.
22. *Ibid.*, 133.
23. *Ibid.*
24. C.C. Redman, "History of State Highway 84," in *History of Dunklin County*, vol. 1 (Kennett, MO: Dunklin County Historical Society, 1951), 22.
25. Doherty, "Missouri Interests," 141–44.
26. *Ibid.*, 163–65.
27. Rhodes, 195.
28. Doherty, "Missouri Interests," 128–83. Documents filed by the various companies with the Missouri Secretary of State's office, 1902–1907.
29. *Dunklin Democrat*, September 13, 1902.
30. Leon Ogilvie, "The Development of the Southeast Missouri Lowlands" (Ph.D. diss., University of Missouri, 1967), 58–59.
31. *Ibid.*, 59–60.
32. Ophelia R. Wade, *Deering Plantation* (Xlibris Corporation, 1999), 32.
33. Ogilvie, "Development," 60.
34. *Ibid.*, 61–64.
35. *The Modern Promised Land*, promotional booklet published by Sikeston real estate agent, C.F. Bruton, 25.
36. Aristia C. Shewey, *Shewey's Guide and Map to the Happy Hunting Grounds of Missouri and Arkansas* (St. Louis: Aristia C. Shewey, Map Publisher, 1892), 13, 15.
37. *Ibid.*, 14.
38. *Ibid.*, 10.

Chapter 7

1. Major James F. Brooks, Chief Engineer to Louis Houck, President, St. Louis, Kennett and Southern Railroad, December 11, 1891, quoted in Edward C. Matthews, *Matthews: The Historic Adventures of a Pioneer Family* (Cape Girardeau: Southeast Missouri State University Press, 2004), 138.
2. Business correspondence of Otto Kochtitzky, Kochtitzky Papers, Missouri Historical Society, St. Louis.
3. Ogilvie, "Development," 101.
4. Bureau of Labor Statistics Twenty-Second Annual Report 1899, Surplus Products, Missouri Counties 1914, 258, 304, 312, 320, 356. The statistics for lumber are reported in two parts, hardwood and pine. In the Bootheel, what is reported as pine may have actually been cypress or other species such as cottonwood since the amount of native pine in these counties was very small.
5. Bureau of Labor Statistics, 1910, 99, 145, 152.
6. Bureau of Labor Statistics, 1918, 414, 415, 437, 440. The Bureau of Labor Statistics reported data for 1917 in the number of rail cars shipped rather than board feet of lumber. The number of board feet was calculated based on a conservative estimate of 6,000 board feet per car.
7. William E. Towel, "Trees of Dunklin County," in *History of Dunklin County*, vol. 1, 233. Randy Carter, grandson of J.A. Hemphill, personal communication, 2007.
8. Doherty, 1960, 44.
9. *Ibid.* Information Sheet, Gideon-Anderson Lumber and Mercantile Co. Papers, 1901–1985, R 290, State Historical Society of Missouri Manuscript Collection, Rolla.
10. Doherty, "Missouri Interests," 44.
11. Matthews, 138.
12. Himmelberger-Harrison Lumber Company Papers, Special Collections and Archives, Southeast Missouri State University.
13. Wade 24–25.
14. *Ibid.*, 34, 38–39.
15. F. R Gadd, "Utilization of Southeast Missouri Lands," *The Harvester World* 3 no. 11 (November 1912), 23.
16. *The Farmer's Guide*, International Harvester Corp., 1905, quoted in Wade, 24.
17. P.E. Gilbert, "Why and How," *The Harvester World* 3, no. 11 (November 1912), 24.
18. "Tall Timber," City of Poplar Bluff Historical Preservation Commission, http://www.butlercountyhistory.org/poplarbluff/html/timber.html (accessed 7/27/16).
19. Matthews, 138–39.
20. Gerlach, 36.
21. Thad Snow, *From Missouri* (Boston: Houghton Mifflin, 1954), 141.
22. *Ibid.*, 139.
23. *Ibid.*, 134.
24. *Ibid.*, 142.
25. Bill Crabtree, "Wardell Writings," *Portageville Missourian News*, July 13, 2000, 3.

26. Ibid., July 27, 2000, 3.
27. Towell, 232–33.
28. Davis, 85.
29. Centers for Disease Control, "The History of Malaria, an Ancient Disease," http://www.cdc.gov/malaria/about/history/index.html. (accessed 7/27/16).
30. Loren Humphrey, *Quinine and Quarantine* (Columbia: University of Missouri Press, 2000), 16–17. Perry McCandless, *A History of Missouri*, vol. II. (Columbia: University of Missouri Press, 2000), 217.
31. Centers for Disease Control, http://www.cdc.gov/malaria/about/history/index.html.
32. Ibid.
33. Ibid.
34. Margaret Humphreys, *Malaria: Poverty, Race, and Public Health* (Baltimore: Johns Hopkins University Press, 2001), 309.
35. National Library of Medicine, http://archive.nlm.nih.gov/fdanj/bitstream/123456789/50820/4/FDNJ16546.pdf.
36. Snow, 136–37.
37. Ibid., 137.
38. K.F. Maxey, "The Malaria Problem of Southeast Missouri: I. General Discussion of the Locality," *Public Health Reports* 38, no. 6 (February 9, 1923), 233.
39. Chart from Ibid., 236.
40. Ibid.
41. M.V. Ziegler and K.F. Maxey, "The Malaria Problem of Southeast Missouri: II A Study of Malaria Prevalence and Some of the Factors Affecting it in the Sikeston Area of Southeast Missouri," *Public Health Reports* 38, no. 6 (February 9, 1923), 237–43.
42. Ibid., 250.
43. Towell, 232.

Chapter 8

1. Amos Stoddard, *Sketches of Louisiana* (Philadelphia: Mathew Carey, 1812), 203.
2. Estwick Evans, *Evans Pedestrious Tour of Four Thousand Miles—1818* (Concord, NH: Joseph C. Spear, 1819), 300–03.
3. *Journal of the Senate, U.S.* 19th Cong., 1st Sess. (1826, 217, 224 and *Report of the Commissioner of the General Land Office Relating to Public Lands in Missouri and Illinois Which are Unfit for Cultivation, U.S.* 19th Cong., 2nd Sess., Senate Document 59, 1827, cited in Leon Parker Ogilvie, "Governmental Efforts at Reclamation in the Southeast Missouri Lowlands," *Missouri Historical Review* 64, no. 2 (January 1970), 155.
4. Ogilvie, "Governmental Efforts," 155.
5. House Report No. 549, 24th Congress, 1st Session, 1836. Cited in McDowell, 187.
6. U.S. House of Representatives, 20th Congress, 1st Sess., *Swamplands in Missouri and Arkansas*, January 13, 1846, 1.
7. Ibid., 2.
8. *Laws of the State of Missouri, Fourteenth General Assembly*, 1847, 227–28.
9. Journal of the Senate of the State of Missouri, First Session of the Fifteenth General Assembly, Appendix, 198–200.
10. Ogilvie, "Governmental Efforts," 159.
11. John H. Nolen, *Swamp and Overflowed Lands and their Reclamation*, Report to the Forty-seventh Missouri General Assembly, January 1913, 6–7.
12. Report of Swampland Commissioners in regards to Making Levees in Southeast Missouri, December 18, 1852, 22, cited in McDowell, 187–88. *Laws of the State of Missouri*, Seventeenth General Assembly, 1853, 108–109.
13. Nolen, 7.
14. *Laws of Missouri of the State of Missouri*, Eighteenth General Assembly, 1855, 154–58.
15. *Laws of Missouri*, Twenty-fourth General Assembly, 1868, 69–72.
16. Nolen, 10.
17. *Loans for the Relief of Drainage Districts*, Hearings Before the Committee on Irrigation and Reclamation, House of Representatives, 70th Congress, 2nd Sess., January 29–February 1, 1929. Cited in McDowell, 102, McDowell, 184.
18. Nathan H. Parker, *Missouri as It Is in 1867* (Philadelphia: J.B. Lippencott & Co., 1867), 174.
19. Ibid. 37–38.
20. *The Mississippi River Floods: Hearing Before the Committee on Flood Control*, House of Representatives, Sixty-Fourth Congress, First Session, March 1916, 61.
21. S.P. Reynolds, "History of the Levees and Drainage in Southeast Missouri," in *Proceedings of the First Conference on Land Utilization* (Columbia: University of Missouri Agricultural Experiment Station Bulletin No. 323, 1933), 39.

22. Reynolds, 40.
23. Appendix E 1928 Flood Control Act, 70th Cong. Sess. 1, Ch. 596, 1928, http://www.mvd.usace.army.mil/Portals/52/docs/MRC/Appendix_E._1928_Flood_Control_Act.pdf. (accessed 7/27/16).
24. Reynolds, 42.
25. McDowell, 232.
26. Reynolds, 42.
27. McDowell, 224.
28. *Ibid.*, 226.
29. Towell, 232.
30. Arthur F. King, "The Dipper Dredge for Drainage Work," in *Missouri's Swamp and Overflowed Lands and Their Reclamation*, report by John H. Nolen, Special Agent Hugh in Land Reclamation, report to the 47th Missouri General Assembly, January 1913 (Jefferson City: Stephen Printing Co., 1913), 138.
31. McDowell, 115.
32. *Ibid.*, 115–16.
33. *The History of Large Federal Dams: Planning, Design, and Construction in the Era of Big Dams* (U.S. Department of the Interior, Bureau of Reclamation, Denver, 2005), 383.
34. *Ibid.*, 385.
35. *Report of the National Conservation Commission*, vol. 1 (Washington, D.C.: Government Printing Office, 1909), 14–15.
36. *Ibid.*, 23.
37. *Ibid.*, 27.
38. Nolen, 130.
39. Guy Elliott Mitchell, "To Farm America's Swamps," *The American Review of Reviews* XXXVII, no. 4 (April 1908), 434–35.
40. McDowell, 122.
41. Kochtitzky, 97.
42. Kochtitzky, 98; Ogilvie, "Governmental Efforts," 108.
43. Ogilivie, "Governmental Efforts," 109.
44. Kochtitzky, 114–15.
45. *Ibid.*, 113.
46. *Ibid.*, 117.
47. *Ibid.*
48. *Ibid.*, 117–118.
49. *Ibid.*, 118–119.
50. Charles Kettleborough, *Drainage and Reclamation of Swamp and Overflowed Lands* (Indianapolis: Indiana Bureau of Legislative Information, April 1914), 20.
51. *Ibid.*

52. Kochtitzky, 121.
53. *Ibid.*
54. *Ibid.* 9.
55. *Ibid.*, 14.
56. *Ibid.* 20–21.
57. *Ibid.*, 77–87.
58. *Ibid.*, 93–96.
59. *Ibid.*, 115–117.
60. *Ibid.*, 134.
61. *Ibid.*, 136.
62. *Handbook of Missouri* (St. Louis: Missouri Immigration Society, 1880), 14.

Chapter 9

1. *Draining and Leveeing Missouri Lowland* (Jefferson City: Missouri Bureau of Labor Statistics, 1910), 15. McDowell, 234.
2. *Ibid.*, 16.
3. Kochtitzky, 139.
4. *Ibid.*
5. *Ibid.*, 140.
6. *Ibid.*
7. *Little River Drainage District: 1907–Present* (Cape Girardeau: Little River Drainage District, 1989), 8.
8. Ogilivie, "Governmental Efforts," 120.
9. Little River Drainage District Collection, Southeast Missouri State University, letter to the Mississippi River Commission.
10. *Little River Drainage District: 1907–Present*, 8.
11. In RE Little River Drainage District, 236 Mo. 94, 139 S.W.
12. *Ibid.*
13. Joel Rhodes, *A Missouri Railroad Pioneer: The Life of Louis Houck* (Columbia: University of Missouri Press, 2008), 264.
14. *The Daily Republican*, Cape Girardeau, Missouri, December 9, 1909.
15. *Dunklin Democrat*, March 4, 1910, 2.
16. *The St. Louis Republic*, July 12, 1911.
17. Bonnie Stepenoff, "'The Last Tree Cut Down': The End of the Bootheel Frontier, 1880–1940," *Missouri Historical Review* XC, no. 1 (October 1995), 70.
18. Kochtitzky, *St. Louis Republic*, July 29, 1911.
19. Houck, *St. Louis Republic*, August 1, 1911.
20. Paper from the Oliver Law Firm in the Little River Drainage District Records, Special Collections, Kent Library,

Southeast Missouri State University, Cape Girardeau.

21. Houck v. *Little River Drainage District*, et al., 248 mo. 373, 154 S.W. 739 (February 12, 1913).

22. Houck v. *Little River Drainage District*, 239 U.S. 254 (1915).

23. *State Ex Rel. McWilliams, Pros. Atty. v. Little River Drainage District*, 269 mo. 444, 190 S.W. 897 (December 21, 1916).

24. Landowner meeting minutes, 1907, Little River Drainage District Records, Special Collections, Kent Library, Southeast Missouri State University.

25. *Ibid.*

26. Kochtitzky, 143.

27. Annual Report of the Board of Supervisors of the Little River Drainage District, 1912. Little River Drainage District Records, Special Collections, Southeast Missouri State University.

Chapter 10

1. Otto Kochtitzky, Annual Report of Chief Engineer of the Little River Drainage District, Cape Girardeau, January 1, 1909, Kochtitzky Records, Missouri Historical Society, St. Louis, MO.

2. Letter from Otto Kochtitzky to J.E. Dunn. Little River Drainage District Records, Special Collections and Archives, Kent Library, Southeast Missouri State University.

3. Letter from Otto Kochtitzky to M. McReynolds, Little River Drainage District Records.

4. Letter to J.E. Dunn, Little River Drainage District Records.

5. Kochtitzky, 1908 Annual Report.

6. Report of the Board of Supervisors, Little River Drainage District, 1918.

7. Larry Dowdy, Chief Engineer, Little River Drainage District, Cape Girardeau, personal communication (8/8/07).

8. Letter from Isham Randolph to Otto Kochtitzky, June 9, 1908, Kochtitzky Papers, Missouri Historical Society.

9. Kochtitzky, 146.

10. Report to the Board of Supervisors, December 20, 1909, Little River Drainage District Records.

11. Annual Report of the Chief Engineer of the Little River Drainage District, published January 29, 1909, in the *Weekly Republican*, Cape Girardeau, Kochtitzky Papers, Missouri Historical Society.

12. Kochtitzky, 143.

13. Bulletin 28, LRDD, February 1922, Little River Drainage District Records.

14. Annual Report of the Board of Supervisors of the Little River Drainage District, December 17, 1912, Little River Drainage District Records.

15. Copy in the Little River Drainage District Records, Special Collections and Archives, Kent Library, Southeast Missouri State University.

16. Bulletin No. 4, August 1915, Little River Drainage District Records.

17. B.F. Burns, *Engineering and Contracting* 48, no. 3 (July 18, 1917), 47–48.

18. *Ibid.*, 47.

19. *Engineering News* 76, no. 8 (August 24, 1916), 345.

20. Charles P. Stivers, "Digging 624 Miles of Drainage Ditches," *The Contractor* 20, no. 11 (December 1, 1914), 31–33; 49–51.

21. Richard W. Stewart, ed., *American Military History, Vol. 2, The United States Army in a Global Era, 1917–2003*, 7–24.

22. *Ibid.*, 23.

23. Nancy K. Bristow, *American Pandemic: The Lost Worlds of the 1918 Influenza Epidemic* (New York: Oxford University Press, 2012), 16–17.

24. *Ibid.*, 21.

25. *Ibid.*, 17.

26. *Ibid.* 23.

27. *Springfield Missouri Republican*, November 21, 1918.

28. Bristow, 44.

29. http://www.flu.gov/pandemic/history/1918/your_state/southwest/missouriindex.html (accessed 7/27/16).

30. http://www.history.com/topics/1918-flu-pandemic.

31. Bulletin of LRRD, December 27, 1918.

32. Bulletin 15, Little River Drainage District, May 1918.

33. Bulletin 25, LRRD, Chief Engineer's Report, November 1920.

34. *Ibid.*

35. Bulletin 32 LRRD, February 1924, Minutes of Annual Meeting.

36. Bulletin 32, Minutes of Annual Meeting. Little River Drainage District Records.

37. Bulletin 36, LRRD February 1926.
38. Bulletin 40, LRRD, February 1928.
39. Bulletin 36, LRRD, February 1926.

Chapter 11

1. David B. Danbom, *Born Country* (Baltimore: Johns Hopkins University Press, 1995), 185.
2. *Ibid.*, 188.
3. http://www.nass.usda.gov/Publications/Trends_in_U.S._Agriculture/Land_Values/index.asp (accessed 6/23/15).
4. Special Bulletin, November 1927.
5. Semi-Annual Bulletin, Little River Drainage District, June 1927, 6–7.
6. *Ibid.*
7. Semi-Annual Bulletin, Little River Drainage District no. 40, February 1928, 14–16.
8. *Ibid.*
9. *Ibid.*
10. Monthly Weather Review, Supplement 29, October 1927 by H.C. Frankenfield, et al., United States Department of Agriculture Weather Bureau (Washington, D.C.: United States Government Printing Office, 1927), 42.
11. Kevin R. Kosar, *Disaster Response and Appointment of a Recovery Czar: The Executive Branch's Response to the Flood of 1927* (Washington, D.C.: Congressional Research Service, 2005), 5.
12. *The Mississippi Valley Flood Disaster of 1927, Official Report of the Relief Operations*, American National Red Cross, 40.
13. John M. Barry, *The Rising Tide* (New York: Simon & Schuster, 1997), 317.
14. *Ibid.*, 389.
15. John M. Barry, "After the Deluge," *Smithsonian Magazine* (November 2005), 3, http://smithsonianmag.com/history-archaeology/pom.html?c=y&page=3 (accessed 7/10/15).
16. Little River Drainage District Bulletin 45, February 1931.
17. *The Mississippi River & Tributaries Project: Birds Point–New Madrid Floodway*, Mississippi River Commission Information Paper, n.d.
18. *Sikeston Standard*, January 20 and January 27, 1928.
19. Otto Kochtitzky, March 31, 1930, *Southeast Missourian*, Cape Girardeau.
20. *The Mississippi River & Tributaries Project*, 7.
21. Little River Drainage District Special Bulletin, December 1927.
22. Ogilvie, "Governmental Efforts," 130.
23. *Sikeston Standard*, February 7, 1930.
24. Little River Drainage District Bulletin 43, February 1930, 8–9.
25. LRDD Bulletin 43, 1930, 7.
26. Larry Schweikart and Michael Allen, *A Patriot's History of the United States*, (New York: Sentinel, 2004), 554.
27. Danbom, 202.
28. Little River Drainage District Bulletin 43, p. 4.
29. *Ibid.*, 7.
30. Snow, 170.
31. National Agricultural Statistics Service, Track Records United States Crop Production" http://www.nass.usda.gov/Publications/Track_Records/croptr07.pdf. (accessed July 27, 2016).
32. Little River Drainage District Bulletin 45, February 1931.
33. *Ibid.*
34. *Ibid.*
35. *Ibid.*
36. Snow, 169.
37. C.E. Willis, letter to the Board of Supervisors and the Bondholders' Protective Committee of the Little River Drainage District. Little River Drainage District Records.
38. Julien Friant, *Loans for Relief of Drainage Districts, Hearing Before the Committee on Irrigation and Reclamation*, House of Representatives, 70th Congress, Second Session, 119, quoted in Gary Lane McDowell, 375.
39. Snow, 161.
40. Letter from John W. Dennison to Little River Drainage District Board of Supervisors, Little River Drainage District Records.
41. Letter from Julien Friant to Russell L. Dearmont. Friant Papers, Special Collections and Archives, Kent Library, Southeast Missouri State University.
42. McDowell, 392.
43. Snow, 209.
44. Floyd M. Clay, *A Century on the Mississippi: A History of the Memphis District U.S. Army Corps of Engineers 1876–1976*.
45. *Sikeston Standard*, January 26, 2937.

46. Snow, 211.
47. Ibid., 209.
48. *Mississippi River and Tributaries Project: Birds Point–New Madrid-Floodway*, 7.
49. Snow, 214–15.
50. David Welky, *The Thousand-Year Flood* (Chicago: University of Chicago Press, 2011), 167.
51. Clay, 150.
52. Welky, 173.
53. *Ibid.*, 167.
54. Clay, 151.
55. Welky, 181–82.
56. Clay, 151.
57. Welky, 174.
58. *Ibid.* 178–79.
59. *Ibid.*, 193.
60. *Ibid.*, 194–95.
61. *Ibid.*, 183.
62. *Ibid.*, 183, 184, 204.
63. *Ibid.*, 203.
64. *Ibid.*
65. *The Mississippi river and Tributaries Project: Birds Point–New Madrid Floodway*, 8.

Chapter 12

1. Missouri Immigration Society, *Hand-Book of Missouri* (St. Louis: Times Printing House, 1880), 18, University of Missouri Digital Library, http://digital.library.umsystem.edu/cgi/t/text/text-idx?page=home;c=umlib (accessed 7/27/16).
2. Ogilivie, "Governmental Efforts," 138.
3. Missouri Pacific Railway Company, *Statistics and Information Concerning the State of Missouri*, 1889, 84.
4. *Prairie Farmer* January 21, 1922, 23.
5. Ogilivie, "Governmental Efforts," 169.
6. *Daily Democrat*, Kennett, MO, January 18, 1924.
7. *Daily Democrat*, Kennett, MO, January 12, 1924.
8. Roy Godsey, "Cotton in Missouri," *Monthly Bulletin of the Missouri State Board of Agriculture* 20, no. 12 (December 1922), 21.
9. Little River Valley Land Company, *Southeast Missouri: The Garden Spot of the Mississippi Valley*, 11.
10. *Ibid.*, 13.
11. C.F. Bruton Real Estate and Investment Company, *The Modern Promised Land*, 15.
12. *Wallaces' Farmer*, March 20, 1925.
13. Ogilvie, "Governmental Efforts 157.
14. *Cut-Over Lands* 2, no. 2 (May 1919), 22, 23.
15. Wade, *Deering Plantation*, 112–13, 118.
16. *Ibid.*, 113.
17. *Ibid.*, 113–16.
18. Snow, 134.
19. *Ibid.*, 135.
20. Matthews, 138–39.
21. Snow, 90.
22. Hugh Studabaker, *What They "Showed Me" in Southeast Missouri* (1913), 9, 19.
23. *Ibid.*, 17.
24. *Ibid.*, 22.
25. Percentages calculated from data in United States Census of Agriculture for years 1890 to 1940.
26. Twenty-Second Annual Report, Missouri Bureau of Labor Statistics, 259.
27. Clyde E. Sorenson, "The Boll Weevil in Missouri: History, Biology and Management," University of Missouri Agricultural Guide, G 4255, Columbia, 1995.
28. http://www.columbiatribune.com/wire/cotton-fields-nearly-clear-of-boll-weevil/article_798a2882-927d-5ffd-9219-eed2c5084c13.html (accessed 6/12/16).
29. U.S. Census Bureau, Statistical Abstracts https://www.census.gov/library/publications/1925/compendia/statab/47ed.html (accessed 6/12/16).
30. United States 1930 Census.
31. Snow, 156–57.
32. Irvin G. Wyllie, "Race and Class Conflict on Missouri's Cotton Frontier," *The Journal of Southern History* 20, no. 2 (May 1954), 186–87.
33. *Ibid.*, 188–89.
34. *Ibid.*, 189–90.
35. *Ibid.*, 192.
36. *Ibid.*, 194–95.
37. *Sikeston Standard*, May 2, 1919.
38. Ogilvie, "Governmental Efforts," 240.
39. *The Weekly Tribune and Cape County Herald*, October 1, 1915.
40. Jama McMurtery Grove, "Uneasy Waters: The Night Riders at Reelfoot Lake, Tennessee, 1908" (master's thesis, East Tennessee State University, 2012), 6–8.
41. Lowell H. Harrizon and James C. Klotter, *A New History of Kentucky* (Lexing-

ton: University of Kentucky Press, 1997), 279–81.
42. *Weekly Tribune and Cape County Herald*, November 26, 1915.
43. *Ibid.*
44. Jarod Roll, "Gideon's Band: From Socialism to Vigilantism in Southeast Missouri," *Labor History* 23, no. 4 (November 2002), 184.
45. John Case in *Missouri Ruralist*, reprinted December 17, 1915, in the *Sikeston Standard*.

Chapter 13

1. *Scott County Kicker*, October 30, 1915.
2. *Ibid.*, December 25, 1915.
3. *Ibid.*, February 8, 1908.
4. *Ibid.*, December 3, 1910.
5. *Ibid.*, September 4, 1909.
6. "Historic Missourians," shsmo.orghistoricmissourians/name/o/ohare. (accessed 5/15/16).
7. Judith Rosenbaum, "Rose Pastor Stokes," *Jewish Women: A Comprehensive Historical Encyclopedia*, March 20, 2000, Jewish Women's Archive, http://jwa.org/encyclopedia/article/stokes-rose-pastor (accessed 5/15/16).
8. Roll, "Gideon's Band," 492.
9. *Justice*, Kennett, MO, January 9, 1914.
10. *Justice*, Gibson, MO, August 7, 1914.
11. *Justice*, Kennett, MO, April 1914; The families Scott references were some prominent Dunklin County residents who owned large tracts of land.
12. *Justice*, Gibson, MO, May 6, 1914.
13. *Justice*, Kennett, MO, April 10, 1914.
14. *Justice*, Kennett, MO, February 27, 1914.
15. *Justice*, Kennett, MO, April 10, 1914.
16. Gary B. McGee, "The Revival Legacy of Charles F. Parham," *Enrichment Journal* (Summer 1999), n. p.
17. Gary B. McGee, "William J. Seymour and the Azusa Street Revival," *Enrichment Journal* (Fall 1999), n. p.
18. Edith Blumhofer, "Azusa Street Revival," *Christianity Today* (March 7, 2006), 20–22.
19. Walter J. Higgins, *Pioneering in Pentecost* (Bostonia, California, 1958), 27.
20. *Ibid.*, 30–31.
21. Roll, *Spirit of Rebellion*, 38.
22. *Christian Evangel*, December 19, 1914, 4.
23. *Ibid.*, 2.
24. *Word and Witness*, August 20, 1913, 4.
25. 1919-1920 *Official Manual of the State of Missouri*, 409–11.
26. Ogilvie, "Governmental Efforts," 183.
27. Roll, *Spirit of Rebellion*, 25.
28. *Ibid.*, 24.
29. H.L. Mitchell, *Mean Things Happening in This Land* (Montclair, NJ: Allanheld, Osmun & Co., 1979), 20.
30. Ray Brassieur, "From Two Mules to Twelve-Row Equipment: An Oral History Interview with Maxwell Williams Bootheel Farm Manager," *Missouri Historical Review* 91, no. 1 (October 1996), 64–65.
31. Louis Cantor, *Prologue to the Protest Movement* (Durham: Duke University Press, 1969), 44.
32. Mitchell, 11.
33. *Ibid.*, 33.
34. *Ibid.*, 47–52.
35. *Ibid.*, 111–12.
36. Roll, *Spirit of Rebellion*, 97.
37. Schroeder and Lance, 123, 127.
38. Gellman and Roll, *Gospel of the Working Class* (Urbana: University of Illinois Press, 2011), 34.
39. *Ibid.*, 37.
40. *Ibid.*, 39.
41. Michael K. Honey, *Sharecropper's Troubadour* (New York: Palgrave Macmillan, 2013), 126–27.
42. Gellman and Roll, 70–73.
43. Cantor, 53–55.
44. *Ibid.*, 33.
45. Cedric Belfrage, "Cotton Patch Moses," *Harper's Magazine* 36 (November 1948), 98.
46. Bonnie Stepenoff's excellent biography provides a detailed look at the fascinating life of Thad Snow.
47. "Preliminary Report on Labor Displacement on Cotton Plantations," cited in Cantor, 43.
48. Cantor, 33.
49. *Ibid.*, 38.
50. Snow, 262–264.
51. *Ibid.*, 248.
52. Cantor, 62.
53. *Ibid.*, 59.
54. *Ibid.*, 64, *Sikeston Standard*, January 13, 1939.

55. *Sikeston Standard*, January 13, 1939.
56. Letter from Albert Beis to Julian Friant, Friant Papers, Box 1094, Folder 7, Special Collections, Kent Library, Southeast Missouri State University.
57. *Sikeston Standard*, January 20, 1939.
58. Letter from R.B. Oliver to Julian Friant, Friant Papers Box 1084, Folder 7, Special Collections, Kent Library, Southeast Missouri State University.
59. Ogilvie, "Governmental Efforts," 293; Cantor, 84.
60. Cantor, 86.
61. *Sikeston Standard*, January 17, 1939.
62. *Ibid.*, March 14, 1930.
63. Lorenzo J. Greene, "Lincoln University's Involvement with the Sharecropper Demonstration in Southeast Missouri, 1939–1940," *Missouri Historical Review* 82, no. 1 (October 1967), 31.
64. *Ibid.*, 34.
65. Stepenoff, *Thad Snow*, 110.
66. *Sikeston Standard*, December 15, 1939.
67. Cantor, 132.
68. *Ibid.*, 135.
69. *Ibid.*, 142–43.
70. B. Mildred Smith, *Delmo: Threshold of Freedom* (Mount Ayr, IA: Paragon Publications, Inc., 2003), 17.
71. *Ibid.*, 22–24.
72. *Ibid.*, 20.
73. *Ibid.*, 46–47.
74. Cantor, 145–46; Smith, 168–69.
75. Smith, 179.
76. Michael J. Meyer, "An Evaluation of the North Lilbourn Group, Delmo Farm Labor Homes Project, on Route D in New Madrid County, Missouri," Missouri Department of Transportation, 2001, 15–16.

Chapter 14

1. Will Sarvis, "Black Electoral Power in the Missouri Bootheel, 1920s–1960s," *Missouri Historical Review* 95, no. 2 (January 2001), 183–84.
2. *Official Manual of the State of Missouri*, 1923-1924 and 1927-1928.
3. Sarvis, 185.
4. *Ibid.*
5. Vic Downing, interviewed by Will Sarvis, October 30, 1996, at his home in Bakersville, MO, transcript, Oral History Program of the State Historical Society of Missouri, Politics in Missouri Oral History Project.
6. Tom Cash, interviewed by Will Sarvis, October 30, 1996, at his home in Kennett, MO, transcript, Oral History Program of the State Historical Society of Missouri, Politics in Missouri Oral History Project.
7. Sarvis, Vic Downing interview.
8. Jack Stapleton, Jr. interviewed by Will Sarvis at his office in Kennett, MO, transcript, June 6, 1997, Oral History Program of the State Historical Society of Missouri, Politics in Missouri Oral History Project.
9. John M. Alford, interviewed at his office in Caruthersville, MO, transcript, June 4, 1997, Oral History Program, The State Historical Society of Missouri, Politics in Missouri Oral History Project.
10. Hal Hunter, Jr., interviewed at his law office in New Madrid, MO, October 27, 1998, Oral History Program of the State Historical Society of Missouri, Politics in Missouri Oral History Project.
11. Sarvis, 69.
12. *Missouri Year Book of Agriculture*, 1919, 550–51.
13. James H. Street, "Mechanizing the Cotton Harvest," *Agricultural History* 31, no. 1 (January 1957), 13.
14. Douglass Hurt, *Agricultural Technology in the Twentieth Century* (Manhattan, KS: Sunflower University Press, 1991), 32.
15. Hurt, 35; John Rust, "The Origin and Development of the Cotton Picker," *West Tennessee Historical Society Papers* 7 (1953), 48.
16. Rust, 53–54.
17. Street, 22.
18. *Ibid.*, 17.
19. Historical Statistics of the U.S. Colonial Times to 1970.
20. Missouri Census Data Center, http://mcdc.missouri.edu/trends/historical.shtml (accessed 6/17/16).

Chapter 15

1. Ogilivie, "Governmental Efforts," 389.
2. *Ibid.*, 385.
3. *Ibid.*, 388.
4. H. Riley Bock, "Formation of a Drainage District," in *Little River Drainage Dis-*

trict: Celebrating 100 Years, 1907–2007 (Cape Girardeau: Little River Drainage District, 2007), 20–21.

5. Little River Drainage District Bulletin, December 1956, 8.

6. Little River Drainage District Bulletin, December 1957, 6.

7. Bock, 21.

8. Little River Drainage District Bulletin, December 1956, 5.

Bibliography

Books

Barry, John M. *Rising Tide.* New York: Simon & Schuster, 1997.

Billon, Frederic L. *Annals of St. Louis.* St. Louis: G.I. Jones and Company, 1886.

Blethen, H. Tyler, and Curtis W. Wood, Jr., eds. *Ulster and North America.* Tuscaloosa: University of Alabama Press, 1997.

Bradbury, John. *Travels in the Interior of America in the Years 1809, 1810, 1811.* Liverpool: Smith and Galway, 1817.

Bristow, Nancy K. *American Pandemic: The Lost Worlds of the 1918 Influenza Epidemic.* New York: Oxford University Press, 2012.

Bryan, Eliza. Letter written in 1816 in *History of Cosmopolite or the Four Volumes of Lorenzo Dow's Journal.* Wheeling, WV: Joshua Martin, 1948.

Burns, Louis F. *A History of the Osage People.* Tuscaloosa: University of Alabama Press, 2004.

Cantor, Louis. *A Prologue to the Protest Movement: The Missouri Sharecropper Roadside Demonstration of 1939.* Durham: Duke University Press, 1969.

Chapman, Carl H., and Eleanor F. Chapman. *Indians and Archaeology of Missouri.* Columbia: University of Missouri Press, 1983.

Cramer, Zadok. *The Navigator,* 9th ed. Pittsburgh: Cramer, Spear, and Eichbaum, 1817. University of Missouri Digital Library (accessed 12/2/14).

Cuming, Fortescue. *Cuming's Tour of the Western Country, 1807–1809.* In Reuben Gold Thwaites, ed., *Early Western Travels,* vol. 4. Cleveland: Arthur H. Clark Co., 1904.

Danbom, David B. *Born in the Country: A History of Rural America.* Baltimore: Johns Hopkins University Press, 1995.

Delcourt, P.A., and Hazel R. Delcourt. "Paleoclimates, Paleovegetation, and Paleofloras of North America North of Mexico During the Late Quaternary." In Flora of North American Committee, ed., *Flora of North American North of Mexico,* vol. 1, chapter 4, 1993.

Douglass, Robert Sidney. *The History of Southeast Missouri, Vol. 1.* Chicago: The Lewis Publishing Co., 1912.

Dunklin County Historical Society, vols. 1 and 2. Kennett, MO: Thrower Printing Co., 1951.

Estwick, Evans. *Evans Pedestrious Tour of Four Thousand Miles-1818.* Concord, NH: Joseph C. Spear, 300–303.

Ethridge, Robbie. *From Chicaza to Chickasaw: The European Invasion and the Transformation of the Mississippian World, 1540–1715.* Chapel Hill: University of North Carolina Press, 2010.

Fisk, Harold N. *Geological Investigation of the Alluvial Valley of the Lower Mississippi River,* Vicksburg: Mississippi River Commission, 1944.

Flint, Timothy. *Recollections of the Last Ten years in the Valley of the Mississippi.* Boston:

Cummings, Hilliard, & Co., 1826. Reprinted, George R. Brooks, ed., Carbondale: University of Southern Illinois Press, 1968.

Foley, William E. *The Genesis of Missouri*. Columbia: University of Missouri Press, 1989.

———. *History of Missouri, Volume I, 1673–1820*. Columbia: University of Missouri Press, 1971.

Foster, J.W. *The Mississippi Valley: Its Physical Geography*. Chicago: S.C. Griggs & Co., 1869.

Fuller, Myron L. *The New Madrid Earthquakes*. Washington, D.C.: Government Printing Office, 1912.

Gellman, Eric S., and Jarod Roll. *The Gospel of the Working Class*. Urbana, IL: University of Illinois Press, 2011.

Gerlach, Russel L. *Settlement Patterns in Missouri*. Columbia: University of Missouri Press, 1986.

Harrizon, Lowell H., and James C. Klotter. *A New History of Kentucky*. Lexington: University of Kentucky Press, 1997.

Higgins, Walter J. *Pioneering in Pentecost*. Bostonia, CA, 1958.

Honey, Michael K. *Sharecropper's Troubadour*. New York: Palgrave Macmillan, 2013.

Humphrey, Loren. *Quinine and Quarantine*. Columbia: University of Missouri Press, 2000.

Humphreys, Margaret. *Malaria: Poverty, Race, and Public Health*. Baltimore: Johns Hopkins University Press, 2001.

Hurt, Douglass. *Agricultural Technology in the Twentieth Century*. Manhattan, KS: Sunflower University Press, 1991.

James, Edwin, *James's Account of S.H. Long's Expedition, 1819–1820*. In Reuben Gold Thwaites, ed., *Early Western Travels*, vol. 14. Cleveland: The Arthur H. Clark Co., 1905.

Kelley, J.E. "The Emergence of Mississippian Culture in the American Bottom Region." In *The Mississippian Emergence*, ed. B.D. Smith. Washington, D.C.: Smithsonian Institution Press, 1990.

Knox, Ray, and David Stewart. *The New Madrid Fault Finders Guide*. Marble Hill, MO: Guttenberg-Richter Publications, 1995.

Kochtitzky, Otto. *The Story of a Busy Life*. Cape Girardeau: Ramfre Press, 1957.

The Little River Drainage District of Southeast Missouri: 1907–Present. Cape Girardeau: The Little River Drainage District, 1989.

Mainfort, Robert C., Jr., and Marvin D. Jeter, ed. *Arkansas Archaeology: Essays in Honor of Dan and Phyllis Morse*. Fayetteville: University of Arkansas Press, 1999.

March, David D. *The History of Missouri*. New York: The Lewis Historical Publishing Co., 1967.

Matthews, Edward C., III. *Matthews: The Historic Adventures of a Pioneer Family*. Cape Girardeau: Southeast Missouri State University Press, 2004.

Mehl, Maurice G. *Missouri's Ice Age Animals*. Educational Series, no. 1. Rolla: Missouri Geological Survey and Water Resources, 1962.

The Mississippi Valley Flood Disaster of 1927: Official Report of the Relief Operations. Washington, D.C.: The American National Red Cross.

Missouri Handbook. St. Louis: Missouri Immigration Society, 1880.

Mitchell, H.L. *Mean Things Happening in This Land*. Montclair, NJ: Allenheld, Osmun & Co. Publishers, Inc., 1979.

Morse, Dan F., and Phyllis A. Morse. *Archaeology of the Central Mississippi Valley*. New York: Academic Press, 1983.

O'Brien, Michael J. *Cat Monsters and Head Pots: The Archaeology of Missouri's Pemiscot Bayou*. Columbia: University of Missouri Press, 1994.

O'Brien, Michael J., and W. Raymond Wood. *The Prehistory of Missouri*. Columbia: University of Missouri Press, 1998.

O'Brien, Michael J., and Robert C. Dunnell, eds. *Changing Perspectives on the Archaeology of the Central Mississippi River Valley*. Tuscaloosa: University of Alabama Press, 1998.

Otto, John Solomon. *The Final Frontiers, 1880–1930: Settling the Southern Bottomlands*. Westport, CT: Greenwood Press, 1999.

Penick, James Lal. *The New Madrid Earthquake*. Columbia: University of Missouri Press, 1981.

Rhodes, Joel P. *A Missouri Railroad Pioneer: The Life of Louis Houck*. Columbia: University of Missouri Press, 2008.

Roll, Jarod. *Spirit of Rebellion*. Urbana: University of Illinois Press, 2010.

Rothert, Otto A. *The Outlaws of Cave-in-Rock*. Cleveland: The Arthur H. Clark Co., 1924.

Saucier, Roger T. *Geomorphology and Quaternary Geologic History of the Lower Mississippi Valley*. Vicksburg: U.S. Army Corp of Engineers, Waterways Experiment Station, 1994.

Schultz, Christian. *Travels on an Inland Voyage*. New York: Isaac Riley, 1810.

Smith, B. Mildred. *Delmo: Threshold of Freedom*. Mount Ayr, IA: Paragon Publications, Inc., 2003.

Snow, Thad. *From Missouri*. Boston: Houghton Mifflin, 1954.

Stanford, Dennis J., and Bruce A. Bradley. *Across Atlantic Ice: The Origin of America's Clovis Culture*. Berkley: University of California Press, 2012.

Stepenoff, Bonnie. *Thad Snow A Life of Social Reform in the Missouri Bootheel*. Columbia: University of Missouri Press, 2003.

Stewart, David, and Ray Knox. *The Earthquake America Forgot*. Marble Hill, MO: Guttenberg-Richter Publications, 2000.

____, and ____. *The Earthquake that Never Went Away*. Marble Hill, MO: Guttenberg-Richter Publications, 1993.

Stewart, Richard. W. *American Military History, Vol. 2. The United States Army in a Global Era, 1917–2003*. Washington, D.C.: Center of Military History, United States Army, 2005.

Stoddard, Amos. *Sketches, Historical and Descriptive of Louisiana*. Philadelphia: Mathew Cary, 1812.

Stone, Barton W. *The Biography of Barton Warren Stone*. Cincinnati: J.A. & U.P. James, 1847. Reprinted in *The Cane Ridge Reader*, ed. Hoke Smith Dickinson and Robert Wesley Steffer. Cane Ridge Preservation Project, 2006.

Hugh Studabaker. *What They "Showed Me" in Southeast Missouri* (1913).

Valencius, Conevery Bolton. *The Lost History of the New Madrid Earthquakes*. Chicago: University of Chicago Press, 2013.

Wade, Ophelia R. *Deering Plantation*. Xlibrius Corporation, 1999.

Welky, David. *The Ohio-Mississippi Disaster of 1937: The Thousand-Year Flood*. Chicago: University of Chicago Press, 2011.

Wetmore, Alphonso. *Gazetteer of the State of Missouri*. St. Louis: C. Keemle, 1837. Reprint, New York: Arno Press, 1968.

Federal and State Government Publications

American State Papers vol. 3: 426–27.

Billington, David P., Donald C. Jackson, and Martin V. Melosi. *The History of Large Federal Dams: Planning, Design, and Construction in the Era of Big Dams*. Denver: U.S. Department of the Interior, Bureau of Reclamation.

Braile, Lawrence W., et al. "Tectonic Development of the New Madrid Seismic Zone." In *Proceedings of the Symposium on the New Madrid Seismic Zone*. USGS Open File Report 84-770, 1984, 204–33.

Clay, Floyd M. *A Century on the Mississippi: A History of the Memphis District U.S. Army Corps of Engineers 1876–1976*. Memphis: U.S. Army Corps of Engineers, 1976.

Draining and Leveeing Missouri Lowland. Jefferson City: Missouri Bureau of Labor Statistics, 1910.

Frankenfield, H.C. *Monthly Weather Review*, Supplement No. 29, "The Floods of 1927 in the Mississippi Basin." U.S. Department of Agriculture Weather Bureau. Washington, D.C.: United States Government Printing Office.

Fifteenth Census of the United States: 1930, *Drainage of Agricultural Lands*. Washington, D.C.: Government Printing Office, 1932.

Godsey, Roy. "Cotton in Missouri." *Monthly Bulletin of the Missouri State Board of Agriculture*, 20, no. 12 (December 1922), 2–23.

Grohskopf, John G. *Subsurface Geology of the Mississippi Embayment of Southeast Missouri*. Jefferson City, MO: Geological Survey and Water Resources, 1955.

Index to the Miscellaneous Documents of the House of Representatives for the Second Session of the Forty-Seventh Congress 1882-83. Washington, D.C.: Government Printing Office, 1883.

Journal of the Senate of the State of Missouri, First Session of the Fifteenth General Assembly, Appendix.

Kettleborough, Charles. *Drainage and Rec-*

lamation of Swamp and Overflowed Lands. Indianapolis: Indiana Bureau of Legislative Information, Bulletin No. 2, April 1914.

Kosar, Kevin R. "Disaster Response and Appointment of a Recovery Czar: The Executive Branch's Response to the Flood of 1927." Congressional Research Service, October 25, 2005.

Laws of the State of Missouri, Fourteenth General Assembly, 1847, 227–28.

Laws of the State of Missouri, Seventeenth General Assembly, 1853, 108–09.

Laws of Missouri of the State of Missouri, Eighteenth General Assembly, 1855, 154–58.

Laws of Missouri, Twenty-fourth General Assembly, 1868, 69–72.

Loans for the Relief of Drainage Districts, Hearings Before the Committee on Irrigation and Reclamation, House of Representatives, 70th Congress, 2nd Sess., January 29–February 1, 1929.

The Mississippi River Floods: Hearing before the Committee on Flood Control, House of Representatives, Sixty-Fourth Congress, First Session, March 1916.

The Mississippi River & Tributaries Project: Controlling the Project Flood. Mississippi River Commission Information Paper, 2007.

The Mississippi River & Tributaries Project: Birds Point–New Madrid Floodway. Mississippi River Commission Information Paper, n. d.

Meyer, Michael J. "An Evaluation of the North Lilbourn Group, Delmo Farm Labor Homes Project, on Route D in New Madrid County, Missouri." Missouri Department of Transportation, 2001.

Nolen, John H. *Swamp and Overflowed Lands and their Reclamation*, Report to the Forty-seventh Missouri General Assembly, January 1913.

Public Health Reports 38, no. 6, February 9, 1923.

Report of the National Conservation Commission, vol. 1. Washington, D.C.: Government Printing Office, 1909.

Report of Swampland Commissioners in Regards to Making Levees in Southeast Missouri, December 18, 1852.

Reynolds, S.P. "History of the Levees and Drainage in Southeast Missouri." In *Proceeding of the First Conference on Land Utilization*. Columbia: University of Missouri Agricultural Experiment Station Bulletin No. 323, 1933.

Sorenson, Clyde E. "The Boll Weevil in Missouri: History, Biology and Management." University of Missouri Agricultural Guide, G 4255, Columbia, 1995.

Stover, Carl W., and Jerry L. Coffman. *Seismicity of the United States, 1568–1989*. USGS Professional Paper 1527. Washington, D.C.: U.S. Government Printing Office, 1993.

Street, Ronald, and Otto Nuttli. "The Central Mississippi Valley Earthquakes of 1811–1812." In *Proceedings of the Symposium on the New Madrid Seismic Zone*, USGS Open File Report 84-770, 33–63.

U.S. House of Representatives, 20th Congress, 1st Sess. *Swamplands in Missouri and Arkansas*, January 13, 1846.

Wear, David N., and John G. Greis, eds. *Southern Forest Resource Management*, Gen. Tech. Rep. SRS-53. Asheville, NC: U.S. Department of Agriculture, Forest Service, Southern Research Station.

Wooten, H.H., and L.A. Jones. "The History of Drainage Enterprises." In *The Yearbook of Agriculture, 1955*. Washington, D.C.: U.S. Department of Agriculture, 84th Congress, 1st Sess. House Document No. 32, 478–98.

Periodical Articles

Barry, John M. "After the Deluge." *Smithsonian Magazine*, November 2005, 3. http://www.smithsonianmag.com/history-archaeology/pom.html?c=y&page=3 (accessed 7/10/15).

Belfrage, Cedric. "Cotton-Patch Moses." *Harpers Magazine* 36 (November 1948): 94–103.

Blum, M.D., et al. "Late Pleistocene Evolution of the Lower Mississippi River Valley, Southern Missouri to Arkansas." *Geological Society of America Bulletin* 112, no. 2 (February 2000): 221–35.

Blumhofer, Edith. "Azusa Street Revival." *Christianity Today* (March 7, 2006): 20–22.

Bradley, Bruce, and Dennis Stanford. "The North Atlantic Ice-edge Corridor: A Possible Palaeolithic Route to the New

World." *World Archaeology* 36, no. 4 (2004): 459–78.

Brassieur, Ray "From Two Mules to Twelve-Row Equipment: An Oral History Interview with Maxwell Williams Bootheel Farm Manager." *Missouri Historical Review* 91, no. 1 (October 1996): 52–85.

Burns, B.F. "Construction Methods and Machinery for Headwater Diversion System of Little River Drainage District." *Engineering and Contracting* 48, no. 3 (July 18, 1947): 47–49.

Cobb, Charles R. "An Appraisal of the Role of Mill Creek Chert Hoes in Mississippian Exchange Systems." *Southern Archaeology* 8, no. 2 (Winter 1989): 79–92.

Cut-Over Lands 2, no. 2 (May 1919).

Dalton, John Hall, Jr. "Dunklin County, Charles P. Chouteau, and the Courtship of the Iron Horse." *Missouri Historical Review* 82, no. 1 (October 1987): 71–96.

Gadd, F.E. "Utilization of Southeast Missouri Lands." *Harvester World* 3, no. 11 (November 1912): 23.

Gilbert, P.E. "Why and How." *Harvester World* 3, no. 11 (November 1912): 24.

Goebel, Ted, et al. "The Late Pleistocene Dispersal of Modern Humans in the Americas," *Science* 319 (2008): 1497–1502.

Greene, Lorenzo J. "Lincoln University's Involvement with the Sharecropper Demonstration in Southeast Missouri, 1939–1940." *Missouri Historical Review* 82, no. 1 (October 1987): 24–50.

Guccione, Margaret J., Roy B. van Arsdale, and Lynne H. Hehr. "Origin and Age of the Manila High and Associated Big Lake 'Sunklands' in the New Madrid Seismic Zone, Northeastern Arkansas." *Geological Society of America Bulletin* 112, no. 4 (April 2000): 579–90.

Grayson, Donald K., and David J. Meltzer. "Clovis Hunting and Large Mammal Extinction: A Critical Review of the Evidence." *Journal of World Prehistory* 16, no. 4 (December 2002): 313–59.

Heincke, Craig and Wayne A. Grove. "'Machinery Has Completely Taken Over': The Diffusion of the Mechanical Cotton Picker, 1949–1964." *The Journal of Interdisciplinary History* 39, no. 1 (Summer 2008): 65–96.

Johnston, Arch, and Eugene S. Schweig. "The Enigma of the New Madrid Earthquakes of 1811–1812." *The Annual Review of Earth and Planetary Sciences* 24 (1996): 339–84.

Kanon, Tom. "'Scared from Their Sins for a Season': The Religious Ramifications of the New Madrid Earthquakes, 1811–1812." *Ohio Valley History* 5, no. 2 (Summer 2005): 21–38.

King, James E., and William H. Allen, Jr. "A Holocene Vegetation Record from the Mississippi River Valley, Southeastern Missouri," *Quaternary Research* 8 (1977): 307–23.

Li, Yong, et al. "Evidence for Large Prehistoric Earthquakes in the Northern New Madrid Seismic Zone, Central United States." *Seismological Research Letters* 69, no. 3 (May/June 1998): 270–76.

Lueckenhoff, Bill. "The Story of a Leaky Lake." *Land and Water Magazine* 47, no. 1 (2003), http://www.landandwater.com/features/vol47no1/vol47no1_1.html (accessed 7/27/16).

Mainfort, Robert C., Jr. "Woodland Period." *Encyclopedia of Arkansas History & Culture*, http://encyclopediaofarkansas.net/encyclopedia/entry-detail.aspx?entryID=543 (accessed 3/25/14).

McGee, Gary B. "William J. Seymour and the Azusa Street Revival." *Enrichment Journal* (Fall 1999), http://enrichmentjournal.ag.org/199904/026_azusa.cfm (accessed 7/7/16).

——. "The Revival Legacy of Charles F. Parham." *Enrichment Journal* (Summer 1999), http://enrichmentjournal.ag.org/199903/068_tongues.cfm (accessed 7/7/16).

Mississippi Valley Magazine, March 1920.

Mitchell, Guy Elliott. "To Farm America's Swamps." *The American Review of Reviews* XXXVII, no. 4 (April 1908): 434–49.

Morrow, Julie. "The Paleoindian Period in Arkansas." *Arkansas Prehistory and History in Review* 331 (July/August 2006): 3–9.

Ogilvie, Leon Parker. "Governmental Efforts at Reclamation in the Southeast Missouri Lowlands." *Missouri Historical Review* 64, no. 2 (January 1970): 150–76.

——. "Populism and Socialism in the Southeast Missouri Lowlands." *Missouri Historical Review* 65, no. 2 (January 1971): 159–83.

Page, T.E. "History of the Pole Road." In *History of Dunklin County*, vol. 1, 15–19. Kennett, MO: Dunklin County Historical Society, 1951.

Rittenour, Tammy M., et al. "Fluvial Evolution of the Lower Mississippi River Valley During the Last 100 K.Y. Glacial Cycle: Response to Glaciation and Sea-Level Change." *Geological Society of America Bulletin* 119, no. 5–6 (2007): 586–608.

———. "An Optical Age Chronology of the Late Pleistocene Fluvial Deposits in the Northern Lower Mississippi Valley." *Quaternary Science Review* 22 (2003): 1105–10.

"River Diversion and Flood Control in Missouri." *Engineering News* 76, no. 8 (August 24, 1916): 342–45.

Robbins, Ruby Matson. "The Missouri Reader: Americans in the Valley." *Missouri Historical Review* v. 45, no. 3 (April 1951) 278–87.

Roll, Jarod H. "Gideon's Band: From Socialism to Vigilantism in Southeast Missouri." *Labor History* 43, no. 4 (October 2002): 483–503.

———. "'Out Yonder on the Road': Working Class Self-Representation and the 1939 Roadside Demonstration in Southeast Missouri." *Southern Spaces*, March 16, 2010, www.southernspaces.org.

———. "From Revolution to Reaction: Early Pentecostalism, radicalism, and Race in Southeast Missouri." *Radical History Review* 90 (August 2004): 5–29.

Rust, John. "The Origin and Development of the Cotton Picker." *West Tennessee Historical Society Papers* 7 (1953), 38–56.

Sarvis, Will. "Black Electoral Power in the Missouri Bootheel, 1920s–1960s." *Missouri Historical Review* 95, no. 2 (January 2001), 182–202.

Savelle, Max. "The Founding of New Madrid, Missouri." *Mississippi Valley Historical Review* 19, no. 1 (June 1932): 30–56.

Schroeder, Rebecca B., and Donald Lance. "John L. Handcox, 'The Sharecropper's Troubadour.'" *Missouri Folklore Society Journal* 8–9 (1989–1987): 123–42.

Shaw, John. "New Madrid Earthquakes." Account of Co. John Shaw. *Missouri Historical Review* 6 (1912), 91–92.

Shoemaker, Floyd C. "Kennett: Center of a Land Reborn in Missouri's Valley of the Nile." *Missouri Historical Review* 52 no. 1 (January 1958): 99–110.

———. "New Madrid, Mother of Southeast Missouri." *Missouri Historical Review* 49, no. 4 (July 1955): 317–27.

Stepenoff, Bonnie. "'The Last Tree Cut Down': The End of the Bootheel Frontier, 1880–1940." *Missouri Historical Review* 90, no. 1 (October 1995): 61–78.

Stivers, Charles P. "Digging 624 Miles of Drainage Ditches." *The Contractor* 20, no. 11 (December 1, 1914): 31–33; 49–51.

Street, James H. "Mechanizing the Cotton Harvest." *Agricultural History* 31, no. 1 (January 1957): 12–22.

Towell, William E. "Trees of Dunklin County." In *Dunklin County Historical Society*, vol. 1. Kennett, MO: Thrower Printing Co., 1951.

Tuttle, Martitia P., et al. "The Earthquake Potential of the New Madrid Seismic Zone." *Bulletin of the Seismological Society of America* 92, no. 6 (2002): 2080–89.

Van Arsdale, Roy B., et al. "The Origin of Crowley's Ridge, Northeastern Arkansas: Erosional Remnant or Tectonic Uplift?" *Bulletin of the Seismological Society of America* 85, no. 4 (August 1995): 963–85.

Wallace's Farmer, March 20, 1925.

Walker, Phillip L., et al. "The Causes of Porotic Hyperostosis and Cribra Orbitalia: A Reappraisal of the Iron-Deficiency Anemia Hypothesis." *American Journal of Physical Anthropology* 139 (2009): 109–25.

Wyllie, Irvin G. "Race and Class Conflict on Missouri's Cotton Frontier." *The Journal of Southern History* 20, no. 2 (May 1954): 183–96.

Dissertations

Braile, William James. "Crustal Structure of the Northern Mississippi Embayment and Reelfoot Rift From Seismic Refraction/Reflection Profiling." Master's thesis, University of Texas, El Paso, 1993.

Doherty, William T. "The Missouri Interests of Louis Houck." Ph.D. diss., University of Missouri, 1951.

Grove, Jama McMurtery. "Uneasy Waters: The Night Riders at Reelfoot Lake, Tennessee, 1908." Master's thesis, East Tennessee State University, 2012.

McDowell, Gary Lane. "Local Agencies

and Land Development by Drainage: The Case of 'Swampeast' Missouri." Ph. D. diss. Columbia University, 1965.

Ogilive, Leon. "The Development of Southeast Missouri Lowlands." Ph.D. diss., University of Missouri, 1967.

Newspapers

Christian Evangel, Findlay, Ohio
Daily Republican, Cape Girardeau
Dunklin Democrat, Kennett
Hayti Herald, Hayti
Justice (Kennett and Gibson)
Portageville Missourian, Portageville
St. Louis Republic, St. Louis
Scott County Kicker, Benton
Sikeston Standard, Sikeston
Sikeston Herald, Sikeston
Southeast Missourian, Cape Girardeau
Weekly Republican, Cape Girardeau
The Weekly Tribune and the Cape County Herald, Cape Girardeau
Word and Witness, Malvern, Arkansas

Collections

Himmelberger-Harrison Lumber Company Records, Special Collections and Archives, Kent Library, Southeast Missouri State University, Cape Girardeau.

Julien Friant Papers, Special Collections and Archives, Kent Library, Southeast Missouri State University, Cape Girardeau.

Little River Drainage District Records, Special Collections and Archives, Kent Library, Southeast Missouri State University, Cape Girardeau.

Otto Kochtitzky Papers, Missouri Historical Society, St. Louis.

Websites

Anderson, Jacob E. "Eighty Years of Transportation Progress: A History of the St. Louis Southwestern Railway." *Cotton Belt News*, October 1957, http://www.ttarchive.com/Library/Articles/Cotton-Belt_80-Years-Progress.html#3 (accessed 7/27/16).

Arkansas Earthquake Center, University of Arkansas. "The Reelfoot Rift," http://quake.ualr.edu/public/reelfoot.htm (accessed 7/26/16).

Central Arkansas Library System. *Encyclopedia of Arkansas History and Culture*. "Quapaw," Joseph Key. http:www.encyclopediaofarkansas.net (accessed 6/21/14).

Centers for Disease Control. "The History of Malaria, an Ancient Disease." http://www.cdc.gov/malaria/about/history (accessed 6/23/15).

"Historic Missourians." shsmo.orghistoricmissourians/name/o/ohare (accessed 5/15/16).

"Influenza Pandemic of 1918." http://www.flu.gov/pandemic/history/1918/your_state/southwest/missouri/index.html (accessed 6/23/15).

"1918 Flu Pandemic." http://www.history.com/topics/1918-flu-pandemic (accessed 6/23/15).

"North American During the Last 150,000 Years." Comp. Jonathan Adams, Oak Ridge National Laboratory, http://www.esd.ornl.gov/projects/qen/nercNORTH AMERICA.html (accessed 1/18/14).

Rosenbaum, Judith. "Rose Pastor Stokes." *Jewish Women: A Comprehensive Historical Encyclopedia*, March 20, 2000, Jewish Women's Archive, http://jwa.org/encyclopedia/article/stokes-rose-pastor (accessed 5/25/16).

"Tall Timber." City of Poplar Bluff Historical Preservation Commission, http://www.butlercountyhistory.org/poplarbluff/html/timber.html (accessed 6/23/15).

"Trends in U.S. Agriculture." U.S. Department of Agriculture, National Agricultural Statistics Service, http://www.nass.usda.gov/Publications/Trends_in_U.S._Agriculture/Land_Values/index.asp (accessed 6/23/15).

Index

Adkisson, M.B. 174, 175
Advance 14, 173
Advance Lowland 11, 12, 14
adzes 18
African American population 169
Agricultural Adjustment Administration (AAA) 185, 186, 189, 191
Agricultural Stabilization and Conservation Service (ASCS) 204
Alabama 88, 166, 168, 208, 214
alfalfa 109, 160, 161, 163, 166
Alford, John M. 200
Allen, Thomas 69
Allis-Chalmers 205, 208
Alton, Illinois 52
American Steel Dredge Co. 129
American Sugar Refining Co. 79, 83, 143
Anderson, M.S. 80
Anderson, William P. 80
Anderson-Poorman Cooperage 80
L'Anse a la Graisse 29, 30, 31
Arbyrd, Missouri 74, 153
Archaic period 17
Archive of Folksong 188
Armstrong, Sam 192
Arrow Rock, Missouri 85
ash 78, 82, 102
Ash Hills 7
Assemblies of God 181, 182
Atlantic Ocean 8
atlatl 18, 20
Azusa Street Revival 180, 181, 228, 234, 235

Baasch, Hans 191
Baker, Charles B. 163
Baker, W.H. 175

bald cypress (cypress) 2, 5, 13, 50, 78, 82, 90
Bankhead Cotton Control Act 189
bannerstones 18
Barnes, Seth 76
Barry, John M. 138, 139
Bastianelli, Amico 86
Bayou Portage 48
beateau 36
Beavers, L.L. 145
Beckwith's Fort 23
Bedinger, Daniel 42
Beis, Albert 194, 229
Bell, John 62
Bell City-Oran Gap 11
Ben Pearson, Inc. 207, 208, 209
Benton, Thomas Hart 90
Benton, Missouri 19, 62, 68, 92
Benton County, Missouri 19
Benton Hills 7, 12, 58
Berry, Hiram M. 206
Berry site 25
Big Lake 38, 46, 47, 108, 123
Biggins, Francis 68
Billington, David P. 97
Bird's Point 38, 68, 154, 157
Birds Point–New Madrid Floodway 140, 141, 152, 153, 155, 157, 158
Bismarck, Missouri 69
bison 14, 16, 17, 29
Black River 12
Black Swamp 101
Blaine, E.S. 126
Blanton, C.L. 194
Blazer, J.M. 109
Bliss, W.K. 145
Bliss Committee 145

239

Index

Block Hole 123, 124
Bloomfield, Missouri 27, 62, 64, 92, 94
Blue, Norman D. 160
Blyth, Wyllis 150
Blytheville, Arkansas 44, 47
board of supervisors (Little River Drainage District) 124–126, 131, 133, 141, 144–149, 212, 213
Board of Swampland Commissioners 92
Bock, H. Riley 212
Boekerton, Missouri 48, 58
boll weevil 167–169, 210, 214
bond sales 125, 126
bondholders' protective committee 145, 147–149
boreal forests 13, 14, 16
Boston, Massachusetts 39, 132, 145
Bowman, Arthur C. 161
Boyle, Blair 126
Boynton, C.A. 74, 79, 80
Bradbury, John 40
Bradley, Bruce 16
Bragg City, Missouri 185
bridges 53, 67, 69, 73, 111, 117, 151
Briney, Kip 204
Brinkley, Arkansas 187
Brooklyn Cooperage 79, 83
Brooks, James F. 78
Brooks site 25, 26
Brown, Clarence 102
Brown, Dwight H. 160
Brown, Harry 203
Brownwood, Missouri 73
Bruton, C.F. 161, 162
Bryan, Eliza 40
Bucyrus 127
Buffington, Missouri 81
Burdick, R.D. 163
Burkett site 19
Burns, B.F. 127
Butler County 7, 23, 59, 62, 83, 111, 118, 125, 143, 197, 199, 213
Byrd, A.R. 74, 79

Cagle Lake site 165
Cahokia 22
Cairo, Illinois 11, 52, 63, 77, 141, 152–154, 157, 158
Cairo and Fulton Railroad 68, 69
Cairo Lowland 21, 24
Callaway County, Missouri 62
Campbell, Angus 215
Campbell, Missouri 12, 65, 74, 75, 136, 174
Campbell site 25
Canada 13, 15, 29, 36
Canalou, Missouri 160, 181
Cane Ridge, Kentucky 51, 181

Caney Creek 134
canoe 45, 58
Cape Girardeau, Missouri 2, 27, 28, 34, 35, 58–60, 63, 73–75, 91, 93, 94, 109, 111, 114–118, 123, 126, 127, 132, 140, 145, 146, 160, 161
Cape Girardeau and State Line Railroad 72
Cardwell, Missouri 153, 166, 179, 181, 182
Caruthersville, Missouri 29, 44, 62, 73, 74, 76, 80, 160, 171, 172
Cash, Tom 203
Casqui 26
Castor River 12, 27, 60, 94, 122, 123, 133
Cave-In-Rock 37
Caverno, Xenophon 160
celts 18, 24
Centennial Road Law 77
Cerrè, Gabriel 29
C.F. Bruton Real Estate and Investment Co. 162
Chalk Bluff 64–66
Charleston, Missouri 52, 62, 69, 155, 160, 195, 196
Charleston, South Carolina 39
Charleston Alluvial Fan 7, 12
Chepoosa River 29
chert 24
Chicago, Illinois 99, 101, 126, 145, 210
Chicago Sanitary and Ship Canal 101, 122
Chickasaw Tribe 26
chill tonic 87
Chilliticaux, Chief 27
Chouteau, Charles P. 70
Civil War 60, 62, 63, 66–70, 104, 184, 202
Civilian Conservation Corps (CCC) 151, 198
Clark, George B. 70, 101
Clark, Henry E. 67
Clarkton, Missouri 62, 63, 67, 74, 75, 121, 174
Clay, Henry 57
Clay County, Missouri 62
Clovis (culture, sites, points) 15–17
C.M. Smith Brothers Land Co. 165
Cobb, Budge 153
Cobb, Charles R. 24
Coker Landing 121
Columbus, Kentucky 63
Commerce, Missouri 5, 38, 62, 74
Common Pleas Court 116
Congress of Industrial Organizations (CIO) 190, 194, 197
Cook, Fannie 197
Cook, Valentine 51
Coolidge, Calvin 137
Cooper County, Missouri 62

cooperage 80, 82, 83
corn 5, 19, 23–25, 33, 35, 49, 50, 59–61, 109, 148, 160–163, 165, 166, 185, 195, 196, 215
Corps of Engineers 140, 141, 152, 154, 157, 213
cotton 3, 5, 35, 50, 59–61, 67, 70, 71, 89, 100, 146, 157, 161, 162, 163, 166–170, 172, 173, 182–187, 195, 198, 199, 204, 206, 214, 215
Cotton Belt Railroad 71, 74, 76, 111, 160
cotton gins 50, 166, 170
cottonwood 78, 82
cowpeas 161
Crabtree, Bill 84
Cracraft, William Cooper 118
Cramer, Zadok 41
Cretaceous Period 5, 8
Crooked Creek 123
Cropperville 197, 199
Crowley's Ridge 5, 7, 9, 11–13, 38, 58, 64, 68, 94, 108
Cuming, Fortescue 29, 34
Current River 73
cut-over land 147, 161–164, 166
cypress 2, 5, 13, 14, 50, 78, 82, 90

Dalton points 17
Darrow, Clarence 177, 186
Davis, John 181
Davis, Mary Smith 85
Dawson, Robert D. 56
Dearmont, Russell L. 26
Debs, Eugene 177, 178
deer 14, 17, 18, 24, 60
Deering, William 81
Deering, Missouri 74, 76, 79, 81, 82, 84, 115, 163
Deering Plantation 163
Deering Southwestern Railroad 76
Delassus, Dehault Charles 29, 33
Delaware Tribe 26, 27, 29, 31
Delmo Housing Corporation 200, 201
Delmo Labor Homes 200
Delta, Missouri 73, 126, 151
Delta Experiment Station 206
Democratic Party 177, 182, 202
dendrochronology 52
Dennison, John W. 145
Dennison Agreement 146, 148
Denton Mounds 25
Department of Agriculture 100, 122, 124, 167, 185, 199
Department of the Interior 100
de Soto 26
Detroit 36, 210
Dexter, Missouri 7, 160
Dillard, A.N. 45
dipper dredge 94, 96, 97, 104, 126, 129, 213

disfranchisement 202
diversion channel 2, 114, 115, 124–128, 133, 134, 136, 140
Dorena, Missouri 134, 137, 196
Douglass, James P. 70
Douglass, Robert Sydney 66
Dow, Lorenzo 40
Downing, Vic 203
dragline 126, 127
drainage districts 2, 95, 96, 98, 103–105, 107, 108, 117, 142, 143, 148, 149, 151, 166
drainage law 95, 103; Section 5538 113, 116, 117
drainage tax 2, 70, 77, 95, 105, 116–118, 126, 136, 140, 142, 143, 147, 148, 150, 151, 163, 169, 186
Dunklin and Pemiscot Plank road Co. 68
Dunklin County 7, 19, 21, 58, 60, 61–63, 67, 68, 69, 70, 79, 80, 85, 100, 110, 121, 153, 159, 163, 166, 169, 170, 174, 178, 179, 181, 182, 203, 214
Dunn, J.E. 121

earthquakes 1, 8, 9, 29, 34, 38, 39, 40–43, 45–56
East, Clay 157, 186, 187, 189
Eastern Lowlands 12, 13
El Camino Real 33
Elder, John 175–176
elk 14, 91
Elk Chute Drainage District 143, 151
Elliott, C.G. 124
elm 82, 102
Emergency Farm Mortgage Act of 1933 149
England 28, 82
Enterprise, Alabama 168
Ethridge, Robbie 22
Evans, James 56
Everglades 101

Fairbanks dredges 129
farm prices 135, 146, 215
Farm Security Administration (FSA) 191, 198, 199, 200
Farmall 205, 208
Fieser, James L. 137
Filetti, Raimondo 86
Filley, John V. 111
fir 13, 16
Fisk, H.N. 10
fissures 40, 41, 43, 44, 45
flat-faced bear 14
Fletcher, James 42
Flint, Timothy 50
floating dredge 131
Flood Control Act 1928 140, 141
flood, 1927 139, 140, 152, 155, 156

flood, 1937 152, 155, 156, 158
Foard, A.I. 160, 161
Folk, Joseph Wingate 109
Folsom points 17
Ford, Henry 205
Fordyce, S.W. 101
Fort Céleste 32
Fort Pit 30
Fort San Fernando 33
Foucher, Pierre 32
France 15, 28, 33, 34, 82, 90
Francis, David R. 99
Franklin, J.E. 74
Friant, Julien 145, 146, 148–150, 162, 194, 195
Frisco Railroad 74–76, 111, 160
Frissell, N.C. 118, 120, 122
Fuller, Myron L. 43–46
Fulton, Robert 54
Fulton, Arkansas 58, 59

Gamble, Dick 30
Gardoqui, Diego de 30–32
Gatewood, James E. 162
Gayoso, Missouri 38, 62
Gazetteer of Missouri 59, 93
General American Life Insurance Co. 185
General Land Office 21, 91, 93
Gerlach, Russel L. 59
Gibbs, W.D. 145
Gibson, Missouri 137, 180
Gideon, Frank E. 80
Gideon, Missouri 74, 75, 89, 80, 163, 174, 185
Gideon and North Island Railroad 75
Gideon-Anderson Lumber Co. 3, 74, 75, 80, 174, 185
Gideon Cooperage 80
Gizzard Creek 123
glaciers, glaciations 9, 11, 15
Glover, Griff 117
Golf, J.N. 182
Gould, Jay 69, 71–73
granite 9
Grant, U.S. 63
Grassi, Giovanni 86
Gray, Dinah 50
Grayson, Donald K. 16
Greasy Bend 29
Greasy Cove 29
Great Depression 3, 135, 144, 145, 185, 206, 210, 214
Great Migration 210
Great Revival 51
Greene, Lorenzo J. 196, 197
ground sloth 14
Gulf of Mexico 8, 26, 28
gum 2, 13, 78, 82, 102

Hadley, Herbert S. 172
Hafner, Phil 176, 177, 179, 182
Haldeman-Julius, Emmanuel 186
Halls, Tennessee 186
Handcox, John L. 187–190
Hanford, George S. 118
Haring, Peter Paul 206
Harty, A. L 117, 161
Harviell, Missouri 197
hauling voters 203
Hawes, Harry 141
Helena, Arkansas 9
Hemphill, J.A. 79, 80, 82
Henderson, Charles W. 118
Henderson, Howard 126
hickory 13, 16, 19, 76, 78, 82
Hickory Landing, Missouri 82
Hidinger, L.L. 125, 133
Higgins, Walter 181
Himmelberger, Issac 81
Himmelberger, John H. 109, 117, 144, 148
Himmelberger-Harrison Land and Investment Co. 146, 162
Himmelberger-Harrison Land Selling Co. 107, 162
Himmelberger-Harrison Lumber Co. 75, 80, 81, 83, 108, 109, 110, 162
Himmelberger-Luce Lumber Co. 75
Hines, Thomas D. 116
Hoecake Site 21
Holocene Epoch 1, 12, 17
honey locust 78
Hoover, Herbert 137, 139, 149
Hornersville, Missouri 58, 62, 76, 153
horses 14, 49, 59, 60, 63, 79, 154, 173, 183, 204, 205
Houck, Giboney 116, 117
Houck, Louis 32, 72, 78, 106, 113, 114, 126, 159, 213
houseboat 130, 131
Howard County, Missouri 62
Hudson River 54
Hughes, Charles Evan 117
Hunter, Hal, Jr. 204
Hunter, Joseph 105
hunting clubs 2, 76
hypsithermal 13, 17, 18

Illinoian glacial period 11, 12
Independent State of Dunklin 63
Indiana Project 30
influenza 131–133, 155
International Harvester 76, 79, 82, 163, 205, 208, 209
International Health Board 88
Inter-River Drainage District 141
Island No. 10 42, 63, 64

Jackson, Claiborne 63
Jackson, Donald C. 97
Jadwin, Edgar 141
Jadwin Plan 141, 157
James, Edwin 35
Jefferson County, Missouri 16
Jenkins Basin 134
John Deere 205, 208, 209
Johnson, Josephine 196
Johnston, Arch 39
Joilet, Louis 26
Jones, P.C. 145
Jones, R. Irl 160

Kankakee 137, 138
Kanon, Tom 50–52
Kansas 180, 186
Kansas City 99, 178, 180
Kansas Tribe 26
keelboats 36
Kelley, J.E. 21
Kennett, Missouri 27, 44, 46, 47, 62, 68
Kennett and Osceola Railroad 74
Kennett and Southern Railroad 73, 78
Kennett Justice 178, 179, 182
Kennett-Malden Prairie 6, 7, 11, 12, 58, 159
Kentucky 30, 32, 33, 51, 52, 57, 59, 62, 63, 68, 84, 152, 156, 164, 166, 173, 181, 195, 214
Kercheval, Roy 150
Kerfoot, A.J. 73
Kersey site 21
Kettleborough, Charles 103
Kimmswick Bone Bed 16
King, Martin Luther, Jr. 198
Kitchen, Solomon G. 67
Knox, Ray 43
Kochtitzky, Oscar 70, 101
Kochtitzky, Otto 3, 70, 72, 78, 101, 103, 105, 108, 109, 113, 115, 118, 120, 125, 141, 160

Laclede County, Missouri 104
Lafayette County, Missouri 62
La Forge, Peter 29, 33, 77
La Forge Project 191–193
Lake Nicomy 47, 74
land sales 58, 91, 126, 162
land tenancy 4, 164, 185
landslides 43
La Salle 28
Lasswell, W.D. 75, 79
Laurentide ice sheet 12, 13
Laveran, Charles 86
Lawrence, Yewell 204
Leachville, Arkansas 74
Lilbourn, Missouri 23, 26, 200
Lincoln, Abraham 62
Lincoln University 196, 197

Lindus Lumber Company 79
liquefaction 43, 52, 53
Little Prairie, Missouri 29, 35, 37, 42, 43, 47, 56
Little River 12, 24, 38, 46, 47, 48, 58, 60, 67, 68, 70, 76, 82, 91, 92, 94, 96, 101, 102, 104, 106, 108, 109, 119, 120
Little River Conservation Area 44
Little River Corporation 145, 150
Little River Drainage District 2, 3, 46, 47, 70, 56, 96, 98, 105, 172, 185, 195, 212, 213, 214, 215; bond sales 126, 127; construction 126, 127–131, 133, 134; default on bond payments 145; incorporation and objections 111, 113–117; planning 121–125; refinancing 146, 148–151
Little River Lowland 21
Little River Valley 94, 106, 108, 109, 119, 120, 122, 134, 159, 214
Little River Valley and Arkansas Railroad 70, 101, 104
Livington, Robert 54
llama 14
locust 78
log skidders 85, 127
Logan, E.A. 205
Logansport, Indiana 81
logging 79, 80, 83, 84, 85, 162, 164, 213
London 36, 86, 186
Long, Stephen 35
Lorimer, Louis 27
Louis XIV 28
Louisiana Purchase 29, 34, 57, 90
Luce, Charles L. 101, 102
Luce Dredging Co. 101

Madison, James 56
Mainfort, Robert C. 20
malaria 85, 86, 87, 88, 89, 91, 166
Malden, Missouri 68, 70, 74–77, 104, 166
mammoth 14, 15
Manila, Arkansas 46, 123
maple 78, 82
Marion Steam Shovel Co. 127
Marked Tree, Arkansas 46
Markham, Edward 158
Marquette, Jacques 26, 28
Marston, Missouri 76, 80
Mason, Samuel 37
Masters, Betsy 41
mastodon 14–16
Mastodon State Historic Site 16
Matthews, A.J. 117
Matthews, C.D. 165
Matthews, Edward C. III 83, 164
Matthews, Jack 105
Mayes, Jewell 205

McCarty, Eugene S. 73
McCay, Robert 29
McCormick Harvesting Machine Company 81
McCoy, Robert 29
McDowell, Gary Lane 1
McGee, J.D. 145
McKay, A.J. 69
McReynolds, M. 121
Meade, Daniel 122
Means, Lewis 193, 194
mechanical cotton pickers 185, 191, 203, 205–211
Meentemeyer, F. 80
Mehlville Ridge 7, 11
melons 161
Melosi, Martin V. 97
Meltzer, David J. 16
Mendenhall Chill and Fever Tonic 87
Mendenhall Medicine Company 87
Mingo Swamp 94
Miró 30–32
Miskel, Riley 175
Miskel, Tude 175
Mississippi County 19, 21–22, 23, 45, 61, 62, 84, 141, 146, 153, 165, 166, 188–190, 195, 198, 200
Mississippi Embayment 6, 8, 9, 43
Mississippi River 1, 2, 5, 9, 11–13, 19, 22, 25–28, 30, 32, 33, 35, 37, 41, 43, 47, 48, 51, 54, 57, 58, 59, 60, 62–64, 67, 68, 71, 74, 77, 84, 91–95, 101, 114, 122–124, 126, 134, 137–141, 144, 152, 158, 162, 167, 198, 213
Mississippi River Commission 95, 124, 126, 140, 141
Mississippi Valley 7, 9, 10, 11, 12, 13, 14, 18, 21, 26, 50, 101, 136, 145, 152, 160, 161, 163
Mississippi Valley Association 163
Mississippian Cultural Period 21, 22, 24
Missouri and Arkansas Railroad 74
Missouri Compromise 57
Missouri Highway Patrol 193, 197
Missouri Historical Society 3
Missouri House of Representatives 117, 203
Missouri Immigration Society 106, 159
Missouri Pacific Railroad 69, 159
Missouri River 26, 58
Missouri State Board of Health 88, 89
Missouri State Life Insurance Co. 163
Missouri Supreme Court 70, 113, 116, 117
Mitchell, Guy Elliott 99
Mitchell, H.L. 157, 186, 189, 190, 102, 201
Monroe, James 57
Morehouse, Missouri 74, 75, 79, 81, 83, 117, 126, 150, 200, 212
Morehouse Braid Belt 11
Morehouse Lowland 11, 12, 14

Morgan, Arthur E. 122, 124, 125
Morgan, George 30, 31, 32
Morley, Missouri 74, 75, 178
Morrow, Julie 16
Morse, Dan 17, 19, 24
Morse, Phyllis 17, 19, 24
Morton, Robert 139
mosquitoes 86, 120, 129, 166
Moss, T.J. 73, 79
mounds, burial 19, 20, 21, 21, 22, 23, 25, 61
mudboat 85
mules 59, 63, 79, 84, 85, 94, 183, 204, 205
Mulholland, William 126
Mumma, M.V. 80
Murphy site 25

Nashville, Tennessee 42
Nashville Dome 8
National Conservation Commission 98, 99
National Defense Act of 1916 130
National Drainage Association 145, 146, 149
National Drainage Congress 99, 100
national drainage movement 96, 100, 101
National Irrigation Congress 99
National Urban League 156
Netherlands, Wood 145
New Era School of Social Action and Prophetic Religion 190
New Madrid 1, 6, 8, 9, 21, 23, 28, 29, 30, 31, 32, 33, 34, 35, 36, 37, 38, 39, 40, 41, 42, 47, 49, 50, 51, 55, 56, 58, 60, 63, 64, 67, 68, 70, 77, 91, 137, 175
New Madrid & Stoddard Canal Co. 92
New Madrid & Stoddard Plank Road Co. 68
New Madrid & West Prairie Road Co. 68, 70
New Madrid County 91, 101, 102, 104, 110, 111, 169, 172, 174, 181, 193, 196, 200, 204
New Madrid earthquakes 34, 39, 41, 43, 45, 47, 49–55
New Madrid Plank Road Company 68
New Madrid Seismic Zone 1, 8, 9, 47, 52–54
New Orleans 29, 30, 31, 32, 35, 36, 37, 39, 54, 55, 99, 103, 137
New Orleans (steamboat) 55
Newcomb, Harry V. 126
Newcomb, Harry V. 126
night riders 172, 173, 174, 175, 176, 179
Norfolk, Virginia 39
North Carolina 104, 168

oak 2, 13, 16, 45, 78, 82, 102
O'Bannon, W.N.O. 68
Obion County, Tennessee 47, 173
O'Brien, Michael J. 17, 18, 20, 21, 24, 25, 26

O'Brien, William A. 125
Ogilvie, Leon 142, 182
O'Hare, Kate Richards 178
Ohio River 9, 10, 11, 13, 26, 30, 31, 37, 55, 59, 152, 157
Old Field Swamp 14
Old Varney River site 19, 21
Oliver, R.B. 109, 117, 118, 195
Oliver law firm 111, 115, 124, 150, 213
Omaha Tribe 26
Osage Tribe 26
Osawatomie, Kansas 98
Osborn, John 175
oxen 14, 79, 82, 84, 85
Ozarks 1, 2, 8, 27, 58, 108, 23, 164, 180, 214

Packard, George 145
Paducah, Kentucky 52, 152, 156, 157
Page, John W. 126
Painton, Missouri 134
PaleoIndian period 17
Paleozoic Era 8
Panama Canal 86, 101, 122, 126, 127, 213
Paragould, Arkansas 71
Paramore, J.W. 70, 71, 101
Parham, Charles F. 180, 181
Parker, Harry 196
Parker, Nathan 93
Parkin Site 26
Pascola, Missouri: arch 8; site 19
Paw Paw Junction 76, 77
pecans 161
Pemiscot Bayou 24, 25
Pemiscot County 19, 21, 38, 61, 62, 74, 80, 94, 110, 118, 166, 169, 172, 174, 200, 203, 204
Pemiscot Railroad Company 74
Pemiscot Southern Railroad 74
Penick, James L. 52
Pennsylvania 16, 32
Pentecostalism 176, 181, 182
Philadelphia 32, 64
Pidgeon, Richard 145
Pilot Knob, Missouri 68, 69
pine 13
Pine Bluff, Arkansas 208
Pinhook, Missouri 190
Pinson Mounds 20
pirogues 36, 38
plan of drainage 11, 116
plank roads 67, 68
Pleistocene Epoch 1, 6, 9, 12, 14, 15, 16, 17
Point Pleasant 30, 37, 67, 92, 95
Point Pleasant and Dunklin County Road Company 67
Pollard, James M. 102
Ponca Tribe 26

Pontiac's War 30
Poplar Bluff, Missouri 62, 69, 79, 83, 160, 197
Portage Bay 38
Portageville, Missouri 30, 38, 76, 194
Post, H.R. 171
pottery 19, 21, 24
Power's Fort 23
prairie wetlands 101
preemption 58, 93, 102
Prescott, Jedediah 205
Price, Theodore H. 205, 208
Progressive Era 97
promotion of farmland 159, 160, 161, 163, 165
Puxico, Missouri 52, 73, 160

Quapaw Tribe 26
Quigg, James F. 145
quinine 85–89, 132

rabbit 14, 17, 154
raccoon 14, 17, 24
racial conflict 3, 171–174, 176, 179
Randolph, Isham 98, 101, 122, 124, 126
Rankin, Quentin 173
Read, Joseph C. 69
Reconstruction 184, 202
Reconstruction Finance Corporation (RFC) 149–151
Red Cross 137, 138, 139, 153–157, 194
Redman, C.C. 73
Reed, M.C. 118
Reelfoot Ceek 47
Reelfoot Lake 47, 173
Reelfoot Rift 7, 47
Rembert, Samuel S. 205
Republican Party 139, 178, 202
retrograde current 42, 48
Reybold, Eugene 153
Reynolds, S.P. 94, 95, 96, 109, 117, 160, 212
Rhodes, Joel 4, 73
rice 5, 215
Richmond, Virginia 39
rift zones and rifting 7–9
Riley, John 172
Ripley County, Missouri 69
Rockefeller Institute 131
Rodinia 7
Rodney, John 91, 92
Roll, Jarod 4, 178, 182
Rome, Italy 86
Roosevelt, Lydia Latrobe 54
Roosevelt, Nicholas 54
Roosevelt, Theodore 97, 178
Ross, Ronald 86
Rust, John D. 206, 207
Rust, Mack 206, 207

saber-toothed tiger 12
St. Francis, Arkansas 137
St. Francis River 12, 24, 46, 48, 58, 64, 65, 66, 91, 134, 136, 143, 153
St. Francis Sunk Land Wildlife Management Area 46
St. Francis Valley Railroad 74
St. John's Bayou 29, 30
St. John's Levee District 95, 137, 141, 151
St. Louis 2, 3, 22, 28, 29, 31, 33–35, 49, 53, 58, 68, 70, 76, 87, 99, 122, 145, 150, 160, 161–163, 172, 178, 191, 193, 194, 197, 199, 200, 210
St. Louis and Gulf Railroad 75, 111
St. Louis and Iron Mountain Railroad 68, 69, 74
St. Louis and Memphis Railroad 76
St. Louis and San Francisco Railroad 75, 111; *see also* Frisco Railroad
St. Louis Committee for Rehabilitation of the Sharecroppers 197
St. Louis, Iron Mountain, and Southern Railroad 69, 71, 111
St. Louis, Kennett and Southeastern Railroad 75; *see also* Cotton Belt Railroad
St. Louis, Kennett and Southern Railroad 73, 78
St. Louis, Memphis & Southwestern Railroad 111
St. Louis, Morehouse and Southern Railroad 74, 75
St. Louis Southwestern Railroad 71; *see also* Cotton Belt Railroad
St. Louis Union Trust Co. 111
St. Louis Urban League 197
Ste. Genevieve, Missouri 28, 33
Saline County, Missouri 62
sand blows 43, 44, 49, 52
sand boils 43, 44
sand dikes 44
sand fissures 43, 45
sand sloughs 45
Sandy Woods 7
Sappington, John 85, 86, 87
Sarvis, Will 202, 203
Saucier, Roger T. 9, 10
Schult, Hina C. 118
Schultz, Christian 35
Schweig, Eugene 39, 43, 47, 52
Scott, John 56
Scott, John G. 178–182
Scott County 1, 59, 60, 62, 68, 69, 80, 83, 88, 89, 94, 115, 117, 133, 166, 169, 170, 173, 174, 176, 177, 178, 182, 183
Scott County Milling Co. 166, 173
Second Great Awakening 51, 181
Senath Cooperage 80

Seymour, William 180
sharecropper system 3, 184, 185, 190, 211
Sharecropper Troubadour 188
sharecroppers 3, 154, 155, 157, 162–169, 171, 176, 183–199, 202, 203, 210, 211, 214
Shaw, John 41, 51
Shawnee Tribe 26, 27, 29
Shead, A.M. 70, 101
Sheppard, L.D. 126
Shewy, Arista C. 76
Shoemaker, Floyd 63
Shope, Richard 131
Sikes, W.H. 160
Sikeston Braid Belt 11
Sikeston Ridge 6, 7, 11, 12, 14, 38, 58, 134, 137, 159, 165
Simmons, Samuel 69
Skelton, R.W. 181
Smith, Mildred 200
Snow, Thad 84, 87, 146, 147, 148, 153, 160, 164, 165, 169, 188, 190, 191, 193
socialism 177, 178, 182, 186, 187
Socialist Party 176, 178, 179, 180, 187, 188
Southeast Missouri Agricultural and Industrial Association 161
Southeast Missouri Agricultural Bureau 160, 161
Southeast Realty Co. 161
Southern Tenant Farmers Union (STFU) 156, 157, 184, 186–192, 194, 201
soybeans 5, 161, 215
Spain 15, 28, 30, 32, 33, 82, 131
Spanish flu 131, 132
Spanish Mill, Missouri 48
Speed, Mathias 41, 42
spruce 13, 16
squirrels 14
Stanford, Dennis 16
Stapleton, Jack 203
Stark, Loyd C. 193, 199
Stepenoff, Bonnie 4, 115
Stewart, David 43
Stinnett, John 175
Stoddard, Amos 34, 90
Stoddard County 1, 14, 27, 59, 60, 62, 63, 68, 69, 80, 81, 88, 89, 91, 93, 110, 118, 125, 133, 134, 136, 145, 169, 172–174, 200, 204
Stokes, Graham Phelps 178
Stokes, Rose Pastor 178
Stone, Barton W. 51
Stoneville, Mississippi 206
Studabaker, Hugh 165, 166
sunk lands 43, 45, 46, 77
surveyors 31, 92, 120
Swampeast Missouri 87, 147, 169, 191
Swampland Act 60, 62, 69, 78, 92, 93, 101
swamps, river 45, 68

Sweet Home Baptist Church 196
syncline 8

Taft, William H. 178
Tallapoosa, Missouri 178
tapir 14
tax delinquency 136, 142, 143, 144
tax sales 146
Taylor, W.H. 173
Taylor, Missouri 52
tenancy rates 178, 183
Tennessee 12, 20, 24, 32, 33, 47, 62, 84, 152, 164, 166, 173, 177, 195, 214
Tennessee and Pacific Railroad 70
Tertiary Period 5, 9
Texas and St. Louis Railway Co. 71
Thebes Gap 11
Thomas, Richard J. 56
Thompson, Jeff 63, 67
Thwaites, Reuben Gold 29
timber camps 181
timber cutters and workers 83, 87, 175, 182, 194

Tiptonville, Tennessee 63
Tiptonville Dome 47
tobacco 59, 70, 173, 195
Towosaghy State Historic Site 23
tractors 183, 205, 208, 211
tupelo gum 13
Tuskegee Institute 139
Tyler Tap Railroad 70
Tyronza, Arkansas 157, 186, 187, 188, 189
Tywappity Bottoms 38

United Cannery Agricultural Packing and Allied Workers of America (UCAPAWA) 190, 197
United States Geological Survey 8, 39, 44–46, 53, 54, 99
United States Public Health Service 88
United States Supreme Court 116
University of Missouri 161
uplifts 43

Vacant Quarter 23, 26
Valencius, Conevery Bolton 49
Vincennes, Indiana 29, 32, 36

Virginia 8, 16, 30, 32, 39, 104, 168
Vogel, John C. 69
vote manipulation 202
voter fraud 202

Walker, John Hardeman 56, 57
Walker, M.L. 124
Wallace, A.J. 175
War Industries Board 130
War of 1812 51, 57, 58
Wardell, Missouri 84, 200
Washington, D.C. 39, 42, 56, 91, 99, 124, 148, 187, 218
Watson, Robert Goah 36, 49, 51
Weems Site 19
Welky, David 154, 156
West Prairie, Missouri 60, 68
West Tennessee Land Co. 173
West Virginia 30
wheat 5, 59, 61, 109, 146, 161, 162, 163, 165, 166, 185, 195, 215
Whitfield, Owen 189, 190, 191–193, 197, 199
Wicker, Grover 163
Wilkinson, James 30
Williams, Claude 190
Williams, Maxwell 185
Willis, C.E. 147
Willoby, Walter 175
Wilson, Mercer D. 111
Wilson, Woodrow 130, 178
Winchell, B.L. 75
Wirt, William 49
Wisconsin glacial period 11, 15
Wisconsin Lumber Company 76, 81, 82, 84, 107, 111, 115, 143, 163
Wolf River 33
Wood, W. Raymond 17
Woodland Period 18–21
Works Progress Administration (WPA) 151, 198, 204
World Health Organization 86
World War I 130, 135, 169, 178, 181, 182
Wyatt, Missouri 191, 196, 200

Yoakum, B.F. 75

Zimmerman, Orville 193

www.ingramcontent.com/pod-product-compliance
Ingram Content Group UK Ltd.
Pitfield, Milton Keynes, MK11 3LW, UK
UKHW041936140426
5217IPUK00014B/511